The Underground Guide to

Computer Security

Slightly
   Askew
      Advice
         on
            Protecting
               Your
                  PC
                     and
                        What's
                           On
                              It

Michael Alexander

ADDISON-WESLEY PUBLISHING COMPANY

Reading, Massachusetts • Menlo Park, California • New York • Don Mills, Ontario
Wokingham, England • Amsterdam • Bonn • Sydney • Singapore • Tokyo
Madrid • San Juan • Paris • Seoul • Milan • Mexico City • Taipei

Many of the designations used by manufacturers and sellers to distinguish their products are claimed as trademarks. Where those designations appear in this book, and Addison-Wesley was aware of a trademark claim, the designations have been printed in initial capital letters or all capital letters.

The author and publisher have taken care in preparation of this book, but make no expressed or implied warranty of any kind and assume no responsibility for errors or omissions. No liability is assumed for incidental or consequential damages in connection with or arising out of the use of the information or programs contained herein.

Library of Congress Cataloging-in-Publication Data

Alexander, Michael, 1950-
  The underground guide to computer security : slightly askew advice
on protecting your PC and what's on it / Michael Alexander.
     p.   cm. — (Underground guide series)
  Includes index.
  ISBN 0-201-48918-X (alk. paper)
  1. Computer security.   2. Microcomputers—Access control.
I. Title. II. Series.
QA76.9.A25A45   1996
005.8—dc20   95-40661
                                                CIP

Series Hack: Woody Leonhard
Sponsoring Editor: Kathleen Tibbetts
Project Manager: Sarah Weaver
Production Coordinator: Deborah McKenna
Cover design: Jean Seal
Text Design: Kenneth L. Wilson, Wilson Graphics & Design
Set in 10 point Palatino by Rob Mauhar, CIP of Coronado

1 2 3 4 5 6 7 8 9 -MA- 99989796
First printing, November 1995

Addison-Wesley books are available for bulk purchases by corporations, institutions, and other organizations. For more information please contact the Corporate, Government, and Special Sales Department at 800-238-9682.

Find us on the World-Wide Web at:
http://www.aw.com/devpress/

Contents

Foreword   ix

Acknowledgments   xi

Read Me   xiii

Chapter 1   **Information Threats and Thieves**   1

Everyone Should Feel Secure   2
We're Our Own Worst Enemy   3
The Threat from Within: Employees   7
The Threat from Outsiders   9
Putting a Value on Information   19
Risk Assessment Test   23

Chapter 2   **Viruses, Worms, and Other Rogue Code**   25

Computer Viruses   25
What in the Heck Is a Virus?   27
How Are PCs Infected?   30
Telltale Signs   31
Search and Destroy   32
Getting Rid of Viruses   35
How to Buy Antivirus Software   36
A Few More Words about Macs   37
Tips for Warding Off Cybermicrobes   39
Worms, Trojan Horses, and Logic and Time Bombs   40
You Probably Want to Ask . . .   42
Antivirus Software Sellers and Freebies   44

Chapter 3   **Safe Desktops and Laptops**   45

Controlling Access to Computer Systems   46
Identification and Authentication   47
The Last Word on Passwords   48
How to Create Hacker-Proof Passwords   54

One Factor, Two Factors   54
Access Control Programs   61
Portable Computer Security   68
Control Over Remote Access   80

Chapter 4   **Networks: 1000 Points of Fright**   87
LAN 101   88
Entering the E-mail Dimension   103
Streamlined Sign-On   105
This Way to the I-way   109
Dialing for Dollars   121

Chapter 5   **Secret Messages and Digital Hancocks**   131
Encryption and Digital Envelopes   131
Digital John Hancocks   135

Chapter 6   **Natural and Unnatural Disasters**   149
Well-Laid Plans of Mice and Men   150
Things That Go Bump Day and Night   151
You've Got the Power, Maybe   159
Let's Get Physical   166
Cover Yourself with Insurance   168
The Agony, Not Ecstasy of Using PCs   169

Chapter 7   **Lose It? Get It Back!**   175
That Backup Religion   176
Why Back Up?   176
Tape Me Up, Tape Me Down   177
If This Is Daily2, Then It Must Be Tuesday   184
Backup Strategies for Home Offices and Small Companies   186
Other Backup Options   188
Diagnostics, Recovery, and Other Useful Utilities   195

Chapter 8   **Taking Care of Business**   199
Make it a Policy to Protect Yourself   200
The Right and Wrong of Using Computers   200
What Else Goes in the Policy?   202
Get the Boss Behind the Program   207

Computer Awareness Training   209
Computer Crime Statutes   217

Appendix A **PC and Mac Antivirus Software**   219

Appendix B **Computer Security Companies and Organizations**   223

Appendix C **Notes from the Virus Front**   229

Index   231

Foreword

Now, more than ever before, it's vital that PC users understand and practice the basics of computer security. While the sexy virus threats steal headlines—and PC users *do* need to learn about the capabilities and limitations of viri—more down-to-earth problems dog PC users every day. How much backup is really enough? How hard is it for somebody on my company's network to go snooping around in my files? Is my private e-mail company property? Is the Net really as insecure as the pundits would have us believe?

Most of all, what can I do about it?

In this book Michael Alexander, one of the world's foremost authorities on PC security, tells it like it is: no pulled punches, no sugar coating. If you're ready for the unvarnished truth about PC security, this Underground Guide's for you.

Enjoy!

Woody Leonhard
Series Hack

Acknowledgments

Read the acknowledgments in the front of most books, and the first thing the authors do is thank their family and friends for their support and patience. I've always wondered about that. What's the big deal about writing a book? It takes a bit of research and you have to spend loads of hours pounding a keyboard, but how hard can it be?

Now I know. Writing a book *is* a big deal and when you're doing it, everyone else pays a price, including your family. In the months that I spent cranking out this book, my wife and daughters seldom saw me for weeks on end and when they did, I was a more than insufferable curmudgeon.

To my loving wife, Lorri, and my beautiful daughters, Jessie and Leigh, I say thank you for your patience and your unyielding support. I love you.

I'd also like to thank Harold Highland, my technical editor on this project. Harold encouraged me to write this book from the start and provided me with invaluable assistance to the end. Harold did his best to keep me honest. Any errors in this book are mine alone.

Read Me

Misfortune, *n.* The kind of fortune that never misses.

Ambrose Bierce
The Devil's Dictionary, 1906

I've had more than my fair share of computer security mishaps and disasters in the fifteen or so years that I have been using personal computers. I've had all sorts of bad computer experiences, ranging from having my computer fried by a renegade power surge to watching my computer go brain dead as a result of a virus. In between, I've had shelves crash down on my monitor, a dog chew through my computer's cable while I was working, and a hard drive crash. In more ways that I can count or even recall, I've lost enough data to fill a black hole.

Most of the bad stuff that has happened to me could have been avoided had I known what I was doing. But I'll admit that even after I finally wised up, I refused to take seriously the many ways that things can go wrong. If there is anyone with the background to write this book, I'm the guy. In fact, I've had so many calamities, my wife calls me Jane.

I don't know if it was destiny or just dumb luck, but I also have spent the last seven years covering computer security for some of the top publications in the computer trade publishing industry. In that time, I have met hundreds of people just like me who have experienced a computer catastrophe of one sort or the other. I've also been fortunate to have met and interviewed many of the world's top computer security experts. And, despite a certain hardheadedness on my part, I've actually learned a thing or two about the many ways that information and computer systems can be folded, spindled, and mutilated.

I wrote this book for people like you and me who rely on their PCs to earn a living. That includes home office workers, telecommuters, mobile office roadwarriors, and small business entrepreneurs.

If your job is to worry about computer security for a multinational conglomerate, this is not the book for you. The Acmes and Amalgamateds of the world have the resources to buy the brains of computer security consultants who know more about protecting mainframes, massive networks, and all of the other information technology in use today than I ever will. Go talk to one of those folks. If you don't know any, get in touch with me through the publisher and I'll give you some names.

I have a broad definition of computer security and this book reflects that. I write not only about protecting computer systems and information, but also about how to protect your privacy, your telephone systems, and yourself from your computer.

Technoshock   It's easy to go into technophobic shock reading about all of the ways that you can lose all of that hard work stored in your computer. Just keep in mind that if you take some basic, common-sense precautions—such as regularly backing up the files that are most precious to you—you'll be all right.

I'm going to recommend to you a whole range of precautions that you ought to take, even though you and I know both know that you probably won't do them all. Heck, *I* don't even follow all of my recommendations (as I said, I am bit hardheaded).

I do only what I feel I must do to protect myself and very little else. I don't obsess about viruses, hackers, and the other misfortunes that could sneak up behind me at any given moment. I know that I could buy nearly absolute fail-safe security, but it would come at a sacrifice of my productivity and sense of well being. It would be like putting ten locks on each door to your house. That would keep the burglars out, but you would have to schlep around a huge key ring, spend five minutes unlocking the front door, and five minutes locking the door after you're inside. Life is too short.

What's sensible for me may not be sensible for you. I have mainly word processing files to worry about. Although I think everything I write is precious, it's not worth nearly as much as that secret formula for the next whiz-bang soda pop that you're probably working on.

Also, I have a pretty good idea of what my exposure is to any given hazard, and I know at all times just how much I can stand to lose before I start thinking about taking a swan dive into an empty swimming pool. If I care deeply about it, I take steps to safeguard it. It's that simple. You should do the same.

While I was writing this book, for example, I made multiple backup copies of every file and carried a set of disks with me every time I left my house. For good measure, I periodically compressed files and uploaded them to my account at an online service. I'm usually not this cautious, but writing a book is time-consuming and just plain hard work. With the tight deadlines I had me to deliver on this book, I couldn't afford to lose even a minute's worth of work!

The Underground Guide to Computer Security Tipsheet

Any fool can make a rule.

Henry David Thoreau (1817–1862)

While writing this book, I found that I kept coming back to certain topics and themes. To make it easy for you to see at a glance just what this book is all about, I've pulled together the following list of computer security tips. Memorize them, inscribe them in your heart and you and your data will live happily ever after, maybe longer. The order in which these tips is arranged is unimportant.

1. Read the manual. Yeah, yeah, yeah, who's got time for that? Seriously, read the manuals that come with your hardware and software. You would be amazed at just how much information is in them. My favorite manuals are ones that start out with phrases like, "Instructions for hasty people," and "If you don't want to read the manual just do this . . .," but I read the long ones too, sooner or later.

2. Back up. Back up your work early and often. Nuff said.

3. Be prepared. I can't count the number of times I have encountered people— really smart people, too—who discounted the need to protect their PCs and information until something bad happened to them. That's probably why you've got your nose in this book, isn't it? Maybe your PC was infected with a virus and now you're wondering what to do to get rid of it. Maybe someone got a look at some important files on your PC and now you want to make sure that it doesn't happen again. Don't wait for disaster to slap you upside the head before you get around to putting on a helmet.

4. Use encryption. Use a brand-name encryption scheme like Data Encryption Standard (better yet, use triple DES) to scramble data that you don't want anyone to read on your hard drive. Use Pretty Good Privacy or RSA Data Security's RSA public-key cryptography to protect your electronic mail. Encryption is the most powerful weapon you have to protect the confidentiality and privacy of your information, and you can get it for free if you look around only a little bit.

5. Use antivirus software. I've heard lots of experts say that the virus problem is overblown and that you haven't got much to worry about. Take it from me, your risk of having a virus infect your PC or Mac is far greater than you may think. I can tell you from personal experience that even so-called benign viruses are a major butt pain to get rid of.

6. Learn to take care of yourself. If you spend several hours a day sitting in front of a computer pounding a keyboard, you need to make sure that your system,

chair, and desk are in harmony. If you work for someone who forces you to use shoddy equipment or irregular furniture, either make them buy you better gear or work somewhere else. When the time comes for you to retire, no one will appreciate or even care that you spent the last 20 years in agony just because you wanted to be a good soldier.

7. Be computer security aware. Many of the problems that you encounter can be avoided if only you used a little bit of common sense. Don't walk off and leave your computer turned on or logged into a network. Don't eat and drink around your computer. Lock your disks in your desk when you go out for lunch. Don't wait until the end of the day to back up important files. If someone telephones and asks for help in logging onto the company's computer system, get their name, rank, and serial number and then call their boss.

8. Treat your password the same way you should treat your toothbrush. Use it every day; change it regularly, and never share it with anyone.

9. Don't trust anyone. Sigh. This is a tough one for me to recommend. Not trusting anyone seems so selfish and cynical. On the other hand, I've seen too many people get burned because their security was based more on trust than on proper security controls. If you're responsible for configuring the security of a local area network, keep the users honest and plug every single loophole you can find.

10. Get online. There's a wealth of security-related information and free to low-cost software on bulletin board systems, commercial online services such as America Online and Compuserve, and on Usenet newsgroups, the World Wide Web, and other Internet sites.

1 Information Threats and Thieves

> I don't trust him. We're friends.
>
> Bertolt Brecht (1898–1956)

A few years ago, when I was a reporter for a computer industry newspaper and still new to the computer security beat, I would try out some of the security evasion techniques that I reported on, just to see if they really worked. The experts had told me early on that most computer users choose passwords that are easy to remember and easy to figure out. To test this theory, I set out to hack my company's computer system.

I choose as my target the account of a young editorial assistant. Let's call her Elizabeth Smith, which is not her real name, to save her from any embarrassment. I already knew Elizabeth's userID was SMITH. The login ID serves to identify a particular person using a system so you can tell who created a file, send them e-mail and so on.

So, to start, I typed SMITH. The computer responded by asking me for a **SEX?** password. Hmm, what kind of password would Elizabeth use? SEX? That's quite common. Naw, I said to myself, she's much too proper for that. She might use the name of her cat, but I don't know that. Let's try her nickname, LIZ.

Two seconds later I'm looking at her personal directory, a list of files that she has created and supposedly only she can read. I logged off and sent SMITH an e-mail note: "You need to change your password. And, by the way, you might want to take that file called RESUME off the system!"

I'm telling you this story to make the point that it's guys like me—employees—who are one of your biggest security worries. Never mind that I meant no harm. What I did would have gotten me fired in many companies because I exceeded my authorization on the system. When all's said and done, unscrupulous employees are the second most fearsome threat to computer security. The first is people doing dumb things, or what the experts call "accidents and omissions."

1

EVERYONE SHOULD FEEL SECURE

There are only two occasions when Americans respect privacy, especially in Presidents. Those are prayer and fishing.

Herbert Hoover
This Week magazine, February 7, 1960

If you care about your own sensitive or private information (or that of your employer) falling into the wrong hands, computer security is what you need.

Computer security defined

So what is computer security precisely? Computer security involves at least three basic tenets:

1. *Integrity*—Making sure that the information that is stored in your computer is accurate and insulated against accidental and deliberate change.

2. *Confidentiality*—Making sure that the information stored in your computer is seen only by you or people who are authorized by you to see it.

3. *Availability*—Making sure that your computer and the information stored in it are available whenever you want them. (These days, for many computer users, that means 24 hours a day, 7 days a week.)

Post a guard

Protecting your computer from intrusion by snoops is easy. Simply take your computer; disconnect it from any network; lock it in a windowless, lead-lined room; and throw away the key. Then post a guard at the door.

Obviously that solution will not appeal to many computer users, perhaps with the exception of military personnel who handle classified data. However, it's the only approach to security that you can be sure of. There's no such thing as fail-safe security but using a combination of common sense and computer security products, you can do a lot to protect yourself against all manner of trouble.

If You Can't Afford to Lose It, Protect It

Though I am not naturally honest, I am so sometimes by chance.

William Shakespeare (1564–1616)

There's no doubt that the risks to computers and information are on the rise. More people, including crooks, are using computers, which also means that more people are capable of learning how to get around security barriers. Computers are being tied into networks, especially the Internet, making it possible for more people to get to your computer. Also, computers are being used for increasingly important information—financial records, secret formulas, and such—so they're becoming increasingly attractive targets to crooks.

One study, conducted by one of those huge, high-priced accounting firms, **Lost money** indicates that more than one in four companies in the United States and Canada lost money in the past two years as a result of security breaches. Just how much money was lost, however, is hard to tell. For one thing, it's difficult to put a dollar figure on intangibles like business disruption and poor customer service that result when information is tampered with or stolen. Even so, the same study suggests that the cost of security failures typically exceeds $100,000. On occasion, more than $1 million is lost as a result of a single security incident.

If you work for yourself or don't care one whit what happens to your employer's computers, you're probably only interested in protecting the stuff that's in your own computer. Only you know what that's worth, but the message is still the same: If you care about it, do whatever is needed to protect it.

Okay, who and what do you have to worry about?

- People like you and me
- Disgruntled employees or co-workers
- Dishonest employees or co-workers
- Hackers, phreaks, industrial spies, and other crooks
- Viruses, worms, and other malicious software
- Hurricanes, floods, and other natural disasters
- Power outages, the kid next door, and other unnatural disasters

WE'RE OUR OWN WORST ENEMY

We have met the enemy and he is us.

Pogo

Most people think that computer security has something to do with keeping **Screwy things** hackers out of computer systems. Although there's some truth to that, battling hackers is only a small part of computer security. The real problem is you, me, and people like us who sometimes do screwy things.

When bad things happen to good people like us, it's usually because we're careless or ignorant about the risks. More computer security failures are caused by accidents and errors than any other problem.

When was the last time you backed up the files in your personal computer? If you're like most people, you've never done it. It's not that you're stupid—you know that it's something that you should do—but you just haven't gotten around to it. Any way, bad computer things happen to the other guy, right? Even if you do backups, say, once a day before you knock off work, how many times have you accidentally deleted a file, or worse, reformatted an entire disk, without having checked to see if backup copies were even usable?

Alexander's Seven Deadly Sins

> Every man is a damn fool for at least five minutes every day. Wisdom consists in not exceeding the limit.
>
> Edgar Watson Howe
> *The Indignations of E.W. Howe, 1933*

1. *Failing to use common sense when choosing and using passwords.* The first line of defense, and the one that is most easily breached, is your password (or passwords, which are increasingly the case). It doesn't have to be that way. In fact, a common-sense approach to choosing and using passwords could be one of your key defenses and not the weakest as is common. If everyone used sensible passwords and changed them periodically, there would be little need for books on computer security. If you do nothing other than follow the simple steps for creating hacker-proof passwords in Chapter 3, this book will pay for itself a zillion times over.

2. *Failing to back up important data and information.* This one seems pretty obvious, doesn't it? Even so, a surprising number of people simply don't bother to back up their information. It's the single best insurance that you have against whatever trouble comes your way. Note I said "insurance," and just like insurance for your car, backups won't prevent accidents, but you'll be happy to have them if you get in a collision. Chapter 6 gives a bunch of backup strategies as well as several tips on creating a set of disks that will help you recover from any disaster, whether it's a hurricane or your nephew stuffing a grilled cheese sandwich into the slot on the front of your PC.

3. *Failing to protect your PC and files from sneak thieves and other rogues.* Millions of dollars worth of computers are stolen every year, according to the experts who keep an eye on such things. In most cases, the thief wants your machine to sell—he's usually not alert enough to realize that the information stored in the computer might be worth a lot more money than the box housing it. However, an increasing number of businesses are reporting that savvy thieves are targeting information, although statistics are hard to come by. Chapter 3 discusses how to lock down your computer and lock up your data.

4. *Failing to take the threats to your PC and files seriously.* Most people aren't worried about hackers getting into their systems. Why should they? The problems caused by hackers are relatively small compared to all of the other

things that could go wrong. But what about a hurricane? Could your system survive the kind of blow out that landed Dorothy in Oz? How about a fire? A power outage? The nosey guy in the cubicle next door? Your teenage son? Your soon-to-be ex-spouse? Somewhere between the extremes of doing nothing and protecting everything is a level of security that is just right for you. Later in this chapter, I'll give you some tips on assessing your risks to a variety of potential security problems and how to determine what is worth protecting.

5. *Failing to use the brains you were born with.* Many computer security problems are the result of stupid human tricks. Here's what I mean (with a nod to TV talk show host David Letterman):

   • Writing down computer passwords on a Post-it note and sticking it on the front of a computer monitor for everyone to see.

   • Putting on a pair of crepe-soled shoes, shuffling the entire length of a carpeted hallway, and zapping the first personal computer you come to with static electricity.

   • Parking your morning's cup of coffee on top of your computer monitor to keep it warm and thinking that it will never spill.

   • While waiting for a plane, asking the stranger sitting next to you in the waiting area to keep an eye on your notebook computer while you grab a hot dog at the snack bar, particularly after making a point of telling him that your computer cost you 3700 big ones.

   • Installing software on your PC and having no clue as to what it's for.

   You get the idea. Sadly lots of these stupid human tricks could easily be avoided by anyone who wasn't hiding behind the door when the brains were being handed out.

6. *Failing to monitor your system for signs of unauthorized use.* There is little point in setting up a security perimeter unless you get out and walk the fence occasionally. A surprising number of people have taken the care to install security controls but never go back and check to see if they are operating as advertised. In Chapter 7 I'll give you the telltale signs of a possible security breach and what to do about it if you suspect one.

7. *Failing to use antivirus software.* There are two kinds of people: those that have been hit by a virus and those that will be hit by a virus. The experts reckon that new viruses are being created at the rate of two to three a day. At last count, 6500 viruses were on the loose, and that's just for PCs. Your PC can be infected in several ways, including commercial, shrink-wrapped software. Chapter 2 tells you more than you ever wanted to know about viruses and what you need to do to protect yourself.

The Only Sermon in This Book

> The trouble with using experience as a guide is that the final exam often comes first and then the lesson.
>
> Unknown

One of the best ways that you can protect yourself from yourself and all of the other possible computer calamities is to develop a reasonable understanding of how to use your PC, peripherals, and programs. That means reading the manuals that came with your equipment. (I know, it's a dirty job, but somebody ought to do it for goodness sake.)

Shoot for trouble
It also pays to know a bit about the kinds of things that can go wrong so that you are able to troubleshoot problems on your own. Knowing if a problem is caused by hardware, which you usually can't do anything about, or software, which you often can do something about, is already a big step in fending for yourself. A wide variety of recovery utilities, diagnostic tools, and other software were designed to help you out of a jam. We'll talk about those in Chapter 6, by the way.

Some Simple Precautions

> It is inaccurate to say I hate everything. I am strongly in favor of common sense, common honesty and common decency. This makes me ineligible for any public office.
>
> H. L. Mencken (1880–1956)

To protect yourself from the ordinary vagaries of everyday computer life you can take some simple common-sense precautions:

- If you must write down your password, store it in a secure place, away from the computer.
- Put write-protect tabs on disks and label them.
- Delete unneeded files stored on your hard disk drive. It only takes a couple of minutes every few weeks to keep on top of these files.
- Keep your workstation area clean. Regularly vacuum the computer and the surrounding area.
- Occasionally clean the heads on your floppy disk drives and tape backup systems. There are inexpensive cleaning kits (any office supply or computer store should have them) that make this job a snap.
- Don't eat or drink around your computer, or anyone else's for that matter. Accidents happen more often that we like to think.

- Smoking is not only harmful to your lungs and heart, but it's also bad for your computer's hard disk drive, keyboard, and other vital parts. If you must smoke, don't do it while seated at your computer.

THE THREAT FROM WITHIN: EMPLOYEES

Men have become the tools of their tools.

Henry David Thoreau
Walden, 1854

Most computer crime—whether it is the unauthorized access to a company's files or the planting of a time bomb designed to destroy programs and data—is likely to be carried out by current or former employees.

Disgruntled Employees or Co-workers

Companies have disgruntled employees to worry about, especially employees who are intimately familiar with the inner workings of their employers' businesses and the computer systems they've installed. A couple of years ago, for example, at General Dynamics Corp.'s space division in San Diego, a programmer, unhappy with the size of his paycheck, planted a logic bomb—a computerized equivalent of a real bomb—designed to wipe out a program to track Atlas missile parts. Fortunately, during a routine check of programs stored on the system, a fellow programmer discovered the logic bomb and removed it before it was activated.

> **Unhappy people**

Most disgruntled people are motivated by some emotional concern. They're unhappy about something the boss said, or a some perceived slight by a co-worker, or because they've lost their jobs as the result of poor performance, layoff, or other reason.

Dishonest Employees

If you would know the Value of Money, go and try to borrow some.

Benjamin Franklin
Poor Richard's Almanack, 1758

Dishonest employees, on the other hand, are greedy. Any employee who has access to computers that run accounting systems could potentially abuse them. How? Usually they'll manipulate data to cover up a theft of dollars or inventory, a technique that is sometimes called data diddling. If there are a large number of transactions involving fractions of cents, they may round down numbers and siphon off the difference, a technique that is sometimes called salami slicing.

> **Crooked people**

Increasingly, employees are using company computer systems to run sideline businesses or to engage in illegal activities. Officials at Charles Schwab & Co. in San Francisco, for example, discovered in 1991 that a cocaine ring was operating among its headquarters employees. It turned out that the drug sales were being arranged via the e-mail system. In another case, this one involving AT&T's London office, three employees were accused of setting up an outside company with a 900 number, which charges anyone who makes the call. They then rigged an AT&T computer to repeatedly call the number, ringing up huge bills, which AT&T paid.

Surprisingly, many companies—even large sophisticated ones—don't worry much about protecting their computers and information. The suits in the boardroom often are unaware of the threats or they're complacent. I'll also be the first to admit that computer security is about as glamorous as running a car wash, and it's often hard to come up with the dough to pay for security measures.

If you run a small company and you have key technical or financial staff members who never take vacations or decline promotions, it may be because they are engaged in computer fraud. These people often are fearful that evidence of fraud may be uncovered by other employees filling in while they are away.

Those Wacky Employees

The number of ways employees are threatening computer security is multiplying rapidly. Here are some of the most prevalent ways:

1. Entering false data to falsify records, say, to cover up the theft of inventory or embezzlement (also called data diddling). It is by far the most common way employees use computers to rip off the boss.

2. Eavesdropping on e-mail and voice mail messages.

3. Using e-mail to anonymously send co-workers sexually explicit, racist, or other offensive messages.

4. Deliberately planting a virus or some other form of malicious software.

5. Stealing a zillion dollars one cent or even a fraction of a cent at a time by rounding down numbers and siphoning off the difference (also called salami slicing). It's not usually worthwhile in most companies, but if you work in a bank or a financial institution that handles lots of financial transactions, it might be something to worry about.

6. Stealing information that can be resold to a competitor or held for ransom.

7. Using the company's computer system to run a business on the side.

8. Using the computer system to engage in illegal activities such as gambling or drug dealing or distributing hard-core pornography.

9. Stealing computers or peripherals or copyrighted software that the company has paid for or created for its own use.

THE THREAT FROM OUTSIDERS

> Never accept an invitation from a stranger unless he gives you candy.
>
> Linda Festa

All sorts of people might want to get into your system. They range from curious computer users who probe the system simply to find out what's in there to outlaw hackers who want to destroy data or cause mischief in other ways. Telephone phreaks want to get inside your phone systems to make long-distance calls on your dime or to use your voice mail as a meeting place with other phreaks where they can swap long-distance credit card codes and other information. There are industrial snoops as well as ex–Cold War spies now working for their countries' foreign intelligence agencies. Then there are crooks who want to steal information that may be useful in committing crimes or that they can hold for ransom.

Info thieves galore

Outlaw Hackers

Outlaw computer hackers have gotten a lot of attention in recent years—probably more than they deserve. They've been featured in movies such as *Sneakers*, starring Robert Redford and Sidney Poitier, and in books such as the *Cuckoo's Egg*, a tale about three hackers who worked for the KBG in exchange for cash and cocaine. Their latest exploits also are chronicled on the front pages of most of the major newspapers in the country. Most recently it was Kevin Mitnick, a notorious hacker, who was captured in early 1995 after being on the run for two years.

According to the FBI, during the years Mitnick was on the run, he allegedly broke into dozens of computers—in one case, downloading 20,000 credit card numbers belonging to customers of an Internet service provider. The company, Netcom On-Line Communication Services, did not know that the theft had occurred until it was contacted by subscribers. Mitnick also is accused of allegedly breaking into the computer of a noted security expert and downloading thousands of security-related files and programs. His eventual capture in Raleigh, North Carolina, made the front page of the *New York Times*. Now, the security expert and and a *NYT* reporter who helped the feds track Mitnick to his hideout have signed a lucrative book deal and also are negotiating with Hollywood for the movie rights. Call it Billy the Kid on the Electronic Frontier. However, just like the tale of William Bonney, it's at least equal parts fantasy and fact.

Fantasy and fact

The Fine Art of the Hack

> Never engage in a battle of wits with an unarmed person.
>
> Unknown

Social engineering

Contrary to the popular view, the average outlaw computer hacker is not Lex Luthor or even some above-average technical wizard. They (and they are almost always young men) don't get the information they need to break into systems by diligently probing the systems' electronic innards and then vaulting the electronic fences designed to keep them out. Most often, they call up an unsuspecting employee and cajole or wheedle them into giving them a password. They'll say they're a new employee and need help logging into the system, or they may masquerade as a service technician and need the employee to help them test the system in some fashion. Hackers call this "social engineering." If that technique fails, they'll rummage through refuse containers looking for computer manuals, diskettes, or scraps of paper with access codes written on them. This decidedly low-tech approach of "dumpster diving" or "trashing" is one of the productive sources of information that hackers and other outsiders can use to penetrate systems.

I'll tell you about some of the techniques that hackers use, but I'm not going to tell you an awful lot here about how to prevent them from getting into your system. Most of that is covered in the chapters about access control and networks and in other chapters. My reasoning is that it doesn't matter who is trying to get into your computer—whether it's a snoopy colleague or the world's most fearsome computer hacker—the techniques for keeping them out are nearly identical. Still, you need to be aware of a few tricks that hackers use, and I'm going to tell you exactly what they are and what you can do to protect yourself.

Not Smart, Just Well Informed

> Education is what you have left over after you have forgotten everything you have learned.
>
> Anonymous

Although it certainly helps to be a whiz kid, most hackers are merely well informed in the ways of penetrating computer systems and simply are more persistent about doing it than you or I would be. They don't mind trying hundreds of different keystroke combinations until a computer door clicks open.

 Also, people are fairly predictable and hackers know this. They know that most people are going to choose passwords that remind them of a person, pet, place, or some personal interest so that they are easy to remember. Try using such passwords as SEX and LOVE to get into half of the computer systems in the country and you'll probably be inside poking around within minutes.

To put that theory to the test, at my job on the computer newspaper, I would periodically try out various combinations of keystrokes while gabbing on the phone or eating lunch at my desk. Working from the menu that allowed users to make some simple system configuration changes, I figured out that by pressing a certain combination of keys, I could read any file—no matter who it belonged to. The only hitch was that I had to know the name of the file that I wanted to look at. I went hunting for filenames named MIKEA, MALEX, and the like. I figured that if the file is about me, it's as much my business as that of whoever created the file. I resisted the temptation to hunt for such files as PAYROLL, SALARIES, and TERMINATE. A real hacker would have danced away with the keys to the kingdom.

Having uncovered the loophole, I never mentioned it to the system administrator or the bosses. Hey, I probably would have been out on the street looking for another job. I don't hack systems anymore, but I'm convinced that it's remarkably easy. If I can do it, I'm sure that anybody can.

Hackers stay on top of the latest developments in their field and they have good tools. Just like many young business professionals these days, eh? Hackers thrive on information in the same way that other people thrive on sumptuous cusine. What sort of information? Stuff like how to crack passwords that open the portals of computers, how to make a red box with which to make free telephone calls, how to masquerade as someone else when you send e-mail on the Internet, and how to boldly go where no one has gone before. Information is a currency in many places in hackerdom. To get a look at some of the better files on cracking computer systems that are stored on bulletin board systems frequented by hackers, you might be asked to first pay up with a long-distance telephone credit card number.

The key to info is info

Frequent alt.2600, an Internet newsgroup that draws hackers, hacker wannabes, computer industry reporters, and other hacker hangers-on, and you'll find all sorts discussions about how to break into various systems, how to phreak telephone systems, how to crack the copy protection on protected software, and where to get the latest hacking tools.

A good place to start is with the FAQ (Frequently Asked Questions) on alt.2600. It's a fascinating compendium of computer hacking tips and techniques. Here's just a sample:

```
How do I crack UNIX passwords?

Contrary to popular belief, UNIX passwords cannot be decrypted.
UNIX passwords are encrypted with a one-way function. The login
program encrypts the text you enter at the "password:" prompt and
compares that encrypted string against the encrypted form of your
password. Password cracking software uses wordlists. Each word in
the wordlist is encrypted and the results are compared to the
encrypted form of the target password.
```

The best cracking program for UNIX passwords is currently Crack by Alec Muffett. For PC-DOS, the best package to use is currently CrackerJack.

Tools of the Trade

> There are a thousand hacking at the branches of evil to one who is striking at the root.
>
> Henry David Thoreau
> *Walden,* 1854

Many of the tools that hackers use to crack computer systems were originally tools for troubleshooting, tweaking performance, and assessing security measures. A "sniffer," for example, is used to evaluate the performance of a local area network (LAN). While it's checking the flow of packets on the LAN, for example, it's also collecting passwords. Then there are program such as CrackerJack and Crack, which are designed to do nothing more than figure out passwords.

 If you run a business that has a local area network, be careful about the sorts of tools that you use on the system for diagnostics and troubleshooting. They can be easily used against you.

The devil made me do it   The day on which this very page you're reading now was being written, hackers glommed on yet another computer security tool, one that may make it easy for the greenest outlaw hacker to bust into a computer. It's called Security Administrator Tool for Analyzing Networks—SATAN, for short—and it was developed by two guys who believe that it will help security administrators poke at their computers to find weak spots. What's more, it's free—can't beat that with a stick, right?

The problem is that SATAN is readily available to anyone who wants it, including hackers who will use it to find ways to break into computers. It's like a security system that constantly monitors all the entry ways into your house and then sends an alert that the front door has been left ajar—to you and the burglars at the same time.

War Dialers

Did you see *WarGames,* the movie starring Matthew Broderick as a teenage computer wizard, released in 1983? Broderick hacks into a military computer system and nearly starts World War III when he starts playing games with an early warning fail-safe system.

In that movie, Broderick used a war dialer, a program that repeatedly dials the telephone looking for the identifying tones of a computer connected on the other end. Later, the hacker can dial the number, find out what computer it is, and if possible, break into it. Currently the best war dialer available for PC-DOS users is ToneLoc from Minor Threat and Mucho Maas. (I found that out by reading the alt.2600 FAQ.)

Such scanning is illegal in some states, but there's not much anyone can do to stop a hacker from doing it. The good news is that there's a lot you can do to make sure that he or she doesn't go any further than getting your number.

Sweet Talk and Social Engineering

> Life is what happens while you are making other plans.
>
> John Lennon (1940–1980)

Despite the whole arsenal of technical tools in their kit bag, hackers often resort to using the telephone to get the information they need to break into your computer. Hackers call it social engineering, and it's one of their most potent ploys to get passwords and collect information about the systems they intend to attack and more. You should be aware of the following social engineering scams.

The New Kid on the Block

The hacker assumes the role of a new employee, unfamiliar with the organization's information systems and procedures for logging into the systems. In this scenario, the hacker calls up and asks for assistance. Perhaps he'll say that, despite his best efforts to understand the organization's log-in procedures, he still needs guidance on what to do. In many instances, the hacker appeals to your ego in hopes that you'll be induced to show off just how much you know about the system.

Danger: Ego at work

Key to this particular strategy is the hacker's asking for specific assistance such as a step-by-step explanation of how to log in. This ploy is often tried just before or right after business hours. That gives the caller what would appear to be a legitimate reason for asking someone outside of his own department for assistance.

The Big Boss

The hacker acts like the man in charge (well, if the hacker is a she, she'll act like the woman in charge if she's smart). In a corporate setting, that person might be a department head or a personal assistant of a chief executive; in a military setting, it's probably a high-ranking officer. Typically the hacker makes angry demands, in expectation that whoever he is talking to will be pressured into doing whatever it takes to get the nasty boss off the phone.

The Helpful Technician

The fix is in   The hacker pretends that something has gone wrong with the organization's computers and he is a technician calling to fix it. In all likelihood, he will attempt to create a sense of rapport, perhaps engaging you in conversation about the infallibility of computers and expressing annoyance at how much trouble they are. Most people can relate to this—nearly everyone has had a problem with his or her computer! Typically the hacker asks you how to log in, what's your password, and similar questions designed to give him ideas on how to break into the systems. The hacker tries to time his call to coincide with a busy period in the day, choosing late afternoon instead of the first thing in the morning, for example.

Social Engineering Scam in Action

> My mother didn't breast-feed me. She said she liked me as a friend.
>
> Rodney Dangerfield

Credit report   Let's say I want to pull your credit report from TRW, which maintains credit
scam   reports on some 170 million Americans (and probably more than a few foreigners). I'll call up, say, an automobile dealer in some sleepy town in the middle of nowhere and ask for the finance department. To whoever answers the phone, I say:

```
"I'm Bob Jones, a technician with TRW, and I'm trying to track
down a problem at the credit report bureau. Would you mind going
through the log-in sequence with me, please, while I monitor what
is happening on my end? Okay log in. What dial-up number did you
enter? All right, now enter your account number. What did you
type? Okay, everything looks good on this end. If you have any
problems, don't hesitate to give us a call. Thanks much and you
have a nice day now." All that remains is for me to dial into the
credit reporting service, and do the job.
```

Do not give out any information over the telephone, even if you believe the other person on the line is legitimate or a fellow employee. If an employee needs assistance logging in, refer him to his immediate supervisor. If an executive or high-ranking officer calls and demands details on how to access the organization's records, politely refer her to the information systems department or to your supervisor. Under no circumstances should you give out your password—or anyone else's.

Dumpster Diving

Another favorite tactic employed by hackers is to go dumpster diving—rummaging through garbage (usually at night) looking for discarded computer manuals, diskettes, and scraps of paper with potential useful information such as a password, instructions on how to log in, changes to the company's computer system, and so on.

The obvious solution is to put a lock on your trash containers and dumpster. In the office, dispose of documents containing sensitive information in a locking trash container—with a slot on top—and have a trusted employee take it out to the dumpster.

Lock on garbage

Now, it's not likely that a hacker will go through your home garbage in hopes of uncovering information that he can use to break into your home office computer. But you should still be careful about what you throw away and how you dispose of it. I regularly throw away old checks, bank statements, credit card receipts, and such that could be revealing to a snoop or might be simply embarrassing if they were blown all over the neighborhood after a dog decided to go through the garbage looking for leftovers. For peace of mind, I tear up most of the personal stuff that I no longer need before throwing it away.

With individual privacy under assault everywhere you turn, I'm beginning to think that it might be smart to buy a shredder for my home use. In any case, I don't trust my neighbors. (I'm paranoid, which, I suppose, is what you would expect from someone whose main purpose in life is to write a book about computer security.)

Rogues' Gallery

> You can't steal second base and keep one foot on first.
>
> An unidentified 60-year-old junior executive
> *Who's Nobody in America,* 1981

In addition to hackers, there are other outsiders who might be interested in getting a look at what's in your computer or using your telephone system to make long-distance telephone calls at your expense.

Telephone Phreaks

Telephone phreaks specialize in plumbing the depths of telephone systems, especially telephone systems that give them a chance to make long-distance telephone calls on someone else's quarter. (When was the last time you only paid a dime for a telephone call?)

Freaky phones

The typical home computer user doesn't have much to fear from phone phreaks, of course, because there's not much they can do with a personal phone account. Still, some phreaks are adept enough to manipulate telephone switches and eavesdrop on your telephone calls. You might want to keep that in mind if you suspect that you might be a target of a dedicated eavesdropper. Also, if you have a long-distance telephone credit card, you should worry that someone will use it to ring up charges, perhaps sticking you with the bill.

Telephone companies have become increasingly alert to this sort of telephone fraud and they will often intercede on your behalf if they suspect there's a problem. You should know, however, that you are liable for calls made with your card.

Radio Shack radios

It's extraordinarily easy to listen in on cordless and cellular telephone calls using a $100 radio scanner purchased from any Radio Shack. Many hackers, phreaks, and other crooks listen to phone calls in order to intercept calls in which a person gives out a credit card number, a voice mail box account number, or other useful information such as the details of an upcoming vacation, which would be an opportune time to break into a person's home.

If you run a small business, you may be particularly vulnerable if you don't take adequate steps to close the loopholes to your private branch exchange (PBX, in other words) and voice-mail systems. Take a look at Chapter 4 for more details on how to keep hackers out of those systems.

If you have a long-distance credit card number, keep the number to yourself and don't give it out to anyone, especially someone who calls on the telephone and says that he's verifying the number of some such thing. When using your card in a phone booth at the train station or in the airport, stand in such a way that a person cannot look over your shoulder to see what you punch in. Shoulder surfing has become a popular pastime with phreaks and call-sell operators—people who sell the use of your long-distance calling card to others.

Telltale Telephone Troubles

Many attacks on computer systems begin with telephone fraud because telephone systems, which are basically little more than dedicated computer systems, are often easy to penetrate. If security on, say, a voice mail system is weak, it is often an indication that security is weak elsewhere. One way to keep hackers, phreaks, and other rogues out is to regularly scrutinize your telephone bills for signs of suspicious activities.

Chapter 4 covers the many facets of telephone fraud and what you can do to protect yourself.

It's Often a Matter of Intelligence

> When I realized that what I had turned out to be was a lousy, two-bit pool hustler and drunk, I wasn't depressed at all. I was glad to have a profession.
>
> Danny McGoorty (1901–1970)

Glasnost may have occasioned a thaw in East-West relations, but many of the spies who have come in from the cold are as busy as ever. Instead of spying on each other, however, foreign intelligence agencies are focusing on industrial espionage, with U.S. companies as one of the prime targets.

Foreign intelligence operators have turned to industrial espionage aimed at helping their domestic corporations better compete in a global marketplace. The FBI estimates that up to 20 foreign nations are actively engaged in industrial spying. Many of those countries such as Japan and France are U.S. allies.

The theft of information gleaned from computers and communications net- **Spies at work** works may be costing U.S. corporations billions of dollars per year. No one really knows for sure. There's no way to find out because information theft is difficult to detect, and companies that find out the hard way seldom publicly talk about it.

You're probably not too worried about foreign spies breaking into your home computer and stealing that valuable formula to a new soft drink that you've been developing. But if you are, you've come to the right place!

Competitive Intelligence Gatherers

Competitive intelligence (CI) operators, for a price, will gather information about a company or an industry, tailor-made for your interests. Partly because of the growth of computer networks, which makes it easier than ever before to collect information, CI is a booming business. CI operators usually can find out an awful lot just by digging through publicly accessible databases, newspapers, market research reports, and a wide variety of other sources.

However, there's no reason to believe that every CI operator is honest and would never resort to illegal or at least questionable practices to get a look at some of your bet-the-business information. Thus the lesson here is the same as it is everywhere else in this book: If you can't afford to lose it, take care of it.

Sorting Out the Cybermicrobes

> Give me health and a day and I will make the pomp of emperors ridiculous.
>
> Ralph Waldo Emerson
> "Nature" in *Nature: Addresses and Lectures,* 1849

There are all sorts of cybermicrobes—viruses, worms, Trojan horses, bombs (both logic and time)—that are capable of trashing your data faster than a New York minute. (I'm not sure just how fast that is, but people say it when they mean really fast.)

Computer viruses are proliferating exponentially—actually, their numbers double every eight months or so—and the chances of your personal computer being infected are greater than ever. One reason is that personal computers and networks also are multiplying rapidly, making it even easier for viruses to spread. Another reason is that virus creators are devising increasingly sophisticated "stealth" viruses that are more difficult to detect and difficult to eradicate once they have been discovered. Chapter 2 covers all you need to know about viruses.

 Ominously, new viruses increasingly are more insidious and more destructive than prior generations.

Natural and Unnatural Disasters

Master of disaster   As if stupid human tricks, disgruntled employees, various sorts of nefarious software, cyberpunks, and spies were not enough to worry about, there are all sorts of natural and unnatural disasters, too. There are earthquakes, hurricanes, floods, fires, power outages, and little Bobby Smith, your son's friend next door, who loves to come over and play games with your computer when you're not looking. Protecting yourself against natural and unnatural disasters is called disaster recovery planning, contingency planning, or business resumption planning, depending on who you talk to. Chapter 6 spells out all of the ways in which you can prepare yourself, and recover from, nearly every bad thing that comes your way.

More Tips for Keeping What's Yours, Yours

Insiders and outsiders often are put off by the basic knowledge that security procedures are in place and that you and other computer users are trained to be on the alert for weird happenings. Still you need to put in place access control mechanisms such as passwords to inhibit break-in attempts.

1. Taking such precautions as locking doors and properly disposing of documents, computer manuals, and other materials that may provide clues to the inner workings of your computer operations is an effective first line of defense.

2. If outsiders regularly access your computer, post an opening banner on the system that says something to the effect of: "This is my system and unless you've been invited by me, stay out." No, an opening banner is not really going to keep a hacker out of your system anymore than a "No Trespassing" sign will keep a racoon out of your corn field. But, if you ever expect to prosecute someone for breaking into your system, you're going to need some evidence that you posted a banner that indicates to intruders that they have crossed the line.

3. If you don't want someone to read files stored in your computer, encrypt them. Several free to inexpensive shareware programs are available that can be used to encrypt your files in such a way that it would take a dedicated team of scientists with a computer large enough to be called "Big Mama" to decipher them. Read Chapter 5 to find out everything you ever wanted to know about encryption.

4. Use a personal identification number or password that cannot be easily figured out. Chapter 3 goes into detail about how to choose hacker-proof passwords. When you use an ATM, shield your password from the people standing in line behind you and even from someone possibly sitting in a car in a parking lot with a pair of binoculars.

Okay, so there are all sorts of weird, malicious, and even cockamamie threats that you need to worry about. Since you can't protect all of your information, you need to decide what is most valuable and put all of your efforts into protecting that.

PUTTING A VALUE ON INFORMATION

> Tim was so learned, that he could name a Horse in nine Languages.
> So ignorant that he bought a Cow to ride on.
>
> Benjamin Franklin
> *Poor Richard's Almanack,* 1758

Have you ever thought of what you would do if your PC suddenly failed to operate or found that all of the information stored in it was trashed by a co-worker or a virus? Just for the moment, forget about the part where you scream and slash your wrists, and think about the real consequences.

Mom and Pop

When computers stop working, revenues stop, too. A study conducted by the University of Texas–Arlington a few years ago found that by the sixth day of a computer outage, a company's revenues drop by 25 percent. By the twenty-fifth day, revenues drop by 40 percent. Not many businesses can sustain losses like these for very long; in fact, most Mom and Pop operations and small-to-medium size companies will go under in only a matter of weeks.

What's It Worth to You?

> Wall Street Lays an Egg
>
> Sime Silverman
> News headline in *Variety,* following the October 1929 stock market crash

Many large companies put a value on information, and even though deciding what something is worth is pretty subjective, it helps them decide what they ought to protect and how much they ought to spend to protect it. If you run a company, even a small one, I suggest that you do the same.

Hardware is small part

It is easy to think about computer security as mainly having to do with protecting the hardware. That's a part of it, true enough, but a very small part when you consider that what's stored inside the computer is almost always worth far more than the hardware.

For example, a lot of time and effort went into researching, writing, editing, and producing this book. The publisher is going to make a fortune on it. I never would have dared to store the manuscript on my computers and not have bothered to make backups. In fact, at any given time, I had four sets of backups handy. (Okay, so I'm paranoid.)

What's it worth?

What about you? Could you afford to lose the report that is stored in your personal computer or in that laptop you bring back and forth between home and office? Your information is worth a lot—a lot more than you might think. And if it's worth a lot to you, how much do you think it might be worth to a competitor, a disgruntled employee, or a soon-to-be-former spouse who has just filed for a divorce? How much do you think an unscrupulous competitor would pay to get a look at marketing plans stored in your firm's computer system?

If you work for yourself and don't have any employees, you can probably skip what I'm about to tell you. It doesn't make much sense for an individual to set up an information protection program. You just need to keep in mind that the more something is worth to you, the more you should want to protect it. Thus you may not care about losing a letter that you sent to Eugenie while she was in summer camp, but you might care an awful lot about the data that you entered into a tax program or a household inventory for insurance purposes created in a database.

Info assets

Smart companies—no matter how small or how large—recognize that information—and not just the computers and other systems—is a strategic and competitive tool. At the same time, top executives at better run corporations also recognize that should company information fall into the wrong hands, the result may lead to lawsuits for failing to protect the privacy of company data, missed marketing opportunities, or even more disastrous consequences.

You Need To Know

The governing rule for access to information is the "need to know." Only those employees who need to know what the information is about should have access to it. That rule applies for virtually all corporate information, whether it is considered sensitive or not. However, even the information that is not considered sensitive should be safeguarded, if only to avoid the inconvenience of its loss or corruption.

One of the additional benefits of the need-to-know rule is that if data is deliberately tampered with, it helps narrow the field of likely culprits. Also, if the damage was caused accidently, knowing who caused it provides the opportunity to train the offender in proper procedures.

What Is Information?

> The craft of the merchant is this bringing a thing from where it abounds
> to where it is costly.
>
> > Ralph Waldo Emerson
> > "Wealth," *The Conduct of Life*, 1860

Information is an asset—one that organizations seldom properly value until the asset is stolen, trashed, or just plain lost. Imagine how much business you could do without such vital information as manufacturing procedures or sales and marketing strategies.

Information, of course, need not be limited to that which resides in a computer or on a computer printout. Your policy needs to define what information is, if not for your employees, in event that your company finds itself embroiled in a lawsuit of some kind. Courts often require that you show that you exercised due care in the handling of such critical information as tax and personnel records.

Not all information needs to be stored behind lock and key. Some information such as spec sheets and press releases are, in fact, intended to be made public. On the other hand, it makes a lot of sense to protect information related to a new product that the company is planning to launch. Somewhere between the two extremes is a level of security that is right for your firm.

The typical company needs to protect only about 5% to 10% of its data. In fact, protecting up to 80% of a company data would use up only 20% of a security budget; it is the final 20% of data that would be most costly to protect.

Protect the good stuff

Information Classification

Classifying information is often the first step in determining how much to allocate to information protection and how to apportion the budget. A lot of companies have developed information protection programs based on the military's model. There are four generally accepted classifications of information: secret, confidential, private, and unclassified. These classifications are defined as follows:

1. *Secret*—This classification is applied to an organization's most sensitive business information that is intended for use within the organization. Unauthorized release of this information would be severely detrimental to the company's plans and future, its stockholders, and its relationship with customers or suppliers.

2. *Confidential*—This classification is applied to an organization's less sensitive business information that is intended for use within the organization. Unauthorized release of this information would be detrimental to the company's plans and future, its stockholders, and its relationship with customers or

suppliers. Disclosing this information outside of a need to know or legal context could result in substantial harm to the company. Examples includes research and development information, manufacturing information, financial forecasts, marketing plans, patents and trade secrets sales, sales information, and cost data.

3. *Private*—This classification is applied to an organization's personal information for use within the organization. Unauthorized release of this information would have have an adverse and serious impact on the organization or its employees. This category applies to personnel information that if disclosed outside of a need to know or legal context could be seriously detrimental to individual employees or the company. This includes information covered by the government's privacy laws. Examples include employee medical records, personal history statements, personnel folders, performance reviews, salaries of individuals, and other information of personal nature provided to the company as a requirement of employment.

4. *Unclassified*—This classification is applied to all other information that does not fit within the preceding categories. This information is intended for use within an organization, but releasing it would not have a negative impact on the organization or its employees. Some organizations include a subset of this classification called "public" that is applied to information specifically intended to be released to the public.

My friend Harold Highland, who happens to be one of the foremost security experts in the world, told me that I should mention here that if you're concerned about protecting only your information, there are only two classifications that you need worry about. The first is "mine, and only mine," and the second "everyone else." Harold says that for the most part those are the only two that ever matter.

Who Is Responsible for Information?

> Pressed into service means pressed out of shape.
>
> Robert Frost
> "The Self Seeker," *North of Boston*, 1914

There's also a basic premise that the person who creates information owns it and is responsible for it. That responsibility includes:

- Designating who can and who cannot access the information.
- Determining what kind of access is allowed. For example, some employees may be allowed only to read the information, whereas others may be allowed to read, change, and even dispose of it.

- Protecting the information using whatever means are available to keep it from falling into the wrong hands.

- Classifying the information and making sure that the classification label is posted along with the information, whether it's on a computer screen or a piece of paper.

RISK ASSESSMENT TEST

Okay, so now you're convinced that you should care about computer security. But where do you start? You start by assessing your risk to hackers, viruses, fire, and myriad other threats. You'll quickly realize that you can't protect everything. You decide then what to protect by classifying what you have at risk. If the information is readily available to the public and is covered in one of the many handouts at a trade show, it's probably not valuable enough to expend valuable resources to protect it. However, a formula for a new paste wax that your company is developing may be worth quite a bit not only to your firm but to one of your unscrupulous competitors.   **Start here**

I devised this small test that you can use to decide what your level of risk is. It's real easy: If you answer "No" to any of the following questions, you flunk:

1. Do you have a backup tape or some other backup medium?

2. Do you back up every day?

3. Do you have a disaster recovery plan?

4. Do you use access control software or hardware?

5. Do you use a full complement of antivirus software on your PC or Mac?

6. Do you write-protect and label all your disks when they contain particularly valuable data?

7. Do you use passwords that are at least six alphanumeric characters long on networked systems and on your personal online accounts?

8. Do you change your password at least every three months?

9. If your system can be accessed remotely, do you use remote access control software or hardware?

10. Do you encrypt confidential information?

2 Viruses, Worms, and Other Rogue Code

Galileo, launched by NASA in October 1989, will be the first spacecraft in history to enter the atmosphere of an outer planet. Come December 7, 1995, Galileo will send a small probe plunging through Jupiter's turbulent and brilliantly colored cloud layers into the hot, dense atmosphere below.

Not everyone was as pleased as NASA to see the nuclear-powered probe up and away on its half-billion mile journey from Earth, however. In fact, an unidentified French programmer was so unhappy about the mission that he created a worm program and sent it coursing through the Internet only a few days after the launch. A worm is designed to travel along computer networks, slip inside computer systems, usually through software loopholes, and then deposit a payload. Sometimes its cargo is benign; sometimes it's not. Within hours, the worm had wriggled into 60 computer systems worldwide from the Riken Accelerator Facility in Japan to NASA's Goddard Space Flight Center in Greenbelt, Maryland. The rogue program didn't do any damage but computer users were greeted with the message "Worms Against Nuclear Killers" instead of the usual system greeting banner when they logged in the following morning.

A variety of artificial life forms can find their way into your computer, cause mischief, and even wipe your hard drive atomic-bomb clean. In this chapter, I'll tell you about all of these alien programs—not just worms, but viruses, Trojan horses, and bombs (which are both time and logic activated).

COMPUTER VIRUSES

> Thousands upon thousands of persons have studied disease. Almost no one has studied health.
>
> Adelle Davis
> *Let's Eat Right to Keep Fit*, 1954

Computer viruses are to PCs and Macintoshes what the Black Death was to millions of Europeans in the mid-1300s. Well, okay, so maybe that's an exaggeration—but it's only a little one. A computer virus can wipe out your hard drive in less time than it takes to read this sentence. Well, okay, so maybe that's an exaggeration, too—but only a little one.

You've probably heard the experts expounding on TV and in the press about computer viruses—usually about every 18 months when the latest scare, for example, the infamous Columbus Day and Michelangelo viruses, comes around. Maybe you've been wondering just what in the heck all the noise has been about. Or maybe you're having difficulty figuring out what's true and what's malarkey in all that you've heard about viruses.

The straight dope This chapter gives you the straight dope and at the same time probably tells you more than you ever wanted to know about computer viruses and then some. But believe me, it's for your own good. Here I'll focus only on the unique problems of viruses on standalone PCs and Macs. Chapter 4 takes a look at the many threats to networks and tells you about viruses on local area networks and the Internet.

It Can Happen to You

> Luck is what happens when preparation meets opportunity.
> Unknown

Don't make the mistake, as I did, of thinking that a virus is something that infects other people's computers. Sooner or later, you're going to find out that you are one of those other people. I got tagged by the CDEF—a Mac virus that fortunately is considered "benign" by those in the know because it doesn't do a whole heck of a lot beyond messing with the desktop file. In some quirky circumstances, it can trash files and crash your machine. (If you lose a valuable file or if your Mac crashes in the middle of a critical process, you'll think this so-called benign virus was spawned by the Lord of the Underworld himself.)

In addition to the files on my machine, files on several of my floppy disks were infected. Although it was time consuming to chase down each copy of CDEF, I easily got rid of it using Disinfectant, a freebie antivirus software utility.

Lucky break I was lucky. If it had been, say, the INIT-M or some other malicious Mac microbe that destroys files and folders, I would have been in a world of hurt. I seldom backed up anything in those days. If one of my files was trashed, as far as I knew it was carted off to the techno-landfill and buried forever. I eventually learned the hard way why one should regularly back up, but not before I lost really important stuff—twice—as a result of some really bizarre mishaps.

The Bug Is Born

In 1983, Fred Cohen was a student at the University of Southern California when he decided to construct what many experts now say is the first computer virus.

Fred told me that he created the virus to demonstrate the need for computer security. These days, no one knows for sure what motivates virus writers, but whatever it is, it must be as alluring as any pheromone.

At last count, in mid-1995, virus writers had whipped up some 6500 different kinds of PC viruses. The top virus sleuths say these nasty cyber-critters are being cranked out at the rate of two or three per day, often outpacing the ability of antivirus software vendors to keep up. **6500 viruses and climbing**

There are far, far fewer different types of Mac viruses on the loose—probably no more than 25. There are some good reasons for that, which I'll get into later in this chapter. That doesn't sound like many, I know, but one is all it takes to make your day.

Why Worry?

The prospect of your PC or Mac being infected by a virus is on the uptick—trust me on this. Aside from there being a heck of a lot of viruses in the wild, with so many computers being stitched into networks such as the Internet (actually a worldwide collection of networks), it's a lot easier for viruses to get around. Also, virus writers are concocting increasingly sophisticated viruses that are harder to detect and more difficult to stamp out when they're discovered. What's scary is that these viruses are more insidious and more destructive than earlier versions. That said, don't make yourself sick worrying about viruses. If you're careful and use the common-sense tips that I'll give you in this chapter, your PC will live a long, trouble-free, and virus-free life. **Scary**

WHAT IN THE HECK IS A VIRUS?

Okay, let's assume that you're sufficiently worried about these high-tech flu bugs, and you're prompted to ask, "What in the heck is a virus anyway?" Fred, the virus god, came up with this definition (and he ought to know what he's talking about): "A virus is a program that can infect other programs by modifying them to include a, possibly evolved, version of itself." What in blazes does that mean? Good question. Basically what Fred means is that viruses latch on to programs like leeches and replicate themselves like bunnies.

Any virus has three basic parts: a mechanism that permits it to go forth and multiply, a trigger that causes it to activate, and a payload—sometimes harmless, often not.

Send in the Clones

Viruses are not programs in the sense that they are able to do things on their own the way real programs do. Computer viruses work the same way as their biological counterparts. That flu bug you caught last month, for example, needed a host (the cells in your body) to thrive. Computer viruses also are like that. They need a host (a program) in order to do their thing.

Typically viruses clone themselves by preying on computer programs, which they use as launch pads to replicate themselves. Some viruses latch onto files ending in .EXE or .SYS; some viruses attack only files ending in .COM; some attack the area called the boot sector on a floppy or hard disk containing the PC's startup instructions; some viruses, called "multipartite viruses," attack both files and boot sectors.

Most viruses fall into one of two categories: those that infect files, latching onto them like parasites; and those that infect the boot sector of a hard disk.

File Infectors

Programs in IBM PCs and compatibles, which use either the MS-DOS or PC-DOS operating systems, are called executable files because that's what they do when they're opened (they execute). File-infecting viruses attach themselves to these executable files, and when the file executes, they go along for the ride. These files for the most part end with .COM or .EXE, although there are viruses that can infect executables that end with .DLL, .SYS, .OVL, .OVR, .PRG, or .MNU.

Boot Infectors

Boot sector viruses infect the area of a floppy or hard disk that contains the information the machine needs to boot or start up. Without a boot sector, what you've got on your hands is a brain-dead computer.

The boot sector is the first thing that loads into memory when the PC is turned on. A boot sector virus replaces a portion of the boot sector with its own code so it will load before DOS when the system is turned on. Usually these viruses load themselves into memory and infect other programs as they are called up. Boot sector viruses get into your system only if you boot from an infected floppy. I would have figured that not a lot of people boot from floppies these days, but I was looking at a list published by an IBM research lab of the fifteen most prevalent viruses, and you know what? They were all boot sector viruses.

Pulling the Trigger

The virus may activate as soon as the program is run or it may wait until a particular date such as March 6 (the trigger date of the infamous Michelangelo virus) or it may activate after a certain number of times a file is accessed or some other activity takes place. During the entire time before the virus delivers its payload, it is busily infecting every program that it comes in contact with.

Delivering the Payload

Okay, a file is infected. What happens next? It's pay dirt, payday, payback, and payload time. If all that viruses did was attach themselves to files, most people wouldn't care much and they'd go on to worry about more important matters. It's what happens when the virus drops its payload that gets everyone's attention.

"Ouch!" says Harold. The Jerusalem virus only attaches itself to a file and nothing else, but it does it over and over again, making the infected program swell like a pregnant lady's ankles at the end of a long walk. Eventually it fills the PC's memory and causes it to crash. Even leeching onto a file can sometimes be bad, but most of the time, it's the payload that is most worrisome.

Different viruses do different things. I'm sorry, I know that's not particularly profound, but it happens to be true. With so many viruses on the loose, there's just no way that I can tell you everything that viruses do. In general (he said, while taking a deep breath), the things that viruses do range from the relatively innocuous, such as displaying a message, to the catastrophic, such as wiping your hard disk clean of programs and data. **Weird things, man**

Here are a few viruses to give you an idea of what some of them do. The Cannabis, a poorly written virus, displays the message: "Hey man, I don't wanna work. I'm too stoned right now." The Ripper, a particularly mean-spirited virus, randomly trades pairs of numbers on an electronic spreadsheet. (Now you know why you haven't been able to get the family budget to balance.) The Friday the Thirteenth virus, which is also know as the Jerusalem, Israeli, PLO, or 1813 virus, displays black rectangles on the screen and erases programs that have been executed on any Friday the thirteenth.

> **By the way, although many viruses are designed to delete files or cause the PC to malfunction, the fact that these beasties can cause damage is not what makes them viruses. In fact, some computer viruses are intended to be harmless pranks—although they're seldom funny to those whose PCs happen to be infected.**

It's Going to Get Worse Before It Gets Better

Virus writers and antivirus software developers are locked in a version of *Mad Magazine's* Spy vs. Spy. Each time the guy in the black hat creates a virus, the guy in the white hat comes up with a way to defeat it. With each round, the viruses and the methods to detect and get rid of them become more and more clever. **Spy vs. Spy**

I'm going to get into the specifics of antivirus software in a minute, but I need to make this left turn and tell you quickly about a type of antivirus software called scanner so that you'll get a bigger kick in the pants from what I am about to tell you. Scanners are the most common type of antivirus software; that's why I mention that type in particular. Still with me? Good. Viruses have unique strings of code that can be used to identify each new virus in just the same way that you and I can be identified by our fingerprints and signatures. Scanners are designed to look for these signatures in viruses.

 Okay, so why is that relevant? Virus writers have concocted two particularly insidious types of viruses—both designed to evade detection by scanners— that are giving antivirus software developers a case of the willies. You're going to be seeing a lot more of these two types of commando-type viruses in the future, so you might as well know what you'll be up against.

Stealth viruses   The first is the stealth virus, which hides its tracks as it slinks along infecting one program after another. Remember I said that viruses latch onto programs and change their file sizes? One form of the virus intercepts attempts by antivirus programs to detect file-size changes and instead sends back to the scanner the original file size so it appears that the file is clean. Another type completely disables virus scanners so they don't work. Still another keeps a copy of the original boot sector as well as a corrupted boot sector containing the virus and directs attempts to read the corrupted boot sector to the area on the disk containing the original boot sector. What you don't see really can hurt you, eh?

Polymorphic viruses   The second of these viruses is the polymorphic virus, capable of camouflaging itself like a chameleon. One type, rather than make identical clones of itself, produces copies, each of which is slightly different. Another scrambles its code to make it more difficult to identify. Still another scatters decoying bits of code in different places in each copy, creating what amounts to a new identity. In all of these cases, virus scanners may be able to detect some, but not every, variation.

Ten Viruses, 95 Percent of the Problem

Earlier I said that the virus sleuths reckon that there are some 6500 viruses in existence and two or three are coming along every day. (See Appendix C, Notes from the Virus Front.) However, the basic rule of thumb is that the 10 most common viruses cause 95 percent of all infections.

In other words, it's the most prevalent ones that you should really worry about. Many of the viruses that are created are not "released into the wild," as the virus researchers say; others are not particularly efficient at propagating themselves, so your chances of encountering them are slim to none.

HOW ARE PCS INFECTED?

The single most frequent way that viruses get into PCs is on an infected floppy disk, but it's also possible to download a program with a virus attached from a bulletin board system or even one of the nationwide commercial online services.

What usually happens is that one of the programs on the disk has been infected. The disk is inserted into the PC, the infected program is open and voilà, the virus scampers off to infect whatever programs resides on the PC's hard disk drive. Stick a disk into an infected PC, and there's a good chance that the disk will be infected, too.

But—listen carefully now—even a blank disk can harbor a virus. Any disk that has been properly formatted contains an executable program in the boot sector. Where there's an executable program, there could be a virus.

Dangerous disks

Any floppy disk—no matter where it came from—should be looked at with an accusatory eye. I've seen viruses on commercial, shrink-wrapped software; on set-up and utility disks that come with modems, printers, and other add-ons; on demo disks from manufacturers; and on disks used by well-meaning fellow employees who shuttle work between home and office. If you're unsure where the disk came from, don't stick it in your machine. Or at least, protect your PC with the different kinds of antivirus software that I'll tell you about soon—I promise.

If your PC or Mac ever craps out and you need to have a repair technician take a look at it, the first thing that you should do when you get your machine back is check it to make sure that it is virus free. I don't know how many articles I have written about PCs being infected by technicians who use diagnostic disks that have been infected. The same goes for PCs that were used by a sales rep to demo a product. I've heard of many instances in which PCs were infected that way.

TELLTALE SIGNS

Virus writers want their creations to spread as widely as they can before they deliver their payloads. Ergo, your machine may be infected by a virus for quite some time before you actually notice that the rogue code has invaded your turf.

Let's say you're pounding the keyboard on your PC, trying to finish up an important project, when suddenly weird things start happening. Here are the telltale signs that a virus is playing footsie with your PC or Mac:

- The size of programs increases dramatically, and you didn't do anything to change them.
- The date or time stamp on files and programs changes, and it isn't what you expect.
- Programs take longer to load or longer to run than normal, or they simply stop working altogether.

- The hard or floppy disk drive starts to spin up although you haven't touched the keyboard for some time.

- You find you no longer have as much hard drive space or memory as you once had.

- You get unexpected error messages on the screen (at least more than the usual amount).

- Strange things start showing up on screen, such as a bouncing ping pong ball, a message that demands you free Eddie, Frodo, or some other person you've never heard of, or worse, you see a message such as, "Your hard drive is being formatted."

- You can no longer print.

- The computer reboots for no reason.

- The computer keeps crashing, and it has nothing to do with those mail-order memory chips that you just installed.

Basically, just a normal day at the PC right?

Keep an eye on your system

Keep a close eye on your system. Look for changes in the PC's configuration displayed in the startup screen. You can also use the MEM or MEMMAKER programs in recent vintage versions of DOS (5.0 and 6.0, in other words) or CHKDSK and PMAP and MAPMEM in earlier version of DOS to look at your memory configuration and disk space. Type DIR and take a look at the size of programs and files to see if they're about what you would expect. You don't even have to know what all the numbers mean, only that there's a big difference since the last time you checked.

Mac users can press the Option and I keys and "Get Info" on files, folders, and floppy and hard disks. Look at the file size and the date that the file was last modified. If you can't explain the change, it might (note, *might*) be a virus. If you really know what you're doing, you can use the ResEdit program to take a closer look at files to see if they have been tampered with. Personally I seldom touch ResEdit because it's easy to botch up a program.

SEARCH AND DESTROY

Four antidotes

The only way you can be sure if the problems you're having are being caused by a virus is to run antivirus software. You'll need to have these four virus antidotes in your kit bag: a scanner, file-change detector, virus-activity monitor, and disinfectant. Why? You want to be able to:

- Identify both known and unknown viruses.

- Stop them before they infect your PC.
- Get rid of those that manage to slip through the radar.

Most antivirus software being sold today offers a combination of these features. For example, some scanners detect and remove viruses and some file-change detectors also include virus-activity monitors. I use the terms scanner, file-change detector, and so on because they're easy to understand, but they're not universal.

Before I go any further, let me dispel any notion that you might have of using Microsoft Antivirus and VSafe, the utilities that are included in DOS 6. Even before the product hit the streets, virus writers were concocting all kinds of ways to defeat it. In every test that I've seen of MSAV, it has ranked at the bottom for accuracy and speed in detecting viruses. Folks, this is a rabid dog of a program and one you should steer clear of. Whew, I'm glad that I got that off my chest. I feel better now.

Different manufacturers have different names for the same software, usually because they sound more effective in advertisements. I mean, a "behavior blocker" really sounds like it does something important doesn't it? It's the same thing as a file-change detector.

Keep in mind that virus writers are getting smarter at coming up with ways to defeat antivirus software. Some viruses can cover their tracks to avoid detection by scanners and others are capable of defeating virus-activity monitors, for example. Having all of the available tools in your back pocket will help you stay a step ahead of the bad guys.

Some pretty smart virus hunters also will tell you to use two antivirus products, such as two scanners, to be doubly sure. I don't think it's such a great idea because the products eventually start tripping over each other. Say one scanner leaves a string of code in memory and the other scanner thinks it's a virus. The result is one false alarm after another until all you want to do is turn off the software and reach for the aspirin.

Scanning for Trouble

Scanners are designed to look in files, boot sectors, and other places where viruses are known to hide for strings of code or signatures that are unique to each virus. Some scanners can pick up on these signatures even if the file containing the virus has been compressed using PKLite or LZEXE, two popular shareware programs to compress and decompress files.

The advantage of scanners is that they are able to tell you exactly what virus has invaded your system, usually before the virus has a chance to deliver its payload.

The drawback is that if the virus is unknown, a scanner will not have in its library the unique bits of code it needs to run an ID. The other problem is that if the scanner has to check thousands of files against its database of thousands of virus signatures, it takes an annoying amount of time before you can actually get to work. Last, a scanner cannot readily detect polymorphic viruses because they are continually forging new signatures. To get around that, antivirus software sellers are working on scanners that use heuristics—an artificial intelligence of sorts—to help detect polymorphic viruses.

A lot of software these days is compressed in order to squeeze those fat programs onto skinny floppy disks. If the program is infected before it is compressed, a scanner may not detect it. Although I think it's always a good idea to scan new software before loading it on your PC, if it has been compressed, you'll have to do it again, after it has been decompressed.

Signatures Need Updates

All scanners are only as good as yesterday's virus

You also need to be able to keep on top of the new viruses as they come along. One way is to periodically download the signatures of new viruses as they are discovered. Antivirus software vendors routinely provide these signature updates as a service to their customers. The updates are usually released quarterly, although some companies such as McAfee Associates release them as often as every couple of weeks. They're either mailed to you if you have registered the software or, better yet, are available for downloading from the vendor's bulletin board system and from online services such as America Online, Compuserve, and Prodigy. Keeping up with the updates can be time consuming and in some cases costly, however.

Detecting File Changes

Looking for changes in file sizes

A file-change detector takes a snapshot of a file's contents using either the unique checksums or cyclic redundancy check characters contained in the file's code. The detector periodically checks to see whether the checksum or CRC has changed, indicating that a virus may have attached itself to the file.

A file-change detector scopes out the entire disk and checks either every program as it launches or just the files that you specify. You want the ability to exclude files that change frequently for legitimate reasons. Otherwise, what happens is that you'll be alerted all the time that something wacky is going on, requiring you to stop whatever you're doing and investigate. Before long, you start to ignore the warnings, and that's when the wolf shows up and eats your lamb.

The beauty of a file-change detector is that it can be used to ensnare unknown viruses. It's one of the very few weapons you have in your armory against unknown viruses, by the way.

Looking Out for Virus Mischief

Virus-activity monitors also act like watchdogs on the alert for the suspicious activity that would signal that a virus is on the grounds. These monitors "Terminate and Stay Resident" in memory, meaning that they sit in memory and check out files before they're run and alert you when executable files are modified, among other things. Most folks refer to them simply as TSRs.

TSR monitors are not all that effective against unknown viruses, so that's one problem with them. Also, because they reside in memory, they may be taking up space that would be better used by applications, and may even slow the system's performance. Worse, they can be outsmarted by a well-designed virus—such as a boot sector virus that kicks in before the TSR has had a chance to load. Like the file-change detectors, virus-activity monitors tend to set off false alarms at the drop of a hat. **Taking up space**

GETTING RID OF VIRUSES

Okay, despite all of your precautions, a virus somehow manages to wriggle into your PC and infect the bejeezus out of it. What now? Throw yourself on the floor, thrash about, scream, and have a good cry. You'll feel better. Next, get out the disinfectant and those backups.

You have backups, right? If not, you had better read Chapter 6 in which I go into all of the ecstasy of having backups and the agony of not having them. For now, it's worth mentioning that the best defense you can have against viruses and other forms of wacky and mean software is your backups. When all else fails, you'll need to erase any programs that have been infected and reload them using the backups. **Backup, backup**

To Disinfect or Not to Disinfect

There's some debate over whether or not you should attempt to disinfect files yourself. Viruses sometimes only partially infect programs, and at other times they damage applications so that they cannot be run at all. To do a good job of removing a virus, you must be able to restore infected files exactly as they were before they were infected. If you can't do that, the programs may not operate properly. Disinfecting programs vary in just how well they restore files. None does it entirely, anyway.

> **Personally, I think running a disinfectant has limited value. Okay, if the file contains info that I can't afford to lose and I don't have a backup for it, that's one thing. But I'll sleep better knowing that I got rid of the infected file completely and replaced it using the originals or backup disks.**

Harold, who really knows his viruses, wants me to mention here that some antivirus products remove only the first infection they find in a program. If the program has been infected by more than one virus, it won't be entirely bug free. He says if you choose to disinfect, do so with extreme care and caution. Once the job is done, scan the drive again, preferably using a different scanner.

What's in a Name? I'll Tell You

Nothing is standard

The Disk Ogre. Joshi. 4096. Jerusalem. These are names of some common viruses. Where do these names come from? They're named after the place where they're discovered; by the date they are set to trigger; by a line of code in the virus that suggests its intent; by the message it delivers; by what it does. Think of a reason, not even a very good one, and that's what's behind many names. Why am I bringing this up now? There is no standard naming convention. Thus when you're using antivirus software, the same virus may be given two different names by two different vendors. The risk is that you may find yourself trying to remove what you think is the Stoned virus, which requires one approach, and the Empire, which requires another. The result is irreparably trashed files.

If you decide to go ahead and do the disinfecting yourself, boot the system using a clean system disk, run the disinfectant, and remove the virus according to the directions (some antivirus programs do it automatically). You'll also have to give every one of your floppies the same treatment, or it won't be long before your machine is infected again.

You can repair the damage done by a boost sector virus by replacing the Master Boot Record on the hard drive using a backup or FDISK/MBR command (from DOS 5 and up), then using the SYS command to replace the DOS boot sector.

HOW TO BUY ANTIVIRUS SOFTWARE

I hate antivirus (AV) software. I can't think of a single product that I've tried—on PCs anyway—that worked as advertised. They take forever to check out the files on your hard drive; they set off false alarms for even the most trivial actions; they often require that you tweak the AUTOEXEC.BAT or CONFIG.SYS file or make some other configuration changes and that, in turn, inevitably causes something else to go awry. That said, using them is the lesser of two evils.

When selecting a package, make sure you choose one that has the following basic features: scanning capabilities for detection of known viruses; a TSR that continuously monitors not only for known virus signatures, but also for virus-like activity; a file-change detector that alerts you when files change; and disinfecting abilities to remove a virus and then help to repair or recover from the attack.

Harold says that AV products that warn you every time files change are so annoying that most people turn them off after about a week. He's got a point. However, I like the option of deciding when to turn it on and off. If I'm loading a new program, formatting a disk or doing something else that might be mistaken for a virus at work, I turn it off. **They're annoying**

The software should be easy to set up and use. It's gotta be a passably efficient memory user. TSRs occupy memory, and memory being what it is (never enough), I look for small, compact code.

I want the option of scanning on demand or according to a schedule that I determine. Scanning must be reasonably fast and be done in the background so that I can get right to work.

Since I have to regularly update the scanner's signatures, the software seller has to make that easy for me. The vendor ought to at least have a BBS or a forum on one of the popular commercial online services where these updates are posted. How often they post these updates is a key concern, too. At the rate at which viruses are being introduced, vendors should release their updates at least quarterly and whenever there is a sudden outbreak of a new type of virus.

Also, I don't want to pay much, if at all, for signature updates. Some companies give them to you for free; others punch holes in the bottom of your pockets.

Take a look at how the checksums are stored when deciding on a file-change detector. Some detectors create a checksum for every program, which tends to take up disk space. Better that they should store the checksums in a single file. The added benefit is that you can store this file on a disk and pull it out if the hard disk is impaired and you need to rebuild your information.

A FEW MORE WORDS ABOUT MACS

Up till now, we've been talking mainly about viruses that infect IBM PCs and compatibles. The overwhelming majority of viruses are of that type.

Thus far, most of the known Macintosh viruses do not seem designed to cause much damage, at least not intentionally. Mac viruses, even benign ones, can be disruptive, however, because they may inadvertently crash computers or trash files. The fact that viruses take up hard disk space and memory is in itself good enough reason to stamp them out.

The total number of Mac viruses is about 25. One reason that there are so few in comparison to PC viruses is that there are fewer Macs in use, making them a smaller target for virus writers. Another reason is that writing Mac viruses is more difficult. Still another reason is that the Mac community has been vigilant about keeping viruses in check. Whenever a new Mac virus is discovered, an informal **Virus vigilantes** group of virus vigilantes hops on the Internet and starts chasing after the virus perps. That's how the writers of the MBDF virus were nabbed and prosecuted.

Free and good   The most compelling reason of all, however, is that there are two very good antivirus programs for the Mac—Disinfectant and Gatekeeper—and they are free.

Disinfectant

Disinfectant consists of an INIT and an application. The INIT is constantly on the lookout for viruses. The application can be used to scan and remove the infection if one slips through.

The latest version of Disinfectant is 3.6. That's the one you should have or an even more recent one if a new version has come out since this book hit the shelves. A variation of the nVIR B virus was designed to circumvent earlier versions of Disinfectant (other commercial antivirus software programs will spot it, however). nVIR B infects the Mac operating system and programs and causes the Mac to beep incessantly or, if you have MacInTalk installed, to say "Don't Panic."

Disinfectant identifies all known viruses except the Dukakis, Three Tunes, and MerryXmas viruses, which were designed to infect only HyperCard stacks. When able, Disinfectant also repairs infected files. Note that it recognizes known but not unknown viruses. Ergo, using Disinfectant is not bulletproof protection against being infected. The author, John Norstad at Northwestern University, has been very good about updating the program when new viruses come along, but you have to get a new copy of Disinfectant each time that happens.

If you have a program such as Fetch or Anarchie, you can pick up a copy of Disinfectant at its official site by FTP: //ftp.acns.nwu.edu/pub/disinfectant/. New versions also are posted to CompuServe, GEnie, America Online, Delphi, BIX, and sumex-aim.stanford.edu, among other places.

Gatekeeper

The other popular freeware program for the Mac is Gatekeeper. If fear of the unknown is what concerns you most, you'll want to use it because it keeps an eye out for suspicious viruslike behavior. Unlike the Disinfectant INIT, Gatekeeper helps to ward off unknown viruses because it is an integrity checker.

Gatekeeper is not updated as regularly as it once was. The author, Chris Johnson at the University of Austin, says he can't find time to keep up with the steady pace of change in the Mac operating system. In any case, he says there have not been any new releases of viruses since the last official release of Gatekeeper 1.3 in 1993. Gatekeeper still protects against new viruses by

keeping an eye out for viruslike behavior. If you decide to include Gatekeeper in your tool kit—and you should if you can't afford to buy commercial software—you'll be warned by a message that constantly pops up indicating that the version you're using may be obsolete. To lose the message permanently, get out your copy of ResEdit and do the following:

1. Make a copy of Gatekeeper to work on; keep your original in a safe place.
2. Launch ResEdit.
3. Navigate to the disk and folder containing Gatekeeper.
4. Select the resource type INIT and open it.
5. Open ID #1.
6. Scroll down to the line that reads: 0008E8 3380 B0AE FEDE 6200
7. Change the 6200 to 6000.
8. Save the file.
9. Quit ResEdit.

TIPS FOR WARDING OFF CYBERMICROBES

Up-to-date signatures

Use antivirus software that scans, detects changes in files, and monitors for viruslike activity. Make sure that you use a scanner with up-to-date signatures. Run the scanner whenever you suspect a problem, load new software, or insert disks of questionable origin. Don't circumvent the antivirus software's system of checks and balance or turn off its features to save time when you boot up.

Watch the shareware

Be wary of shareware and other software that has been downloaded from bulletin board systems (BBSs) because you can't be sure that they're clean. And stay away from pirated software. Aside from the fact that using it violates someone's copyright, you have no idea where the software really came from.

Write-protect your disks so that there's no way a virus can attach itself to a program on the disk. Store the disks in a secure place when they're not being used. It's still worthwhile checking these disks from time to time. Someone may have removed the write-protect tab, or the disk may have become infected before the tab was put on.

Write-protect documents, directories, and operating system files. If a virus tries to modify a file, it will trigger an error message alerting you that something might be awry. Use ATTRIB to make all of your .EXE and .COM files read only. This protects you from many poorly written viruses. *Caution:* Some programs do not work in the read-only mode.

Track it back

If you manage to spot a virus before it causes damage, try to trace it back to its source and close that entry point. That's not always possible, of course, because many viruses will have been lurking undetected for months. But, if it turns out that the infected disk came from your next door neighbor or the guy in the next cubicle at work, you'll know that he should be treated like the low-life scum he really is. (Okay, so he's a nice guy; just don't let him near your machine, that's all.)

 Consider the prospect that the antivirus software itself has been infected. Some viruses specifically target antivirus software (after all, they're programs too), and some virus creators think it's funny to upload to BBSs copies of an antivirus shareware in which they have embedded a virus. Top-shelf antivirus software will do a self-check for viruses. If yours does not, get one that does, Harold and I say.

Although it helps to purchase software only from a reputable vendor, that is by no means a guarantee of getting a virus-free disk. Microsoft, Aldus, Novell, and countless other companies have distributed shrink-wrapped software that was infected by a virus. (It often happens while the disks are being duplicated at an outside disk-duplicating service.)

Never copy software from other computers, because you don't know where that software may have come from.

Scan before backing up   You run the risk of backing up a virus at the same time you're backing up everything else. If the backups are infected (and it happens a lot), you're outta luck and maybe outta business. To be safe, do a full scan of the hard disk right before every backup to make certain that your backups are virus free.

If you run a small company, do what big companies and universities do: Set aside a PC solely for examining newly purchased software and disks brought in by visitors, employees, or students.

WORMS, TROJAN HORSES, AND LOGIC AND TIME BOMBS

Viruses are not the only sort of malicious software that you have to worry about. Fortunately the other forms of cybercritters are relatively rare, and you'll only run into one on a really rotten day.

Trojan Horses

You know the story about the mythical Trojan horse, right? There's a type of malicious software called a Trojan horse that ostensibly is useful but also contains hidden functions such as a virus, a trapdoor that permits intruders to enter a system, or a time or logic bomb that causes damage when triggered. The most famous, if you can call it that, was the "AIDS Information Introductory Disk, Version 2.0" that was distributed free with copies of a U.K. computer magazine.

That program was designed purportedly to help a person evaluate his or her susceptibility to being infected by the AIDS virus. It did that, but it also contained a virus that in some cases destroyed data and programs; in other instances, it altered filenames and shifted them into hidden subdirectories. The Trojan horse was activated randomly after it had been installed on the user's hard disk drive.

If you have the unlucky happenstance to plug a Trojan horse into your PC or Mac, there's no telling what will happen and there's no telling just what you should do about it. If the Trojan is carrying a virus, you should be able to detect and remove it using any of the popular antivirus programs on the market. However, the Trojan may do something else such as lock or scramble files unless you register the program or send money or something else. In many cases, Trojans do their damage the minute they are run, so you may not have much opportunity to react. What you may have to do is erase a few programs and reload them from your backups. (That's what the backups are for, Bunky.) Luckily, you don't see many Trojan horses on the loose.

Instant carnage

Worms

A worm is yet another type of potential nasty cybercritter, but you already knew that, didn't you? Worms differ from viruses in at least one significant regard: They're living, breathing programs that don't need other programs to help them deliver their payloads. They tend to travel networks, like the Internet, and are sophisticated enough to try different password combinations and to look for loopholes in programs that are running on the targeted system. They don't infect other programs, although they may carry a virus that does. You don't see a lot of worms in the wild, and if your PC is not connected to a network, it's not likely that you ever will.

The most notorious worm is the Internet worm, released back in November 1988 by Robert T. Morris. The then–Cornell computer science grad student created the worm, he said at his trial, as an experiment. He intended to deposit one copy of the worm in each system into which the worm was able to wriggle. However, as a result of a programming error, the worm replicated itself wildly until it clogged the memories of computers that it had attacked, causing them to shut down.

There's no standard "this is what you should do to get rid of a worm." In the case of the Internet worm, the solution simply was to turn off the machine and disconnect it from the network to keep it from returning.

Harold accuses me of being overly simplistic here. He says that I should also mention that no one has written a worm that will target PCs, although it can be done. When worms get to be a problem on PCs and Macs, I'll come back here and tell you all about it. That should keep Harold happy.

Logic and Time Bombs

Here's a true story. A programmer created a customized database under contract for a small importing company. Sometime during the project, the programmer began to suspect that he wasn't going to get paid for his work, so he planted a set of instructions that, when activated, would wipe out his program. Evidently the importing company was not satisfied with the work and refused to pay the programmer the entire amount that had been agreed upon. One day, the programmer telephoned the company and under the pretense of making some final adjustments to the program, directed one of the employees to activate his hidden instructions. In a matter of minutes, the custom database program and all of the company's data that had been laboriously entered into it was wiped clean. The programmer had planted a logic bomb, one designed to activate under a precise set of circumstances.

The logic of bombs   A logic bomb monitors the system's activity, and when a defined event takes place—such as your opening a particular file x number of times—it detonates. Most often, it causes damage, but not necessarily. A time bomb is a variation of the logic bomb—the difference is that it detonates at a certain time or date. There may not be a lot you can do to stop a logic or time bomb from being planted in your system. They're seldom easy to detect, for one thing.

YOU PROBABLY WANT TO ASK . . .

It is better to ask some of the questions than to know all of the answers.

James Thurber
"The Scotty Who Knew Too Much," *Fables for Our Time,* 1940

Can a PC Virus Infect a Mac?

PC viruses infect PCs, and Mac viruses infect Macs. PC viruses, however, cannot infect Macs. It's not impossible, but it's not likely that someone will bother to write such a virus. If you run a DOS program on a Mac in emulation mode, however, the virus may be executed. What happens then is that the virus will try to infect programs, but it probably won't get very far because the operating systems are incompatible.

Can DOS Viruses Run on Windows PCs?

Most of the DOS viruses can't run under Windows because they aren't compatible with the memory management in Windows. However, most of the current viruses will damage Windows-based applications if they try to infect them. The application stops working, a major tip-off to you that something has bollixed up the works. In nearly every case, you'll have to delete the program and reinstall it.

What About Viruses on OS/2 and Windows 95 PCs?

There aren't any viruses (yet) that specifically target applications running under OS/2 or Windows 95, the two emerging 32-bit operating systems. That doesn't mean if you're running either of those two operating systems that you'll be safe from virus attacks.

Existing DOS viruses are not likely to spread on OS/2 and NT machines. However, try booting one of these machines with an infected disk, and a boot sector virus will infect the hard disk. What happens after a few starts and shutdowns is that the boot sector becomes damaged and the machine no longer starts up. The way to remove the damage is to do a reinstallation with the setup disks.

OS/2 can run DOS programs, including any that have been infected by viruses. If a virus targets, say, .EXE files, like the Sunday virus, it's not going to know whether that file is a DOS or an OS/2 program. (It ain't gonna care either.)

Of course, it's only a matter of time before OS/2- and Windows 95-specific viruses turn up—they'll eventually prove seductive to virus writers.

If you decide to upgrade to Windows 95 and your machine is already infected with Anti-exe, Stoned, Monkey, or several of the other more prevalent viruses, good luck. You'll get an error message when you insert the second of Win95's 13 disks indicating that something is amiss. The viruses attempt to install themselves on the second disk and in the process ruin the disk. There's no getting around it; you'll have to replace the disk. Microsoft has set up a special hotline (800-207-7766) for buyers who need a replacement disk.

The obvious thing to do is scan your PC for viruses before trying to upgrade to Win95. You can also slide open the little window in the upper left-hand corner of the disk, called the "write-protect tab," and that will prevent the virus from insinuating itself on the disk. In fact, it's always good practice to open that little write-protect tab whenever you load new software on your machine, not only to hinder viruses but simply to guard against accidently erasing the disk. Not every program will allow you to install software with the write-protect tab open, however, because the program may need to write to the disk during installation.

Of course, you always make backup copies of all your new software, right? Yeah, I bet. I can't blame you for not wanting to jump right in and load that new software without stopping to make backups. And geez, Win95 comes on 13 disks: who's got time to make backups, or even has 13 disks lying around to use? Well, if you think making backups is a drag, try getting through to any company's technical support line—then you'll really know what a drag is. Trust me, make the backups. It will save you lots of time and long-distance telephone calls in the event you have trouble.

Oh, you won't have this problem if you load Win95 from a CD-ROM. Once data has been stored on a CD-ROM, nothing can alter it short of cooking it in a frying pan.

If and when you upgrade to Windows 95, you'll also need to upgrade your antivirus software because it will not work with Win95. The reason is that existing antivirus Windows programs scan for something called Interrupt 21, a sort of doorway in DOS through which new files must pass. Win95 is a replacement for DOS, hence there is no Interrupt 21. Antivirus software programs designed for Windows and DOS are not going to be able to find viruses.

What, No UNIX Viruses?

Virus writers have not bothered creating viruses that attack UNIX workstations, servers, and mainframes. Again, it's not impossible to write such a virus, but it just hasn't been all that appealing thus far. In fact, the Internet worm had sufficient virus qualities that it would be easy to argue that it was, in fact, a virus and not a worm. The virus would have to be reasonably complex to be able to circumvent the access controls common to UNIX machines and mainframes. Like I said, it ain't impossible, but it would take a very motivated (and talented) virus writer to pull it off successfully.

Fortress   I managed to find one company that actually makes an antivirus package for UNIX machines. The product is called Fortress, and the company is Los Altos Technologies Inc., 2111 Grant Rd., Los Altos, CA 94024; (800) 999-UNIX.

ANTIVIRUS SOFTWARE SELLERS AND FREEBIES

I originally thought that it would be useful for you if I were to list all of the available antivirus software and tell you want each one does. But the software scene is changing so fast that I'm reluctant to tell you much about the specific features of each antivirus program. That information will be outdated in only a few months, especially if you're running Windows 95. Instead, I list the companies producing the most popular commercial software, shareware, and freeware and some product names in Appendix A at the back of the book. You'll also find some information sources that will come in handy if your machine is hit with a virus and you're uncertain as to how to proceed.

Freeware is also available for the Macintosh, and if you have access to the Internet, commercial online services, or bulletin board systems, the software is easy to find. (If you don't have some way of getting online, get it—you'll want to have ready access to signature updates and to find out about new viruses that may be particularly bothersome.)

At the same time, I'm going to give you a piece of advice that will carry you through all your years: Shop around. The price of antivirus software runs from nothing to more than $100. With the basic guidelines that I've already given you about what to look for in software and by reading a few of the reviews in the top computer magazines, you'll be able to take care of yourself. That's a promise.

3 Safe Desktops and Laptops

Experience is a good teacher, but she sends in terrific bills.

Minna Antrium
Naked Truth and Veiled Allusions, 1902

I have a friend who works for a privately owned company with revenues of several millions of dollars a year. My friend keeps the books and handles other financial affairs for the company. If you were to look over her shoulder while she worked, you would be privy to the company's most valuable secrets, including its financial data, the names of its customers, bank account numbers, and more. Not only that, you could generate checks and authorize the transfer of thousands of dollars into your own Swiss bank account if you were so inclined.

Do you want to know what my friend's password is? B. Yep, B. How long do you think it would take someone to crack that? I'd guess a nanosecond, give or take a couple bajillionths of a second.

This kind of revelation really makes my brain swell. My friend should have never told me her password (Underground Guide to Computer Security Tip Number 8), even though she trusts that I'm not going to crack her company's system and cook the books.

I asked her why the company permitted such laughably insecure passwords. She replied that no one in her company knows any better and the employees were merely using the passwords set up by an outside computer contractor. If I were the owner of this business, I would horsewhip the contractor with the biggest horse I could find and then fire him. Thousands of dollars and the livelihood of many employees ride on this company's computer system, yet the only thing standing between that and financial ruin is a one-character password. Ouch!

CONTROLLING ACCESS TO COMPUTER SYSTEMS

Thou shalt not steal.

Exodus 20:15

There are lots of reasons that you might want to set limits on who can use your PC and what they can and can't do once they've been given access. On my home machine, I don't want my kids reconfiguring my business programs or inadvertently trashing my files. Should a thief make off with my computer, I don't want the scoundrel to also have the audacity to read the woeful checking account balance that I usually maintain in Quicken.

Nobody's business but my own
On my office machine, I don't want my co-workers to look at anything on my computer. It's not that I don't trust them, but I don't want anyone going through my computer files any more than I want them to rifle the drawers of my desk. Everything that my co-workers need to see is on the server, which is public. The rest, frankly, ain't none of their business. Of course, the company probably doesn't see it that way—it's their PC, after all. But I likes my privacy as much as I likes my security.

The main aim of desktop security is to allow authorized people (you and anyone else you decide can use your computer) to do what they're supposed to do and to stop everything else. The experts call that access control. The main reasons that you want access control are:

1. To protect the confidentiality of business information such as secret recipes for fried chicken coating and computer-aided designs of a bomb sight that you hope the military will buy from you.

2. To protect the privacy of personal information such as employee evaluations, medical records, and family finances.

3. To protect the integrity of your information to ensure that no one can willy nilly change numbers in the massive spreadsheet that has become your life's work.

4. To protect the availability of information so that it's there when you want it and not in the electronic dumpster where you'll never see it again.

Access control also extends to putting limits on the specific applications you can use and the files you can read, write to, copy, and even delete once you're on the system. Without those controls, an unauthorized person can use your machine, and an authorized person can use your machine improperly. (Is that heavy or what?)

The trick is to allow you or anyone else you designate to use your system enough freedom to work productively but at the same time make some reasonable attempt to protect your company's data. If the guidelines are overly stringent, they'll inhibit you from doing whatever it is that you bought the computer to do in the first place. On the other hand, if they're too loose, some rascal is going to steal data or tamper with your PC in other ways.

Simple Is as Simple Does

The first line of defense is to put your computer behind a locked door when you're not there to look after it. The second line of defense is to make sure that no one uses or steals your machine in the event that the door is left unlocked or the locked is picked. Not enough people have what I call "the watchdog and guard in the tower" mentality. There's nothing sophisticated about it—it's only nuts and bolts. I cover a lot of physical security issues in Chapter 6, but in this chapter, I'm going to give you some additional physical security tips to help you hang onto your portable computer at home and while on the road.

> **Here's a security tip that will cost nothing yet provide you with as much security as posting an armed guard at your front door. You see that little keylock on the front of your PC? Go find the key that came with the PC, stick it in the keylock, and turn it to the right. Got that? That lock may not look like much, but it's quite effective for keeping snoops and schnooks out of your machine.**

Defense, defense

IDENTIFICATION AND AUTHENTICATION

I have had just about all I can take of myself.

S. N. Behrman, on reaching the age of 75

In this chapter, I'll tell you all you need to know about creating and using passwords as well as the primary ways in which you can control exactly who can access your system and the sorts of things they can and cannot do once they get on. I'll cover the basics of protecting both standalone desktop and portable PCs. Additional security measures that you can take when your computers are stitched together in networks are covered in Chapter 4.

If you have used an ATM, you know that after you insert your card, you must enter a personal identification number, or PIN. The card contains information that identifies who you are by your name and bank account number, and the PIN confirms that you are who you say you are because it is a password that supposedly only you know.

That two-step process is called identification and authentication and is fundamental to logging in to any computer system that has access control. Assuming that you've properly entered your userID and password, the door to your computer clicks open.

Knock, Knock

> I have a new philosophy. I'm only going to dread one day at a time.
>
> Charles Schulz

Who's there? How does a PC's access control system know you are who you say you are when you come knocking on the security door? Well, after identifying yourself, you can authenticate yourself in three ways:

1. Enter into the computer something you know, such as a password.

2. Use something you have such as a card with a magnetic stripe.

3. Use something that is unique to you, such as a fingerprint.

A number of factors Using one of these methods—like keying in a password—is called a one-factor security system. Using two of these methods is called a two-factor security system. You see where we're going with this, right? Using an ATM card is a two-factor security system. You own the ATM card (one factor), you stick it into a money machine and enter a personal identification number (two factors).

The more, the merrier Your passport is a three-factor security system. Can you figure out what the three factors are? Factor one is the passport itself. Factor two is your signature. Factor three is your photograph. Think about it.

Of course, one-factor systems are not as secure as two-factor systems, and two-factor systems are not as secure as three-factor systems. Most security systems in use today are one-factor systems based on using passwords, but we're slowly inching toward two-factor security systems because of the added protection that these systems offer.

THE LAST WORD ON PASSWORDS

> A thing worth having is a thing worth cheating for.
>
> W. C. Fields (1880–1946)

Say the magic word . . . Using passwords is the most common way of authenticating yourself to a computer. The idea is that if you know the secret password for an account, you must be the rightful user of that account.

The problem is, however, that even well-composed passwords are vulnerable to being cracked or intercepted by today's more sophisticated system attackers. Let's look at the primary ways of compromising passwords and how to defend yourself against these attacks. Some of these techniques only apply if your computer is attached to a network that you log in to, however.

Easy to Remember, Easy to Crack

> We do on stage things that are supposed to happen off. Which is a kind of integrity, if you look on every exit as being an entrance somewhere else.
>
> Tom Stoppard
> *Rosencrantz and Guildenstern Are Dead,* 1967, Act 1

Most people create passwords that are easy for them to remember. That's a natural thing to do—natural, but dumb, as you'll see. They'll use ALEX, PAM, or similar nicknames. They'll use LOVE, AMA (Latin for "love"), or something else they think is cute. They'll use SEX, the F word, or something else they think is mischievous.

You know what? Hackers—and just about any Jack and Jill with common sense—know that people are apt to use common words like these as passwords. They know, for example, that if your name is ELIZABETH, there's a good chance that you'll use LIZ as a password. Why do you think that breaking into computers is so easy that a hormonally challenged, teenage hacker or that dullard Bob in the office across the hall from you can do it within mere minutes?

Then there is that group of people who think that passwords are a waste of time, so they'll use a single character as a password—you would be surprised how often people use a carriage return for a password!

Look, if you're using your nickname, the name of your favorite pet, ABC, 123, or PASSWORD as your password, you must change it. Later in this chapter, I'll give you some tips on creating passwords that are virtually hacker-proof, yet are easy to remember.

Time for a change

I Spy

> You observe a lot by watching.
>
> Yogi Berra, on his qualifications to be a coach

One of the easiest ways that someone might discover your password is by watching you log on and then repeating the same steps. That's certainly one of the most common ways in which passwords are compromised in offices. One of your co-workers will watch you enter a password—you may not even mind that they're looking over your shoulder as you key it in.

Private eyes are watching you . . .

> **Some thieves have taken to sitting in parked cars outside of ATMs and using binoculars to watch patrons withdraw money from their accounts. You walk out of the ATM, they rob you of your cash and take off. Soon after, they'll use your card to get whatever is left in your bank account. Talk about adding insult to injury!**

The solution is obvious: Don't permit anyone to watch you as you log on to your account, any more than you would let a stranger look over your shoulder when you enter your PIN into an ATM machine.

ATM Security Tips

Since I brought the subject up about getting robbed at ATMs, I'll give you a few quick tips on how to take care of yourself:

- Use ATMs only in well-lighted and well-traveled areas.
- If you see someone hanging around, split or use the ATM service telephone to call for assistance.
- Stand so that someone behind you cannot see your PIN as you enter it.
- Withdraw your cash, count your cash quickly, and pocket it.
- Fill in your deposit slip before you go to the machine to avoid having to do it at the machine itself.
- When possible, ask a friend to accompany you.

Okay, back to passwords.

Share and Share Alike

> Gifts are like hooks.
>
> Martial (40?–102?)

Some of the most serious computer crimes have come about because employees shared their passwords with each other. If you work in an office, you probably know some of the passwords of fellow employees. It happens all the time. Before Bob goes on vacation for two weeks, he gives Alice his password so that she can access his e-mail or handle some of his chores while he's snorkeling down in the Caymans.

 Other times, an employee who has shared his password with fellow workers, leaves the company, but the employees keep right on using his password because the system administrator neglects to close the access.

Shocking story   Only a few weeks before I started work on the chapter, for example, a convicted child rapist, working at Newton-Wellesley Hospital in Massachusetts, allegedly used a former employee's computer password to rifle through nearly 1000 confidential files of patients for telephone numbers. He used those numbers to make obscene phone calls to girls. The shocking story made the front page of the *Boston Globe*.

Often, employees share their passwords without even being aware of it. It's quite common for employees to write down their passwords and post them where anyone can see them. Here's another true story. The Government Accounting Office found that computer security at the Drug Enforcement Agency was amazingly lax, especially given the law enforcement mission of the DEA. It seems that DEA employees were routinely writing down their passwords on Post-it notes and sticking them on the front of their computer monitors. Employees were rummaging through computer files and even checking to see whether friends, former boyfriends/girlfriends, and relatives had ever been a target of investigation.

> **Don't share you password with anyone and don't write it down and post it where anyone can see it. If you're a system administrator, don't forget to shut down the accounts of employees when they leave the company.**

Crackerjack Password Programs

> Genius, that power which dazzles mortal eyes,
> Is oft but perseverance in disguise
>
> > Henry Willard Austin (1858–1912)
> > *Perseverance Conquers All*

You could sit at a computer and try every word that comes to mind and you might hit on someone's password. It might take you a few years, but you could probably find one eventually, especially in companies where employees use one-character passwords. But why bother? Let the computer do it for you.

The most popular (with hackers, anyway) password-cracking programs contain minidictionaries of words that are commonly used as passwords, and they'll throw these words at a system one at a time until one of them matches up with a real password. CrackerJack, for MS-DOS machines, and Crack, for UNIX systems, are two such programs that are widely available on the Internet and underground computer bulletin boards.

Pocket dictionary

This is called a dictionary attack, as you might have guessed. Your key defense is to not use any word that might be found in a dictionary and instead use a random series of characters, numbers, symbols, and so on. You're not going to find a password like B1ToP@Hp in any dictionary!

Brute Force Attack

> Ya gotta do what ya gotta do.
>
> > Sylvester Stallone
> > *Rocky IV*, 1985

Program a computer to try every letter in the alphabet starting with A, and then every two-letter combination starting with AA, and then every three-letter combination starting with AAA and so on, and eventually a word will line up like tumblers in a combination lock and the door will click open. That's called a brute force attack.

What about time?   It takes seconds to crack a one-character password, minutes to crack a two-character password, and hours to crack a three-character password. The time it takes depends on speed of the computer being used to do the job, of course. A Pentium isn't going to waste much time cranking though every three-letter combination, and a supercomputer will do it in less time that it takes to stifle a yawn.

Brute force attacks work well, but only up to a point. As soon as you start using four, five, and more characters for passwords, it takes days, weeks, months, and even years to crack them. Moral: Longer passwords are inherently more secure than short passwords.

Three strikes and you're out   Also, don't permit an attacker to hammer repeatedly at your system's door. Install an access control package that will lock out someone if he or she fails to enter the correct password after three attempts. Most of these access control programs also maintain an activity log and will alert you if someone has tried to use your machine.

Password Grabbers

There are a few ways for someone to snag your password, either when you log in or transmit the password over a network. The basic approach to this attack is for an insider to load a phony log-in program onto your machine when you're not looking and for either an insider or outsider with access to your LAN to "sniff" the passwords as they travel across the network.

Beware of Geeks Bearing Gifts

When I was a kid, the story of the Trojan horse was one of my favorites. The Greeks had been laying siege to Troy for several years, and it finally occurred to them that there had to be a better way to get inside the walled city. They decided to build a great big wooden horse, put some well-armed men inside of it, and pull it up to the gates. The Trojans, who were evidently not too bright, dragged the horse into the city, thinking that it was a gift. That night, the Greeks sneaked out of the horse and slaughtered everyone in their sleep (well, maybe they didn't kill everybody, but when you're a little kid, it makes for a more exciting story).

Rude awakening   There's a password-cracking program that, like the Trojan horse, seems to be one thing but is really something else (usually sinister). It works like this. The attacker plants a program that acts just like your regular log-in program. You enter your userID and password, but instead of getting access, the system displays an error message and asks you to reenter the information. Thinking that you mistyped your ID or password, you key them in again, and this time you're admitted. The first program was the Trojan horse and the attacker has just captured your userID and password. Like the Trojans, you're in for a rude awakening.

The first step you can take to protect yourself against this type of attack is to lock your computer, as I mentioned earlier. For added protection, install an access control program—one that prevents unauthorized people from logging in to your computer and installing programs. I'll give you a rundown on access control packages in a minute. You can also adopt a two-factor authentication system, one that requires a person to have a special card or device called a password generator. More about that, too, in a minute.

Sniffers

No matter how clever you are at coming up with a password, if you transmit it over a network, it may be intercepted by a sniffer, network analyzer or other tool designed to troubleshoot networks. Sniffers and other such programs can also be used to harvest passwords as users log in to the system.

> **Encrypt passwords before they are transmitted and it won't matter much if someone intercepts them.**

Passwords by Default

Some computers, like those that are used to power networks and office telephone systems, come with default passwords that are set by the factory. These passwords are pretty standard (like TEST, DEFAULT, and FIELD) and are intended for use by field technicians to set up and test the system, or to perform diagnostics and even repairs from long distances.

Each manufacturer has its own default passwords that it regularly uses, and they're widely known to even rank computer crackers. Surprisingly, not all manufacturers bother to tell their customers that these default passwords even exist, let alone that they should change them. That's not something that you'll have to worry about if you buy a desktop PC, of course, but it's worth keeping in mind if you own a business or your business really takes off and you start to expand your computer system.

> **Slipping into computers using default passwords is one of the most common ways that hackers penetrate systems. Change the default password to something that is hard to figure out and you have just about won this battle.**

HOW TO CREATE HACKER-PROOF PASSWORDS

There is nothing scientific about creating hacker-proof passwords. It's much more a matter of common sense. Here are some guidelines:

- The more you have to lose, the longer the password should be. I would use a four-character password if all I wanted to do is keep my teenage daughter from logging in to my machine to play games when she really ought to be doing her homework. On the other hand, I would use an eight-character password to protect my account on a commercial online service. Bottom line: Choose a password that is at least six characters long and that should cover you fairly well. Keep in mind that not every system will allow you to enter, say, a 12-character password.

- Mix upper- and lowercase characters and symbols like @#$%^&* to add an additional level of protection.

- To make your password easy to remember but tough to crack, use an acronym or pass phrase. For example, TA5WTLYL is easy to remember if you know that it stands for "There are 50 ways to leave your lover!" For even stronger security, create a pass phrase such as "ShepicksSHEllsbyTheCshore."

- Some people create passwords by picking out a pattern on the keyboard. Hackers know that many people like to use patterns like FRED and QWERTY, so you need to be particularly imaginative and try something like 1=q]a'z/g (figure it out).

- Don't give out your password to anyone.

- You shouldn't write your password down, but if you do, don't put it on a Post-it and stick that on your monitor or tape it to your desk.

- Do change your password at least every 90 days. Change it immediately if you suspect that your password has been compromised.

- Don't key in your password while someone watches.

- Don't use the same password for all of the computer systems that you use, whether it's your ATM, commercial online account, desktop, or laptop computer.

- Don't allow an unlimited number of attempts to crack a password. There are password programs that shut someone out after three unsuccessful attempts to enter the correct password.

ONE FACTOR, TWO FACTORS

Relying solely on passwords is not necessarily bad, even though there are ways of getting around them. If you use an access control program and a password that is at least six characters and digits long, you'll be reasonably well protected. That's called a one-factor authentication, as I mentioned earlier.

However, if you have a lot to lose or if you're responsible for protecting a company's computer systems, there are additional ways to strengthen the identification and authentication process using two-factor authentication. You also have to acknowledge that the universe is increasingly security unfriendly. Passwords as a primary protection for computer security are slowly becoming a thing of the past.

Double up for safety

All Types of Tokens

> You just gotta save Christianity, Richard! You gotta!
>
> Loretta Young to Richard the Lionhearted
> *The Crusades*, 1935

Back in the old, old days, a messenger from a king to a general on the battlefield would carry a royal seal or some other object as proof that he was indeed the king's representative and not a spy or other mischief maker. Along with the royal seal, the messenger might also give a secret handshake or say a special phrase. These days, we call that transaction two-factor authentication.

The modern equivalent of that royal seal and secret handshake is a token and a password. There are all sorts of tokens, each providing various levels of security.

Token

On one end, there are credit and debit cards with a magnetic stripe on the back on which has been recorded some basic information, such as your name and account number. On the other end of the spectrum is the password generator, a small calculator-like device that generates a new password every 60 seconds and provides nearly foolproof security. In between, are smart cards, PCMCIA cards, and at least one smart disk.

Magnetic Stripe Cards

> Never invest in anything that eats or needs repairing.
>
> Billy Rose (1899–1966)

You go to an ATM, you insert your debit card with the magnetic stripe on the back, and the machine asks you to enter your password (actually your PIN, or personal identification number). Push a couple more buttons and out pops your dough.

Poppin' fresh dough

That's about as simple a two-factor authentication scheme as you can get. You have the card and you know the PIN. Someone may steal your card, but if he or she doesn't know the PIN, it won't do much good. Conversely, if someone knows your PIN but doesn't have the card, that's not going to do much good either.

However, there are ways around magnetic stripe cards. For example, they may be stolen from your mailbox (or even before they get to your mailbox) and used before you have any clue that someone else is using your card. That's one reason you don't see many magnetic card security systems for computers, although you often see them used as access control devices to enter data centers, buildings, parking garages, and so on.

Smart Cards

> The difference between genius and stupidity is that genius has its limits.
>
> Unknown

A smart card looks like an ordinary credit card but is about twice as thick. Embedded into the card is a microprocessor and other circuitry that can be programmed to do a wide variety of tricks (not just identification and authentication). Cards may be programmed with a certain amount of credit and used to make telephone calls, purchase goods from a vending machine, or pay for parking meters. Other cards are being used at hospitals to store and transport medical records and at large companies to pay for meals in the company cafeteria, parking, and other applications. The information is retrieved from the card by swiping it through a smart card reader.

Get smart!   Smart cards that are used for computer security can be programmed with a userID and password, as well as the right to access files, directories, and such peripherals as disk drives and printers. Some cards are capable of encrypting and decrypting so that passwords and other information stored in them can be securely transmitted over a network.

Smart cards are not perfect, however. Having to swipe the card through a reader and entering a userID and password provides a fair amount of security. The drawback is that an employee could lose the card or someone could steal it. Also, they're an expensive way to protect computers if you have to provide cards and readers for lots of employees.

Not a lot of companies are making smart cards and readers for security applications. In fact, smart cards for all purposes are far more popular overseas than they are in the United States. That's changing, but not as fast as some dreamy futurists have predicted. In the meanwhile, expect to pay $500 or more for a smart card, reader, and software. Stoplock's Stoplock V Smart Card, for example, costs about $500 and consists of a smart card and reader that mount inside a disk drive bay or as an add-on box. The card holds such information as your access rights to files and directories.

The Dynamics of Passwords

> My mind is an open as a forty-acre field, but that doesn't mean that I'm
> going to change it.
>
> Everett Dirksen
> *Dirksen: Portrait of a Public Man,* 1970

Security Dynamics, one of the top security companies, markets a password gen-erator that operates like other tokens, although the company insists on calling it a smart card. No matter what it's called, it offers exceptional security because it does away with having to rely on passwords that you use time and time again and replaces them with dynamic passwords that change every 60 seconds. **Passwords by the minute**

The SecureID card, made by Security Dynamics, contains a powerful micro-processor that generates a new, unpredictable password every 60 seconds. The password is used only once and then discarded. The card displays this unique password, which is different for each card, on a liquid crystal display on the face of the card. To log in to a system, the card owner simply enters his or her password or PIN and the number displayed at that moment on their SecureID card. The computer checks the time, compares the number that you typed with the one the card should be displaying at that moment, and if everything lines up, you're in.

Challenge and Response Password Generators

You've probably seen more than a few movies where a soldier is making his way back to camp at night and the guard yells out, "Who goes there?" The soldier replies with something like, "Tango, Foxtrot, Delta." If the guard is really the suspicious type, he'll ask something that only one of the good guys might know, such as, "Who won the 1914 World Series?" If the soldier replies "the Boston Braves," he's allowed to pass, but if he answers "How in the heck am I supposed to know that?" he gets shot. **Boston Braves?**

All of that back and forth stuff is called "challenge and response" by security types. That same premise is put to work for identification and authentication, but in this case, the system issues the challenge and you provide the response.

Token Password Generators

> I'm in a phone booth at the corner of Walk and Don't Walk.
>
> Unknown

A token looks like a pocket calculator, complete with a numeric keypad and a small liquid crystal display. The token generates and displays a number that is unique to each card and one that varies every time the card is used.

Challenge and response   The session starts with your indicating to the computer that you wish to log in. The computer responds with a challenge. That challenge is nothing more than a series of numbers. You key your PIN and the challenge number into the token and the token responds with yet another series of numbers. Enter those numbers correctly into the computer and you're admitted.

PCMCIA and Other Tokens

> Immature artists imitate. Mature artists steal.
>
> Lionel Trilling
> *Esquire,* Sept. 1962

The PCMCIA (shorthand for Personal Computer Memory Card International Association) slot in laptops and some personal computers is a growing standard that can be used to accommodate add-ons such as modems and flash memory on credit-card–sized cards. Several companies are starting to market security devices on PCMCIA cards. Telequip's Crypta card can be programmed with log-on userID and password sequences, configuration data, RSA encryption for passwords and files, and anything else you can manage to pack into the card's flash memory (up to 16 MB of data). The card itself is protected by a pass phrase.

National Semiconductor, for example, has something that it calls the PersonaCard that provides both encryption and digital signatures for computer messages. The card sells for about $250. If you don't have a PCMCIA reader, NatSemi will sell you one for about $209.

Devices such as PCMCIA cards and other products that use encryption cannot be legally taken outside of North American, even for personal use, without an export license. As I explain later in Chapter 5, the federal government classifies encryption as "munitions" and takes a pretty dim view of anyone exporting such "weaponry" as decoder rings and other scrambling widgets.

Smart Floppy

> I have always depended on the kindness of strangers.
>
> Tennessee Williams
> *A Streetcar Named Desire,* 1947, sc 11 (Blanche's final words)

SmartDisk Security markets a nifty little device called SmartDisk for PCs and Macs that looks nearly identical to a 3.5-inch floppy disk but actually is a security computer. It works in conjunction with SafeBoot software to encrypt and decrypt files. It sells for about $165 (less, if you buy lots of them).

Tokens provide a high degree of security but they are not perfect. They tend to be expensive, especially if you have lots of employees using them. Although they're not fragile, they'll break, even with casual handling. They're small, and thus easy to lose. They're reliable but may not always work as expected, which is frustrating.

I know of one company that purchased tokens by the carload, only to give up on them when employees complained that they were not reliable and hindered productivity. Using them added several more steps to the log-in process that the employees found tiresome. If you have several employees using them, someone must administer the tokens, assign passwords, issue tokens, arrange for replacement if they are lost or broken, and take on many other administrative burdens.

Several more steps

Get Smart Technology

> You can tell a lot about a fellow by his way of eating jelly beans.
>
> Ronald Reagan
> *New York Times,* Jan. 15, 1981

Everyone has characteristics that make him or her unique. My fingerprints are not the same as your fingerprints, and the back of your right eyeball is not the same as the back of my right eyeball. Several companies market authentication schemes, called biometric systems, that make use of these unique characteristics for identification and authentication.

Biometrics

> Every man sees in his relatives a series of grotesque caricatures of himself.
>
> H. L. Mencken (1880–1956)

Let me tell you up front that biometrics is not all that popular for computer security, except with the Mission Impossible and military crowd, but I wouldn't be doing my job if I didn't at least tell you about some of the available systems.

Mission Impossible

Biometric security devices examine the physical actions or traits that make each individual unique. Six types of devices are currently available and at least a few more are under development. They work in a similar manner. A biometric portrait of the subject is scanned or read by sensor devices, converted into digital data, and stored in a database. It usually takes several attempts to enter a profile before the system finally learns to recognize it. On the authentication side, the subject's handprint, voice, or other trait is compared with the stored profile. If

Got a match?

there is an identical—and I mean really identical—match, you get access. The six types of biometric devices include:

- *Retina Scanners*   The back of a person's eyeball contains tiny blood vessels arranged in patterns that are as unique as fingerprints. Retina scanners read the size, location, and pattern of blood vessels in the back of the eye.

- *Signature Dynamics*   Forgers can mimic the appearance of a signature, but a biometric pen or pad measures signature dynamics: the pressure exerted by the writer on the pen point and the motion used in writing, for example.

- *Keystroke Analysis*   Keystroke analysis compares the individual patterns and rhythms of typing repetitive character groups.

- *Hand Geometry*   Hand geometry systems measure finger length, skin translucency, and palm width and shape, among other characteristics.

- *Fingerprint Analysis*   Even junior G-men know that no two fingerprints are identical. Fingerprint or thumbprint identification systems analyze the unique arches, loops, and whorls of a person's finger or thumb.

- *Voice Verification*   Voice verification maps the actual physiology that produces speech, not merely sounds or pronunciation.

Under development are other biometric methods such as one that makes use of neural network technology in a device that aims to recognize faces and another that analyzes a person's genetic pattern, or "DNA fingerprint."

I smell a rat!   Just to show you to what extent some companies are taking biometric technology, let me tell you about Scentinel, a "smell-O-rama" biometric system developed by Bloodhound Sensors. Wave your hand under a special sensor and the device registers each person's unique odor as an "Odorgram." Honest, I'm not making this up! When you want to use a system protected by the Scentinel, pass your hand under the sensor once again and if your smell is in a database, you're allowed access. Don't worry if you're particularly stinky one day or change your perfume. Bloodhound says its system will ignore those "extraneous" smells. I'm usually wont to say, "Only in America" when hearing really wacky things like this, but Bloodhound happens to be a British company. Heck, it might even work for all I know, but I haven't actually seen the smell-O-rama in action.

Character Flaws

> It is sometimes expedient to forget who we are.
>
> Publilius Syrus, c. 42 BC

The problem with biometeric systems is that although they're extremely reliable for ID-ing a person, you can't always count on them to work. That's not as much of a contradiction as you may think. Because each person has unique characteristics, it's impossible to fool a retina or fingerprint scanner. Well, maybe James Bond can, but most of us can't. Ideally the system must be precise enough to reject unauthorized users, but it should also adapt to slight changes in a person's physical characteristics.

However, the systems are not always reliable. A handprint geometry reader may reject an authorized user who recently cut her fingernails, and a voice verification system may reject a user who has clogged sinuses because of an allergy, for example. Using biometrics systems for that reason can be frustrating.

Still, biometrics is slowly coming into use, as the price of the technology goes down and the accuracy goes up. Several companies market fingerprint readers for PCs for about $100. That's not too bad. They are more secure than a password and not easily lost or damaged like a token or smart card.

Price down, accuracy up

Okay, we've covered everything worthwhile knowing about identification and authentication, which is only the beginning of what access control is really all about. You want to keep unauthorized users off your system, but you also want to restrict what they and authorized users can do once they're on the system.

ACCESS CONTROL PROGRAMS

A door is what a dog is perpetually on the wrong side of.

Ogden Nash
"The Turtle," *Hard Lines,* 1931

Access control programs range from those that do nothing more than protect a PC or Mac by requiring that you first enter a password to programs that are packed with features such as password protection, file and directory locking, encryption, compression, virus detection, and more. I like the combo packages because you get several useful security features in one box and they're remarkably flexible. The price of the combo packages is right, too. They range between $100 and $200. If you were to buy a password program, encryption, and compression as separate programs, you would pay a lot more.

Right now, I go into these features of access control programs. In Appendix B, I'll list the companies that market them (as well as other products).

Built-In Password Protection

If one cannot catch the bird of paradise, better to take a wet hen.

Nikita Khrushchev
Time, Jan. 6, 1958

An increasing number of programs—screen savers, word processors, databases, hard drive setup utilities, and so on—are marketed today with password protection as a secondary feature. The password protection offered in these programs is useful for deterring casual snoops, but they're not really all that secure.

Screen Savers

So you like that screen saver that came with Windows, eh? Didn't cost anything extra and that's good. Better yet, it's even got a security feature that will keep the snoops from nosing around. All you have to do is go into the control panel and create a password. Then write a message that says something to the effect that: "This PC protected by the Super-Duper Security Crypto Lock. Security clearance required." and you're covered, right?

 Dream on. Window 3.1's screen saver is about as secure as attaching a bicycle lock to your keyboard. It looks good, but it doesn't do squat. Simply rebooting the computer and restarting Windows is all anyone needs to do to get a peek at that résumé you've been working on when no one was looking.

Left in the lurch   In fact, an intruder could change your password to something that you would never guess and where would that leave you, eh? The password is stored in the CONTROL.INI file. The password is encrypted, but the label PASSWORD is not. Go figure. Anyone could change the order of the characters following the equal sign and make up a whole new password. The only way to get around that, if some miscreant decides to mess with your machine, is to change the line PWProtected=1 (in CONTROL.INI) to 0, delete the Password= line, and save. After you restart, you can create a new password, although Lord knows why you would even bother.

Security as a Feature

Lots of word processing, spreadsheet, and other mainstream applications come with a password option these days. You can protect a documents in Microsoft Word 6.0 and Excel 5.0, for example, by selecting Options from the Tools menu and then entering a password (up to 15 characters long). Sticking a password on a document so that no one else can look at it or tamper with it makes you feel as though you've struck a blow for security, I'll bet.

Don't go to sleep just yet, unless you plan to keep one eye open. Lots of commercial and freeware password-cracking programs available that will get you into Word and many other programs.

AccessData, for example, markets a set of password recovery utilities that will crack passwords used to lock files in popular software applications within seconds. The company's Password Recovery Utilities can be fired at passwords in Novell's WordPerfect, Microsoft's Excel, Lotus Development's Lotus 1-2-3, and several other programs. Each module sells for about $185. New Visions' MasterKey ($185) works with both Excel and WordPerfect. These products were not developed so that hackers and other intruders could go around and make everyone's life miserable, by the way. Rather, they were developed so that people who forget their passwords can recover their files.

Some access control programs that lock files do not happily co-exist with the file protection schemes that databases and other applications use. You may have to resort to using the database protection feature instead of the access control package's. Not only is it not as secure, but who's going to remember before long that you should use one scheme in the database and another for everything else? The net result is data locked with two different methods. That's not data you're likely to retrieve either.

Hard Drive Setup Utilities

Setup programs bundled with hard drives often feature password protection. You typically have the option of dividing the drive into partitions or volumes and protecting them with a password. You could store sensitive data in one partition and protect that. That would also speed up the process of backing up because all you would have to do is back up the partition instead of the disk.

However, a clever computer user could remove the password protection using a disk editing utility. Also, the hard drive setup utilities I've tried have been quirky, no doubt because the password feature is added as an afterthought.

One program would only accept my password if I typed it in all caps, although I had created the password in lowercase letters. Another one would allow me to access the hard drive after four failed attempts at entering the correct password. I also found that in some cases I could circumvent the password protection by booting from a floppy or by using the hard drive setup disk. Based on personal experience, I would only rely on this kind of password protection if I wanted to deter casual snoops and couldn't afford to buy something more substantial.

Good for casual snoops, only

Bob

If you're a PC user, you've probably heard all about Bob, Microsoft's friendly user interface that is designed to help novices use PCs. In addition to providing instructions for doing all sorts of user-friendly things like how to open files, it's even got a password protection feature designed to keep the anti-Bobs at bay.

Bob may be a fun-loving type of guy, but Bob is an idiot. If you enter the password incorrectly three times in a row, Bob asks you if you want to change it to something easier to remember. I'm all in favor of user friendliness, but this is ridiculous!

CMOS Setup

Recent vintage PCs permit you to password-protect your machine by creating a password in the CMOS setup screen. Just how to do that varies from machine to machine, but in many instances, you'll have to hold down the F1 or Del key at startup or use the setup disk that came with your desktop or laptop machine. Creating a password in CMOS is not industrial-strength security, but the only way to get around it is to take the cover off the PC and reset a jumper on the motherboard or remove the battery, which powers the CMOS. Not many people know enough to do either, and if they do, it's not something they are likely to try in front of an office with a bunch of people standing around.

Hard Drive Protection Programs

> Open sesame.
>
> Aladdin
> *The Arabian Nights*

No ticket? No laundry Several basic password protection programs on the market are designed to keep the bad guys out of your machine mainly by locking the hard drive. Install one of them, and it kicks in during the boot process and demands that you enter a password. Quite simple, really.

Programs such as Symantec's DiskLock for PCs and Macintoshes, ASD Software's DiskGuard for Macs, and COM&DIA's DiaLOCK Boot PCs lock the hard drive, offer basic password protection, and work exceedingly well for keeping out all but the most persistent of snoops. They range in price from $100 to $250 (some do other things beyond hard drive locking such as alerting you to attempted security violations and checking for viruses).

Some caveats: A clever computer user can get around most of these programs, often by merely booting from a floppy startup disk or from a second hard drive. These programs do not protect removable media, including floppy

disks, Syquest and Bernoulli cartridges, tapes, or optical disks. They also do not protect hard drives that use driver-level compression such as Stacker and TimesTwo.

I've also experimented with several shareware and freeware password protection programs. Many of them are rudimentary and not difficult to crack (you can get around many of these programs by booting from a floppy). That said, the price is right. Password protection shareware costs between $5 and $15. For the PC, there's Hard Pass ($5) from Data Tech, Lock 'M Up ($15) from Bill Travis, and Password ($12) from Ray Dittmeier. For the Mac, there's Simply Everything from Deadbroke Software ($9.50 and requires Hypercard) and Sentinel from Brian Booker ($5). These are programs that I have looked at recently; there may be others that are more secure or better in some other way. If you have access to the Internet or to one of the commercial online services like CompuServe and Prodigy, you'll find lots of programs like these.

Protecting Files and Directories

If you share a machine with co-workers or family members, there's a good chance that you are less interested in keeping people off the machine and more interested in keeping them out of your personal files or from messing around with your system's configuration, files, directories, and folders.

For Windows-based PCs, you have a least couple of choices. The first is TriTech's WinBolt ($35) and Cetus Software's WinGuard ($15). Both will keep someone from trashing program items, rearranging icons, and the like. Winbolt is a commercial program that can be used to keep someone from rearranging your icons. You can also hide programs and files to fool the snoops. WinGuard is a shareware program that offers seven levels of protection starting with blocking someone from making changes to the Program Manager to removing the File menu from Program Manager.

Stop messing around

The protection files reside on the machine where a savvy computer user can get at them. For added security, Cetus also offers Storm Windows ($15), a version of WinGuard, that you can use to set protection levels but store the files on a diskette PC for safekeeping.

There are several of these file and folder locking programs for the Mac, including At Ease ($37) from Apple Computer, FolderBolt Pro ($130) from Kent Marsh, Mac Control ($59) from BDW Software, MacPerfect ($61) from Hi Resolution, and On Guard ($57) from Power On Software. Kent Marsh's FolderBolt Pro gives you the option of keeping people out entirely, restricting them to read-only access, or letting them add files but not open the folder. The problem with FolderBolt Pro and many other packages like it is that they won't put off a professional attacker. They're relatively easy to get around, so they don't belong on the top shelf of security.

Also, these programs jigger with the hard drive's file directory (it's like moving items on a table of contents around). Diagnostic utilities and antivirus software programs spot these changes and think that the directory has been corrupted. To run the utility, you must disable the security package, which might not be even possible if you're in the middle of trying to fix a real problem.

All-in-one Programs

Sometimes simple password protection isn't enough. Maybe you also want to permit guest users on your machine but don't want to give them the keys to the kingdom. Maybe you also think that encrypting your files will help you sleep better. Go for a full-featured access control package. Here is a quick roundup of the primary features:

Password Protection

As you know by now, one of the key ways in which you can limit or control access to a machine is through the use of passwords. The popular access control packages have a minimum and maximum number of alphanumeric characters that you can use to create a password.

Plain dumb   Some packages permit you to enter a single character or digit for a password, which is plain dumb; others require a minimum of 5 or 6. If you have employees, for example, you might want to require that they use 6, 8, or even more complex passwords. The maximum is between 16 and 256 characters, so you can create pass phrases that are easy to remember, yet difficult to crack. They're usually case sensitive, meaning that they distinguish between capital and lowercase characters. A few packages permit you to set a password expiration period, forcing the system's users to change passwords every few days, weeks, or months. That's a worthwhile feature.

Encryption

You gotta encrypt   If you want to set up a security barrier of the sort that foreign intelligence agencies and federal law enforcers cannot hope to crack, you must encrypt your files. Several of the full-featured access control programs use Data Encryption Standard (DES), Triple DES, or some encryption that is equally secure.

These programs also encrypt passwords so that if they are transmitted across a network and are intercepted, they can't be used to against you. The password file is typically stored on an area of the hard disk that is inaccessible to all but the owner or administrator of the machine.

Access Control Levels

Someone administers the system and someone uses it. Even if it's a shared machine, like the one that I share with my kids, I'm the administrator and I determine who gets access to the two hard drives that I use and to the applications, directories, and files that are stored on them.

An access control package allows you to determine exactly what files can be modified. A secondary benefit to locking files this way is that it helps contain a virus if one should infect your system. Viruses must attach themselves to programs in order to execute, and if you lock the program, the virus will be unable to latch on and modify it. Keep in mind that if you give yourself the ability to modify files and you infect the system, the virus will have the same level of access to programs that you have. The access control program will hinder the virus from spreading, but it is not a fail-safe antivirus solution.

Contain a virus too

Guest Accounts

Once installed, the access control system permits people to log in as guests for specified time periods and to access certain applications and files. If you have a newsletter publishing business, for example, you may need to permit a freelancer to come in and use your machine to design pages. This is then a feature that you would find particularly useful.

Useful feature

Timed Lockout

The administrator has the option of determining exactly when someone is allowed to use the system and locks out any attempts to use the system outside of those hours. The problem is that when this feature is implemented in software, it's a trivial matter for the user to reset the clock.

Time out

Show User Last Time and Date

The system creates a log of each person who logs in and the log-in time. If you log in on Monday, after being away on vacation for a week, and you notice that someone has logged in the previous Friday, you should suspect that an impostor is at work.

Log in, log out

Token Compatibility

Software that is packaged with most tokens features password protection and little else. If you want to control access to files and directories and also use a smart card or token, you'll need an access control package like Watchdog SecureID from Fischer International or PC/DACS from Mergent International.

Token talk

Shredder

Gone, but not forgotten

When you delete a file, it really isn't gone—only the filename is. The actual file lurks on your hard disk until other files are written on top of it (and that may take quite a while). Meanwhile, anyone with MS-DOS 6.x's UNDELETE or Norton Utilities can restore the file in less time than it takes Speedy Gonzalez to cross the street. To prevent supposedly trashed files from being recovered, you need to run them through the electronic equivalent of a paper shredder.

Floppy and Hard Disk Storage Lockout

Lockout

If you don't want someone accessing a hard drive or offloading data to a floppy disk, you can determine who can do that and who can't. If you have two hard drives, one may be your secure drive, containing all of your valuable data, and the other can be used only by guests on the system.

Keyboard Lock

Disable Crtl-Alt-Del

If you would like to prevent the unauthorized use of your keyboard in specific circumstances, say, while the screen saver is running or in the event that the security software has been tampered with, look for a package with keyboard lock. You can use it to disable Crtl-Alt-Del to keep someone from rebooting the machine in an attempt to get around the access control package.

PORTABLE COMPUTER SECURITY

Show me a good loser and I'll show you an idiot.

Leo Durocher

RAF Wing Commander David Farquhar ordered his driver to stop his staff car in front of a used car dealer's lot in London so he could take a look at some of the cars on sale. Farquhar, a decorated veteran of the Falklands War, needed a new automobile and a Range Rover had caught his eye. While he and his driver were checking out the mileage on the fancy four-wheel drive, a thief made off with three briefcases and a laptop computer that had been left in the trunk of the senior officer's staff car. The laptop contained top-secret U.K. Desert Storm war plans—plans that were so sensitive they "could have lost the war," according to a military officer who later testified at Farquhar's court martial. Police found the briefcases in a parking garage less than three hours later, but the computer didn't turn up until more than two weeks later when it was mailed to police, apparently by the thief. The loss of the laptop was serious enough to prompt the U.K. Defense Ministry to invoke a 75-year-old press censorship rule and prohibit U.K. news organizations from publishing anything about the computer theft until it was recovered.

Farquhar, as a military man, should have known better than to leave valuable secrets unprotected. What he obviously did not know is that leaving a laptop computer unattended in an automobile is a sure way to lose it to a thief.   **He wuz robbed.**

Data Protection

> I never travel without my diary. One should have something sensational to read.
>
> Oscar Wilde (1854–1900)

Portable computers are great for taking your act on the road. In fact, I never leave home without my Apple Powerbook. It's got my database of important contacts, telecommunications software for keeping in touch by e-mail and fax, spreadsheet software so that I can track my expenses as well as massage my meager investments, and word processing for whatever articles, books, and other stuff I happen to be working on. My data is valuable to me and I wouldn't want anyone to see my personal financial affairs. The laptop was expensive—$2800 plus 18 months of credit card charges. All in all, I am particularly careful with my notebook computer, and I never let it out of my sight.

I still worry, however, that something will happen while I'm on the road that will cause my information to take a powder. I also worry about it being stolen, although the people who keep track of such things tell me that my laptop is more likely to be stolen from my home or office than when I'm on the road. I also worry more that something bizarre might happen, like my hard drive going up in smoke only minutes after I saved the last iteration of the Great American Novel that I plan to write some day.   **Lost laptop**

When I travel, I can't be bothered to take along instruction manuals and lots of disks with original software, an array of diagnostics software, a printer, extra batteries and cables, and all of the other useful items that I have back in the office. I know I should be better prepared, but I sneer at those business travelers who carry, in addition to their laptops, troubleshooting guides, extra batteries and cables, printers, and all of that other stuff that turns a 5-pound notebook into a 20-pound, airport arm stretcher. I'm one of those run through the airport and throw the bag in the overhead bin kind of guys. I don't check bags unless someone holds a gun to my head.

That doesn't mean that I park my common sense in the airport parking lot along with my car. I trade off what I really should carry for absolute protection for an acceptable level of risk. I have a pretty good idea of all the bad things that could happen, and I try to cover myself for the likeliest of trouble.   **Tradeoffs**

I use an access control package to keep snoops out of my laptop and to make it utterly useless if a thief snags it; encryption to make the data unreadable; and an antitheft device. The latter works something like a bicycle lock if I decide to leave my laptop in my hotel room instead of schlepping it to a trade show, meeting, or some other place where it won't be used.

Survival Kit

> Being in the army is like being in the Boy Scouts, except the Boy Scouts have adult supervision.
>
> Blake Clark
> *The Tonight Show*, Feb. 8, 1984

I put together a sort of survival kit when I travel. I have a disk containing an all-in-one program for word processing, database, spreadsheet and communications. I don't normally use it, but if something should happen to one of the key programs I use, at least I can keep on working. It beats having to take backups along for four programs. I also take along a disk containing an operating system and basic tools. In addition, I have a disk containing a variety of small diagnostics programs that can be used to retrieve lost files and repair minor hard disk drive damage. Last, I carry a couple of blank disks for storing data and backing up key files.

In Chapter 6, I describe how to create a set of emergency disks. I'll go into some of what that entails here so you can create a set of rescue disks that you can take with you when you hit the road.

Disks to the Rescue

These boots were made for walking First you've gotta make an emergency disk or two containing all of the valuable little (and some not so little) utilities and files that you'll need if you get in a jam. Start by sticking a floppy disk into drive A: of your PC and type: FORMAT A: /S. That gives you a bootable disk. Make two, although you may not need both just yet.

Next, copy to one or maybe more disks the following files (exactly which files you'll copy depends on which version of DOS you're running):

- SCANDISK (MS-DOS 6.2) or CHKDSK.EXE (earlier versions)—Gives you an update on the status of a disk, including the number of files on it, whether there are lost file clusters, and more.

- FDISK.EXE—Prepares the hard drive for formatting if the worst happens and Godzilla trashes your hard drive.

- FORMAT.COM—Formats a disk so you can use it.

- SYS.COM—Puts DOS system files on a disk; it's what makes a disk bootable.

- UNFORMAT.COM-Does the opposite of FORMAT.COM.

- UNDELETE.EXE-Snatches your files back from the dead.

- HIMEM.SYS—Extends memory

- EMM386.EXE—Expands memory

- MEMMAKER—Does what HIMEM and EMM386 do but without making you work for it.

- WIN.INI and SYSTEM.INI—Provides backups of your Windows configuration files which saves you time and a lot of effort getting everything back shipshape.

Copy any other special files that you think you might need such and PCMCIA and print drivers.

If you have Norton Utilities or PC Tools for Windows, use the "rescue" disk utility to automatically create an emergency disk. Running Norton Utilities, for example, creates a disk with the following files:

To the rescue

- CMOS values, which provide information about the hard drive.

- Boot record, which consists of the BIOS Parameter Block, which provides information on how the disk is laid out, and the bootstrap loader, which determines where to load the operating system.

- Partition tables, which is a record of how the hard drive has been divided.

Mac users can make a copy of the Disk Tools that came with the MacOS bundle of disks. That disk contains a bare-bones system folder, a First-Aid disk repair utility, and a hard drive utility. If you have Norton Utilities for the Mac, you can create a couple of emergency disks with a variety of file recovery and diagnostics utilities.

Utilities

A compression utility is handy to have (if your access control features it, so much the better). You can compress files to save space, obviously, but it's also useful for transmitting large files back to the office or to your home machine as backup. Also, if you get in a jam and you need to offload files to floppy disks, this may be the only way you're going to pack the critical files onto a few disks. If your access control package does not feature compression, get a copy of PKZIP, the hugely popular and widely available shareware program. The program is also handy to use because you can create self-extracting files.

If You're Forgetful Like I Am

I also write down useful information such as local access numbers for online services in the state where I'm headed, special characters or conventions that I might need to upload a file to a publication, and setup strings for my modems. If I send an article to the newspaper that I regularly write for, for example, I have to put something like this at the top of the file: {ET{SLHOMTEC01{QUHOM-COP{BYALXNDR{BT. Although I've been doing this dozens of times a year for nearly 10 years, sometimes I forget a character or two, and the system bounces the article, and my editor wonders if I forgot about my deadline. Dullard that I am, I always check my little crib sheet to make sure that I didn't forget anything. Also, if I have quickstart guides for software that I am still trying to get the hang of, I bring those along. I also have photocopied setup instructions and troubleshooting tips from some of my software and hardware manuals, and I carry these along as part of my kit.

Telephone Tapping Tools

> Be prepared.
>
> Boy Scout motto

After checking into a hotel room, I first check the hotel's telephone connections to see what I need to do to hook up my laptop and modem. Sooner or later, I'll want to check my mail, upload files, and so on.

Behind the headboard
    Many modern hotels are business traveler friendly and have readily accessible modular phone jacks for computer hookups. The rest of them think that life is made more interesting if the telephone is hardwired into a phone jack that is behind the headboard of a bed that has been bolted to the floor. For some reason, that's the kind of hotel that I always get booked into. After several years of struggling to plug into hotel telephone systems, I have assembled a kit that makes life a heck of a lot easier. In this kit go:

- Two sets of phone wires with RJ-11 clips at each end to connect the hotel's telephone to my modem and the modem to the wall phone jack. You can also use a duplex phone adapter, which allows you to plug the phone and modem into the same wall jack.

- RJ-11 clip adapter with an RJ-11 plug on one end and alligator clips on the other. If I find myself in an old hotel without modular phone jacks, I unscrew the cover plate on the wall or the mouthpiece on the telephone's handset and go for the wires. Most of the time, you attach one alligator clip to the red wire and the other to the green one. It doesn't matter which clip you connect; there's no right or wrong way. Some hotel phone systems use the yellow and black wires, although it's rare. If you want to cover yourself, Radio Shack has a $7 adapter that permits you to switch between the two pairs.

- RJ-11 coupler, which is useful for connecting two lengths of phone wires, or the RJ-11 clip adapter and enough phone wire to work comfortably at a desk or table.

- A small, cheapo plastic flashlight that I picked up for free at a trade show booth. It's come in handy when I have to peer into a telephone box to find the right wires.

- A Swiss Army knife in case I need a screwdriver, or a corkscrew, for that matter.

You can get all of this stuff at any Radio Shack or similar electronics parts store for only a few bucks.

Digital Destruction

> I will always cherish the initial misconceptions I had about you.
>
> Unknown

A growing number of hotels have digital telephone systems. Meanwhile, however, your modem is an analog device. The phone system and the modem don't speak the same language, so you can't just plug in and go to work.

Remember the red and green wires that I told you were okay to connect to just a minute ago? Well, I lied. You don't always want to do that with a digital system because those wires carry power instead of a telephone signal. Make the wrong connection and you'll have a silicon barbeque within seconds.

Some newer modems, like the Supra that I use, have built-in protection against digital telephone destruction. Check with the maker of your modem to see if it has a defense mechanism.

IBM, TeleAdapt, and Radio Shack market "modem savers" that detect digital lines. They sell for $7 to $30. The top-priced IBM is more reliable than the two cheaper alternatives.

Modem savers

Another way around the problem is to use an acoustic coupler that attaches to the telephone handset. Konexx sells a kit that includes the acoustic coupler and other gear for about $150.

Yet another alternative is to purchase and use a handset adapter, a device about the size of a deck of cards that connects between the handset jack and the laptop. The Konexx company also sells a handset adapter for $100.

Last, you can ask the hotel's telecommunications administrator.

If none of these approaches appeals to you, take a look at the phone itself. Analog phones have what's called a ringer-equivalence number, which is abbreviated as REN. If there's a REM and a number marked on the underside of the phone, it's analog and you can use your modem. If it's not, you're outta luck.

Protecting Your Data From Disaster

Traffic signals in New York are just rough guidelines.

David Letterman

On the road   Business travelers often forget or don't want to bother to back up the data stored in their laptops while on the road. I suppose the logic is that backing up is something you do back at the office using a tape backup drive. Perhaps they think that if you can't do the job properly, you might as well not do it at all. The truth is that the chances of your losing data are just as great (even greater) on the road than back at the ranch.

The first security step to take is to back up to floppies. This protects the information from some quirky loss, but it won't do much if a thief bags your carrying case and the disks. Keep the backups in your briefcase or some place other than the computer carrying case.

Send files to yourself   Send the files to yourself as an e-mail message. For added security, you can encrypt them first. If the files are large, compress them to save time. Harold, my technical editor, says that I should also tell you that you may not always be able to encrypt and compress files. Some encryption and compression programs produce ASCII characters that are not transmittable as e-mail. If you work for someone and have remote access to a server, you can upload the files for safekeeping as well.

Access Control for Laptops

I've been in more laps than a napkin.

Mae West (1892–1980)

Obviously the same software that is used to lock up files and encrypt data on the desktop can be used with laptop computers. Still, it's certainly worth mentioning that there are access control packages especially for laptop computers. In addition to the password protection, encryption, and other features that I have mentioned, they also have battery management to eke out every drop of power in a rechargeable battery, file synchronization to keep files on the laptop and desktop current, and remote access that helps speed connecting to a network.

Some programs like these that come to mind include M&T Technologies' MicroSAFE laptop Information Security System ($50) for PCs and ASD Software's PB Guard ($59) for Apple PowerBooks.

Limiting Access

If you run a small company and your employees use the company's laptops when they travel, you might want to consider removing the floppy or at least inserting a disk-locking mechanism so that data can't be offloaded and unauthorized software loaded onto it. That's a radical solution, I'll admit, but if they're carrying around secret plans for a perpetual motion machine that you're getting ready to introduce, it's a thought.

Conserve Batteries

> Never mistake endurance for hospitality.
>
> Unknown

Create a RAM disk on your portable, load your favorite program and data, and run it from there. This will substantially reduce your use of the battery-sucking hard drive. Turn off backlighting when you can. Turn off virual memory on your Powerbook and 32-bit disk access on your PC portable to also reduce the power drain.

Set Up a RAM Drive

You can use part of your portable's memory as if it were a hard disk drive. It's called a RAM drive because it resides in random access memory. RAM drives operate just like hard drives but they're lots faster (most of the time) and that's one of their good features. The main advantage of a RAM drive in this instance is to reduce the number of times that you have to access a juice-guzzling hard drive, thereby conserving battery power.

I know lots of people who hate RAM drives; in fact, they hope that RAM drives remain a closely guarded secret from now until the Apocalypse. The reason is that it's easy to lose your work if you don't know what you're doing. Whenever you turn off or restart your computer, everything that is in RAM goes kablooey!

These same people will tell you that it's better to use SmartDrive that came with DOS, which also uses a portion of memory as a cache. SmartDrive is easier to use, and there really isn't any significant difference in performance. They're right. But what they don't know is that I'm also going to tell you to turn SmartDrive *off* when you're on the road.

Now I'm going to tell you how to set up a RAM drive and the heck with everyone else. Information wants to be free! When you set up Windows, the setup program puts a copy of RAMDRIVE.SYS in your Windows directory. Here's what to do:

1. If you haven't done it already, add the HIMEM.SYS command line to your CONFIG.SYS file. HIMEM is a memory manager that permits you to use extended memory. If you have DOS 6.x, MEMMAKER will do the configuration automatically.

2. Make a system disk and put a copy of your CONFIG.SYS file on it.

3. Open CONFIG.SYS with a text editor (use the Notepad, if you like).

4. Add the following command line right after the HIMEM.SYS command line: device=c:\windows\ramdrive.sys 256 /e. That specifies the location of RAMDRIVE and allocates 256K of extended memory to the RAM drive. You can allocate more or less RAM. It depends on how much RAM you have to begin with and the size of the program or file you want to stuff into the RAM drive.

5. Save.

6. Restart.

Get a Mac   If none of this is making any sense, get a Macintosh. Go to the memory control panel, click the On button under RAM drive, slide the little dohickey to the right to allocate the percentage of available memory to allocate to the RAM drive, click the Off button under virtual memory, and close. You're done.

Common Sense with SmartDrive

Windows 3.1 and MS-DOS 6.2 come with SmartDrive, a disk-caching program that is automatically installed and turned on when Windows or 6.2 is installed. SmartDrive saves information that is read from your hard drive in a disk cache in memory. SmartDrive also saves information that is to be written to the hard drive in the same way. Windows and DOS run faster when using a disk cache. If you should suddenly run out of battery juice before the disk writes are executed, you'll lose data.

Here's how to turn SmartDrive off when you're packaging your portable if you have DOS 6.2. (SmartDrive is installed with the delayed writes turned off by default.)

1. From DOS, type: C: SMARTDRV /S

2. Go the field that says "write cache," and make sure that it says "No."

If you have an earlier version of DOS, do this:

1. Open AUTOEXEC.BAT with Notepad.

2. Add C- at the end of the SMARTDRV.EXE line to disable delayed writes on drive C:.

Physical Security

> A kleptomaniac is a person who helps himself because he can't help himself.
>
> Henry Morgan
> *Infinite Riches,* by Leo Rosten, 1978

While John Labatt, the Canadian beer maker, was a takeover target in 1995, a thief broke into the company's Toronto headquarters and stole five laptop computers belonging to senior executives. Investigators on the case suspected industrial espionage because the thief ignored cash that could have easily been taken. The thief apparently spent five hours in the building collecting the laptops and rifling the offices of the president, CEO, and other top executives. When he was ready to leave, the brazen thief called security and asked them to help carry out a bag containing the laptops!

Laptop theft is up

Theft of computer equipment—especially notebook computers—has risen dramatically in recent years. It's easy to understand why that's so: Notebook computers are plentiful, they're small and easy to steal, and they're worth a lot of money.

Although the theft of computers is nothing new, it now appears to be more organized, several law enforcers say. Previously the main reasons for microcomputer theft were for money, either for drugs or other purposes. Now, however, computers are being stolen for competitor intelligence or to access data on local area networks or mainframe computers through modems. After many of the latest thefts, thieves logged on to networks and rifled files.

Computer bicycle lock

Although more laptops are bagged from homes and offices, I'm not about to forget that someone could very easily steal my laptop from my hotel room. When I travel, I take along a security cable system that works like a bicycle lock. One end attaches to the computer, the other loops around an immovable object like a radiator pipe, and back to the computer. I use one made by Z-Lock, but several companies make them. They sell for about $15 to $30.

Powerbooks always have had a slot built into the back to attach a latching device and cable. Now, a few PC makers—AST, Compaq, and Toshiba come to mind—have the same feature.

Lockdown Devices

Vendors offer several options for securing equipment. Most of them work like bicycle locks and consist of attaching a strong cable to the laptop and looping it around a radiator pipe or other immovable object and then back to the computer.

Some locks attach to the computer with adhesives; others fit inside a floppy drive door or a special security slot on the back of the laptop. Anchor Pad Products, Compu-Gard, Kensington Microware, PC Guardian Security Products, Qualtec Data Products, and SecurTech (to name but a few) make these devices. Most sell for about $25 to $35.

SonicPro International markets the unimaginably named Model LT128 ($90) motion-activated alarm for laptops. The device as a little keypad for arming and disarming it. Set it and if someone picks it up, the alarm sounds. It attaches with bonding tape and has adjustments for sensitivity and alarm volume.

Displaying Unbecoming Behavior

> Ladies and gentlemen, the captain asks that you please refrain from using your portable computer, radios, or other electronic devices during takeoff and landing.
>
> Every U.S. airline that I've ever flown

Business travelers who are concerned about guarding the information in their laptops think twice before using their laptops at any time during a flight. In close quarters, it's too easy for fellow passengers to get a close look at the laptop's display.

I almost never use my laptop on a flight unless I have a row all to myself. I don't know how many times some overly curious traveler has poked his nose into my business. Heck, it's not that my work is all that private, but I just can't stand someone reading my stuff as I write it. It makes me nervous. Instead I spend time sneaking peeks at other people who insist on working on their computers. I keep hoping that I'll read something that is really useful, like a comprehensive plan being developed by Acme who is planning a hostile takeover of Amalgamated. I could make a small fortune—or at least enough to buy braces for one of my kiddies—on the stock market with inside info like that!

If you insist on taking care of business on your laptop, here's something to consider buying. A few companies have released antiglare, privacy screens for notebook computers. 3M, for example, markets a privacy filter that weighs less than one pound and fits most notebook computers.

With a filter in place, the person sitting next to the user can't view the data unless he or she is directly in front of the screen. The filter also reduces glare from light and improves contrast, 3M says. It has a suggested retail price of $119. Kantek markets a similar screen called Secure-View. When viewed from an angle, an onlooker sees a blurred image of the display. It has a suggested retail price of $99.

X-ray Machine Myth

Okay, I know you want to ask this, so here's the answer. No, running your laptop through an airport X-ray machine will not hurt your laptop. In fact, it's probably better to send it along the conveyor belt than to carry it through the metal detector, which gives off an even greater magnetic field than the see-through machine. Personally I worry more about taking it out of the carrying case and showing one of the security guards that the blasted thing is powered up and working. Although I always keep it charged up and ready to go, what if it didn't work? I'd probably get arrested as a suspected terrorist and miss that all-important convention in Las Vegas.

Portable Protection

> When you have got an elephant by the hind legs and he is trying to run away, it is best to let him run.
>
> Abraham Lincoln (1809–1865)

What follows is every single decent idea that I have ever had about protecting laptop computers (and in no particular order):

1. Don't let your portable computer leave your hands. Carry it with you at all times. That means don't check it with luggage at the airport and don't put it down while you search for passport, tickets, and so on. Don't let it be carried into or out of your hotel on a baggage cart. Thieves often use the busy activity of a major hotel lobby to conceal their actions.

2. Be especially careful of your portable computer while at airports waiting for your flight. If you sit down, place the portable where you can always keep an eye on it. Take it with you if you need to talk to a ticket agent or go to the restroom. Never ask anyone, particularly a stranger, to keep an eye on it.

3. If possible, store the portable in your briefcase rather than use a portable computer carrying case, which is easily identifiable to thieves. If you must use a carrying case, use one that does not have a computer-company logo or other identifying symbol. Never leave the laptop carrying case unattended. Laptops are easy to spot and are prime targets for theft.

4. Make sure that you leave home with a well-charged battery, and if you're planning to work coast to coast, make sure that you have a spare.

5. Encrypt everything on your laptop, especially if you, like I do, store personal stuff like addresses and credit card numbers on it.

6. If you decide to leave your laptop in your car, lock it in the trunk. Don't leave it on the seat where it can be seen.

7. When you leave your hotel room, lock the laptop in your luggage, use a lockdown device, or stow it in the hotel safe.

8. In the office, the laptop should be secured in a locked office or locked furniture, or secured to the work surface.

9. If you regularly access a remote system, don't use an auto-logon program. If someone steals the laptop, you've also made it easy for him or her to get into your system back at the office.

10. Do not write down your userID and password; if you do, don't leave the note with the laptop.

11. Lots of portables have a power-on password protection. In the absence of anything else, use it.

12. Watch out for shoulder surfers and anyone else who might be able to read the information on the laptop screen. Do not read or enter confidential information on airplanes or in public places where the screen is visible.

13. Scan floppy disks and laptop hard drives for computer viruses.

14. Periodically back up the hard disk to floppy disks, and store the floppy disks someplace other than in the laptop carrying case.

15. Use encryption software to scramble confidential and proprietary information that must be kept on the laptop, and remove information that you no longer need.

16. Check to see whether your insurance policy covers your laptop, and if not, get a rider to cover it. If the laptop is stolen, report it to the police, hotel, and airport security to establish your insurance claim.

CONTROL OVER REMOTE ACCESS

> No tin hat brigade of goose-stepping vigilantes or Bible-babbling mob of blackguarding and corporate-paid scoundrels will prevent the onward march of labor.
>
> John L. Lewis
> *Time*, Sept. 9, 1937

These days, folks want to work wherever they happen to be and "wherever" is increasingly everywhere but the home office. There are the roadwarrior types who schlep their laptops and cell phones from one client's office to another; and there is that growing cadre of people who work at home, either because they want to get ahead or they're telecommuters. I've also met small groups of entrepreneurs who operate as a single business unit, yet each member of the team works out of a home office. They only get together every few weeks for some valuable face time.

In any case, these folks also need to have the option of remotely connecting to the company LAN. They can connect to the LAN in different ways, but they share one common concern: security. After all, if you give employees a way to get into the company system, what's to stop some dastardly hacker from doing the same? How are remote systems attacked? Let me count the ways.

Security is the concern

War Dialing

The first way is to use a war dialer, which I told you about in Chapter 1. The war dialer goes through a list of telephone numbers, dialing each one and listening for the high-pitch signal given off by a computer modem picking up the line on the other end. The phone numbers of these computers are entered in a database. Later the hacker will dial into these numbers individually to see what's on the other end and probe these systems for security weaknesses.

To minimize the prospect of being hit on by a war dialer, set your network modems to answer after several rings, not immediately.

While you're at it, the telephone numbers that you use for data connections should not be the same or even similar to those used by the rest of the company. Hackers often look at the telephone numbers used by a company for consecutive numbers and then dial the numbers immediately before and after that sequence in hopes of hitting on a data line. Use data line numbers that are out of the range of company phone numbers.

Brute Force Attack

The second way a hacker is going to try to get into your system is by hammering on passwords until the door caves in. If you use hacker-proofing techniques such as pass phrases, limited attempts to enter passwords, and two-factor authentication, you can do an awful lot to keep intruders on the outside.

Other Possibilities

A technically sophisticated intruder will go for the network operating system itself or attempt to circumvent security in other ways. When all else fails, he or she may pick up the phone and con someone into revealing a password.

Setting Up the Barricades

One common way to keep the vandals and visigoths from storming your company's network is to use a modem with security features that limit who can dial into your network, when they can dial in, and from where they can dial. Here are some types of security-conscious modems.

Call Me Call-back

You dial in, the computer answers the phone, you enter your userID and password, and then you hang up. The computer calls you back, using a previously agreed-upon telephone number. That's why they call it a call-back modem.

Not for everyone   Not everyone can use call-back modems. It's one thing if you're a telecommuter who seldom leaves your house, but if you're a traveling salesman, using a call-back modem is impractical. Call-back modems are a less effective safeguard; they require advance programming of the remote user's phone number, so this approach is not appropriate for mobile users. They also authenticate only the location, not the user.

Glaring   Hackers use a technique called glaring to fool simple call-back systems. The hacker, for example, transmits a fake dial tone and the call-back is tricked into thinking that it's made a connection. The hacker seizes the opportunity to slip in while the call-back modem is waiting (or glaring) for a signal or answer sequence.

If you want to use a call-back modem, get one that uses separate lines to answer and call back to prevent glaring.

Secure Modems

Another alternative to use is a secure modem that makes the connection with a random password and also encrypts data before transmitting it as well as performs other security tricks. The U.S. Secret Service uses these secure modems for communications between field agents and headquarters in Washington, D.C.

Smart Cards, Etc.

Some call-back modems, such as LeeMah DataCom Security's TraqNetwork, operate in conjunction with a password generator. TraqNet consists of a small device that sits between the modem and the computer, intercepts all calls, and requires authentication before passing a call on to the modem. As an option, the TraqNet dials back an authenticated user at a preset number. The system's pricing starts at $950 for a one-modem port box.

Communications Devices makes a mobile security system called WinGuard Access that turns a pager into a password token. If you use the product, you dial into the network and enter a personal identification number. In response, the system generates a one-time random number and transmits that to your pager. If you enter that number into the system, you're allowed to pass through the security portals. The company says it works in a matter of seconds. They also say WinGuard works with Ocean Isle Software's Reach Out, Microcom's Carbon Copy, and Symantec's Norton PC. Anywhere. I can't vouch for either claim, but if it works as advertised, it's a nifty idea.

Who's Calling Security?

> Talk is cheap because supply exceeds demand.
>
> Unknown

Caller ID and other calling-party identification services that most phone companies now offer can be used to enhance dial-in security. Better yet, they don't cost much either. The big idea is to use these services to identify who is calling before the caller is given access to the network. **Are you the party to whom I am speaking?**

The long-distance carriers offer automatic number identification (ANI) with 800- and 900-number services. The ANI is a code unique to each telephone circuit and can be used by the call recipient to identify the caller before answering. The ANI is quite secure and cannot be tampered with by outsiders.

A growing number of local telephone companies offer Caller ID within their regional calling areas (it works like ANI). This is an option that you might want to consider if most of your employees and others who dial in to your network are based in the same region as your company.

The caller has no way of knowing whether the call is being screened by ANI or Caller ID screening. If the caller's number jibes with that of an authorized employee, the call goes through; if it doesn't, the call is bounced.

No Trespassing Sign

> After I'm dead I'd rather have people ask why I have no monument than why I have one.
>
> Cato the Elder (234–149 BC)

Many systems have opening banners that greet users as they dial in. These banners typically read something like, "Welcome to Acme's friendship computer system, where we keep our customers happy every day. Please enter your userID and password." Many security experts will tell you that you shouldn't use a welcome banner because it provides potential hackers with clues about the system. There's a lot of truth to this, but I'm not opposed to using an opening banner.

In fact, I recommend it. What I suggest is that you post a No Trespassing banner on your system that warns anyone dialing in that the system is for private **No trespassing** use and if you are not authorized to use the system, stay the heck out. Then, for good measure, install the electronic equivalent of scattergun that will keep prowlers from getting into the system (more about how to do that in a minute, but now, back to that No Trespassing sign).

Everywhere there's signs

The following warning banner was developed by the U.S. Justice Department and is widely used by federal government agencies. I got it from a computer system that I have access to that is operated by a very secretive federal government agency that knows more about computer security than just about anybody else in the entire world. If it works for them, it will work for you:

```
To protect this system from unauthorized use and to ensure
that this system is functioning properly, system administrators
monitor the system. This system is for the use of authorized users
only. Individuals using this computer system without authority,
or in excess of their authority, are subject to having all of
their activities on this system monitored and recorded by system
personnel. In the course of monitoring individuals who improperly
use this system, or in the course of system maintenance, the
activities of authorized users may also be monitored. Anyone
using this system expressly consents to such monitoring and is
advised that if such monitoring reveals possible evidence of
criminal activity, system personnel may provide the evidence of
such monitoring to law enforcement officials.
```

Not such a corny idea

This is a carefully worded banner, as you can see. It is very specific about what is going to happen if you use the system. At the same time, it doesn't provide any clues to an outsider about who the system belongs to. This No Trespassing sign isn't going to keep a hacker off your system anymore than a real sign will keep raccoons out of your corn field. But, it's a much more valuable security tool than you might think. Here's why.

Oops, gotcha

Let's say a hacker breaks into your system and in a bid to nab him (or her), you begin to monitor his activities. You set up your electronic stakeout, record all of his illegal activities—perhaps even bait him with phony files—and then track the intruder back to his lair. With evidence of skullduggery in hand, you call the computer crime cops who then go off to bust the hacker. Sounds good, eh? You forgot something. It's against the law for you to monitor the hacker's activity on your system without his consent. Oh, irony of ironies—that hacker you just nabbed could sue you for invasion of privacy!

The Electronics Communications Privacy Act (ECPA) is very specific about who can monitor another person's electronic communication and under what circumstances. The ECPA says that although you own the system, that doesn't give you the right to eavesdrop; for that you need a court-approved wiretap. Think of the telephone company in your area. They own the system, but it's against the law for them to listen to you playing phone footsie with the person next door.

Posting the No Trespassing sign on your system warns the intruder that you will monitor his activities and that if he insists on going beyond that point, he expressly consents to this monitoring. Sometimes, strange times demand strange measures.

A sign of the times

4 Networks: 1000 Points of Fright

A good scare is worth more to a man than good advice.

Edgar Watson Howe
Country Town Sayings, 1911

One November morning in 1988, I strolled into work at *Computerworld*, where I worked as a senior editor. I was the first reporter to arrive that morning, and the only other person in the news room was the news editor. As soon as he spots me, he yells out, "Alexander, get into my office. There's a problem on the Internet and we've got to get the story in by noon." It was Friday, the day that we shipped the newspaper out to the printer in the Midwest. If the paper was to start dropping on desktops around the country the following Monday, we had to transmit the newspaper to our printer in the Midwest by noon.

"What's the problem?" I ask.

"I'm not sure, but it has something to do with a worm."

"Right boss, I'll get right on it. Uh, boss, what's the Internet?"

"It's some network. Now get going."

"Right boss, I'll get right on it. Uh, boss, what's a worm?"

"I dunno, it's some virus thing. Now get to work!"

"Right boss, I'll get right on it."

I learned what the Internet was, how to tell the difference between a virus and a worm, and more stuff than I ever thought possible in only a few hours. What I learned was that Robert Tappan Morris, a brilliant Cornell University computer science graduate student, had injected a worm program onto the Internet to test a pet theory on computer security. His experiment went awry and, as a result of a programming error, caused the shutdown of some 6000 computers on the global matrix. Some months later, Morris found himself on trial in a federal courtroom in Syracuse, New York, where he became one of the first ever to be prosecuted under the federal government's Computer Fraud and Abuse Act of 1986. I knocked out the story by deadline (it made the front page), and nearly seven years later, I'm still chasing stories about computer security.

Experiment gone awry

More than you'll ever know

I have to confess, there is no way that I'm going to be able to tell you everything you might want to know about network security in one chapter. It's a complex topic, and you would need to read a book or two before you could start to get a handle on it. Also, computer network security is not a do-it-yourself sort of job unless you're a technical wizard (in which case, why are you reading this book?).

You'll be dangerous

What I aim to do is give you enough information to make you dangerous. I'll give you an overview of what you can do to protect your LAN from attack by disgruntled insiders and outlaw intruders. I'll also give you a rundown on connecting to the Internet and offer some tips on what you must do to protect yourself. I'm also going to tell you about telephone networks and how to protect yourself from all manner of dial-tone bandits and phone scam artists.

LAN 101

> Just because your voice reaches halfway around the world doesn't mean you are wiser than when it reached only to the end of the bar.
>
> Edward R. Morrow (1908–1965)

Link a bunch of PCs together and you have the rudimentary makings of a local area network. LANs are set up in one of three basic ways, which the tech folks call bus, ring, and star topologies. In a bus topology, the workstations are strung together like pearls on an unclasped necklace. A ring topology is similar to a bus topology, except that the necklace is clasped to complete the circle. In a star topology, the workstations are connected like the spokes of a wheel to a central device called a hub. No matter the topology, the big idea of networking PCs is that they are able to share files, applications, printers, scanners, modems, and other devices.

Small companies, with 5 to 20 users, typically set up a bus topology. It's relatively cheap and easy and works well if the data traffic on the network is not too heavy. In more complex setups, one computer, called a server, acts as a central repository that houses applications and files that everyone can access. The server also functions as a sort of traffic cop, controlling all of the interaction between it and the workstations. You'll have to forgive me if all of this seems spectacularly obvious, but I've visited a lot of small companies that weren't even aware that they had LANs.

> The higher a monkey climbs, the more you see of its behind.
>
> General Joseph "Vinegar Joe" Stilwell (1883–1946)

Security is not seamless

In the early days, LANs were used primarily for exchanging files and for sharing databases and peripherals. One of the most common applications then and now is electronic mail. Over time, LANs have become much more sophisticated, with powerful servers handling databases, financial transactions, and a wide variety of other complex applications. Meanwhile, some companies have been tying their LANs together and hooking them up with mainframes and other systems. Eventually all of this grew into one massive network that many companies now call a client/server architecture.

Out of all of this topology, and client/server stuff has come one of the most pressing security issues facing systems administrator and computer security chiefs. Patching together a variety of PCs, Macs, and workstations; running a bunch of different applications and network operating systems like Novell NetWare and Microsoft Windows NT Server; and trying to perform all the other computer tasks that are supposed to make your business leaner and more competitive is a real feat under any circumstance. Making sure that everything fits together seamlessly so that there are no security loopholes is about as hard as building the Great Pyramid without an instruction manual.

Get Physical about Server Security

> Always do right—this will gratify some and astonish the rest.
>
> Mark Twain
> "The Man That Corrupted Hadleyburg," 1890

I've visited lots of companies where the servers were tucked into utility closets. That's not good enough. If an unauthorized person can get to the server, no amount of access control is going to prevent him or her from stealing trade secrets or even blasting your data into oblivion. It takes but minutes to reboot the server from a disk and install a Trojan horse to collect passwords, for example. And that's only the beginning of a long list of bad things that could happen.

Secure the server under lock and key. Give some thought to whether it is also **Lock it up** adequately ventilated and not susceptible to water or anything else that might harm the equipment. Also, make sure that you use an uninterruptible power supply (see Chapter 6 for more details about power protection) to guard against blackouts and other power-supply problems.

> **If you yank the wiring out of the average LAN, it would stretch from Timbuktu to Venus, or something like that. A lot of that wiring is exposed, allowing an intruder to tap into the LAN's cable and siphon off data.**

Copper wiring is especially vulnerable to eavesdropping because it's easy to connect to (and it doesn't always require a direct connection to the wire). Fiber cabling is less susceptible because tapping in requires special connectors, but it is vulnerable nonetheless. It's not likely that you can protect every inch of your LAN's wiring, but take care to protect it in the out-of-the-way spots where it is most likely to be attacked.

Some Novel Ideas for NetWare

> Distrust any enterprise that requires new clothes.
>
> Henry David Thoreau (1817–1862)

Novell's NetWare is by far the most popular of the LAN operating systems. The company says that about 70 percent of all LANs use some version of NetWare.

There are several of versions of NetWare, including NetWare Lite, Personal NetWare, and NetWare 2.x, 3.x, and 4.x. There's no way that I can tell you about all of them in any detail, and I'm not even going to try. Instead I'll tell you about the main points of securing Novell 3.x, one of the most popular network operating systems for small companies.

LAN basics   Even if your company is using something other than NetWare, you'll find this part useful. The fundamentals of NetWare 3.x security apply to all of the LAN operating systems—Banyan Vines, IBM LAN Server, and Microsoft Windows NT Server—although the terminology and ways of setting up security obviously differ.

LAN operating systems—at least the mainstream ones—have in common the ability to:

- Identify and authenticate people who log into the LAN.

- Restrict the access of each user to specific files and applications.

- Track the activities of LAN users and spot attempts to breach security.

Personal NetWare and NetWare 3.x have lots of security features, enough that the typical employee would be hard pressed to get inside and bollix up the works.

 The problem is that NetWare's security features can be difficult to configure properly, especially if the LAN administrator is not particularly security savvy.

NLMs   NetWare can be enhanced with NetWare Loadable Modules (NLM) that run on the server with the same privilege level as NetWare. NLMs are generally more functional than products that run on workstations because those products lack the same privileges as the network's operating system. NLMs also can be security risks because they have these same privileges.

Jackie Gets the Job

> The two hardest things to handle in life are failure and success.
>
> Unknown

Someone has to oversee the installation and administration of the LAN. In large companies, the job is assigned to a terribly bright person with a computer science background and years of experience overseeing and managing information systems. In small companies, the job is given to the mailroom clerk because no one else wants it or has a clue about what to do. That's a key reason LAN security is woeful in small companies.

Here's one of those common-sense-should-tell-you tips: Establish a relationship with an outside computer consulting firm that will help set up your LAN and fix it when it dies (and it will always die when you need it most). Yes, it's going to cost you more money than it would take to buy a newly discovered Fabergé egg, but it's worth it. In fact, it's worth whatever value you place on your company.

Okay, so you're not going to listen to me and you've decided to appoint Jackie in the mailroom as the LAN supervisor. So, what's the job going to entail?

Captain of the *Enterprise*

> We all can't be heroes because somebody has to sit on the curb and clap as they go by.
>
> Attributed to Will Rogers

The LAN supervisor is the equivalent of Captain Katheryn Janeway on the bridge of the *Starship Enterprise*. She determines how the LAN is set up, what rights and privileges each user gets, which files can be read and changed by each user, and countless other tasks. She performs lots of other nonsecurity tasks, too, as part of her administrative duties, but right now all we care about is getting Jackie squared away on securing the LAN. If she needs to know about all of the other headaches of LAN management, she'll have to read someone else's book.

When NetWare is installed, it creates a SUPERVISOR account and a GUEST account. If the SUPERVISOR is the equivalent of Captain Janeway, then GUEST is a visiting Ferengi dignitary who has been locked in his room for trying to steal dilithium crystals from engineering.

Untrustworthy guests   In fact, GUEST is so untrustworthy, no one one really wants the sneak thief hanging around. The GUEST account is what gives an outsider the same access rights as everyone else. This is an account that most LAN supervisors should delete as a security precaution. Not all do, however, because there may be legitimate reasons for a nonemployee to access the LAN. That's certainly true if you have freelancers or other contractors working temporarily on site. In that case, you want to make sure that you give the GUEST account the minimum access rights to do the job and nothing more (as the SUPERVISOR you can do anything you want).

Captain, I Cannae Give You More Power!

> I don't know the key to success, but the key to failure is trying to please everybody.
>
> Bill Cosby

A LAN supervisor can be too powerful, however. Imagine the trouble the captain could cause if suddenly she were afflicted by a space spore that made her want to lock everyone out of the LAN while she goes off to count how many cans of strawberries there are in the galley.

What's needed is a watchdog for the watchdog. One of the ways that's done is to give two people LAN supervisor status and let each of them oversee only a part of the LAN or divide the duties in other ways so that not one person holds all of the security keys. Even that is not foolproof because this approach is done through policy and not a set of technological locks and keys. Both people will still have unlimited access to the LAN.

I once worked as a magazine editor for a small publishing company that also was in the business of training people how to configure their LANs and secure them. The company's top trainer also happened to be our LAN supervisor, so you've got to bet that the guy really knew his stuff, right? He was constantly changing things around on the LAN and I don't know how many times weird stuff happened because of his finagling.

Dumb mistake   Once, I found that I inadvertently had been given read and write access to the president's personal directory. For three days, I resisted the temptation to read the boss's own files as well as the personnel reviews, employment contracts of co-workers, and lots of other confidential and sensitive data. I knew the LAN man would eventually figure out that he had done a Swiss cheese number on the LAN's security and do something about it. Had there been two LAN supervisors, with one keeping an eye on the other, that sort of dumb mistake probably would not have happened.

It's just as bad to have too many people with supervisory status than too few. I've been in plenty of companies where several people—far more than are necessary to administer the LAN—have supervisory status. Users with supervisory status are free to roam the LAN and have unrestricted access to sensitive information that can be read, tampered with, or improperly handled.

Supervisors should create two accounts for themselves. The first is SUPERVISOR status, of course. The second is the same account as all of the other employees get. The SUPERVISOR account is used for those things that supervisors need to do, and the other account is used for everyday work.

The reason is that supervisors, although omnipotent, are far from perfect. In fact, they are just as likely as anyone else to screw something up, except that a screw-up by a supervisor is a far bigger deal than a mistake by you are me.

Suppose Jackie has been out all night with a bunch of her friends, celebrating her elevation from mailroom drone to supervisor. Jackie comes to work with a hangover and bleary eyed, accidentally deletes an entire directory of valuable files. She's the only one who has the power to do something like that (at least she is if the LAN is properly set up). Had Jackie used her regular account, she wouldn't have been able to delete much of anything.

More Words About Passwords

> When ideas fail, words come in very handy.
>
> Johann Wolfgang von Goethe (1749–1832)

NetWare comes out of the box without requiring that any passwords be used on the system. You should first make sure that passwords are needed to access the system. As I explained in detail in Chapter 3, passwords ought to be set at a minimum length, be difficult to crack, and all of that. NetWare has loads of password protection features. All you have to do is turn them on.

NetWare permits you to create passwords with as many as 127 characters. That's a lot, huh? Bet not even Superman could crack a 127-character password. Let me give you a tip: Don't create a 127-character password. In fact, don't create any password that is too long to be practical. A 15-character pass phrase ought to be enough. (If it's not, the National Security Agency probably wants to have a talk with you about those secrets you're keeping.)

NetWare has its own burglar alarm, called Intruder Detection (ID), which is designed to protect the LAN against password cracking. This is another feature

Built-in burglar alarm

that you must turn on. Once configured, ID counts the number of times a person attempts to log in to the LAN. After a preset number of failed attempts, the user account is locked out for a time specified by the LAN administrator.

Surprisingly, Intruder Detection often is turned off by LAN administrators who find it inconvenient to reset the disabled accounts of legitimate users. My friend, Robert Kane, a NetWare security expert, likens not using Intruder Detection to having a house with a fancy burglar alarm system but leaving the front door wide open.

Savvy NetWare insiders who are aware that Intruder Detection is enabled will make several attempts to log in as supervisor, causing the account to lock out the real supervisor. Do that enough times and the supervisor may disable ID simply to get rid of the administrative headache.

NetWare has two other options for passwords. The first is the Periodic Change in Passwords options that requires that passwords be changed every 90 days. The second is the Unique Password Option that keeps track of the last eight passwords each person has used and prevents them from using those passwords again. Both of those options should be turned on (they are by default, but someone may have changed them).

**Disable
userIDs** When employees leave, their userIDs and passwords should be immediately disabled as part of their termination process. Inactive userIDs are an open invitation for disgruntled employees and hackers to enter the system.

Passwords on LANs running NetWare 3.x (and 4.x) are encrypted before being sent across the network. If someone were to intercept the password, they would not be able to use it without first decrypting it (not something an intruder could do easily, if at all). On earlier versions of NetWare and other LAN operating systems, passwords are sent in plaintext, which means that anyone can read them if they are intercepted.

Not Too Tight, Not Too Loose

> You appeal to a small, select group of confused people.
>
> Fortune cookie message

Because insiders pose the greatest threat to security, you need to minimize the opportunities to make trouble either accidentally or deliberately and set limits on what activities are permitted. You can set the limits as loose or as tight as you want; you can apply those limits just on Ralph in auditing, whom no one likes, or on everyone in the company.

The trick is figuring out just what the limitations should be so that they are effective yet don't get in the way of everyone doing their jobs. They also must reflect the importance of the data that you're trying to protect. You can put the tightest controls where you need them the most and probably not hinder the work of too many employees.

Remember in Chapter 1, I talked about setting limits for information and providing access to that information on a need-to-know basis? To recap, not all employees need to access all information on a local area network. The marketing VP probably does not need access to an accounting person's personnel records, for example. All access stems from this need to know. That should be one of your underlying principles when you set up your LAN.

Need to know

Supervisor Gets Attributes

> Three may keep a Secret, if two of them are dead.
>
> Benjamin Franklin
> *Poor Richard's Almanack*, 1735

NetWare comes with a variety of options for assigning attributes to files and directories. They're something akin to a parental lockout that keeps young teenagers (like my daughter Leigh) from vegging out on MTV's Bevis and Butthead for 24 hours at a stretch. These attributes determine what files can be read, changed, deleted, renamed, and so on. The LAN supervisor can permit LAN users to do some of these activities at their discretion and, if she wants tighter security, require that these activities be mandatory.

Attributes

A user with discretionary access control might be allowed an unrestricted ability to read and change files. Nothing prohibits that same employee from copying a file to a floppy disk or putting it in a directory that can be accessed by other employees who are not able to access the original file. This is basic level security.

A user with mandatory access controls, on the other hand, might be allowed to read the file but would be prohibited from copying the file and storing it where someone else with lesser access rights could get at it. The LAN supervisor also could require users to log in from a specific workstation and may even control the time of day during which that access from that workstation is allowed.

Mandatory access controls all sound pretty Draconian, but it's for a noble cause. If nothing else, you want to prevent users from logging in to the network more than once. This stops them from logging in to multiple locations and then walking away, which is a one of the most common ways that insiders are able to jump security fences.

Batten Down the Security Hatches

> Being too good is apt to be uninteresting.

> Harry S. Truman

NetWare has several attributes that can be used to batten down the security hatches. Here is a rundown on some of the main attributes that security-minded LAN supervisors are likely to use:

- Copy Inhibit—Users are not able to copy files with this attribute. It prevents users from installing or copying unauthorized software like games, bootleg copies, and other software by preventing the copying executable files (those ending in .EXE and .COM). Harold wants me to mention that this feature will keep people from copying files, but that does not mean the information is safe. There are several programs that will take a snapshot of each screen. Given enough time, anyone can copy a file this way.

- Delete Inhibit—Users are not able to delete files or directories with this attribute.

- Execute Only—Programs can be run, but they cannot be copied or tampered with in any way (that's good for helping to minimize the spread of viruses). The problem is that once set, this attribute cannot be undone. You'll need to delete the file and reinstall it from the original disks. Also, programs that modify themselves will not work with the Execute Only attribute turned on.

- Hidden—This attribute hides files and directories so that they cannot be called up with the DIR command. What users can't see, they can't mess with.

- Read Only—Just what you think it means.

- Read/Write—Users can read and change files with this attribute. (It's the default setting, by the way.)

- Sharable—Most of the time, you don't want two or more users working on the same file simultaneously because one does not know what the other is up to. But there are files, such as databases, that several users may need to look at, all at the same time. Sharable makes it so.

You Got Rights

> Women who seek to be equal with men lack ambition.

> Timothy Leary

NetWare supervisors give LAN users certain rights. Although all LAN users are created equal, it's the supervisor who determines just who is more equal than everybody else. The way that's done is with these rights:

- Access Control—You have the right to say who else gets to see your directories and files.

- Create—You have the right to create directories and files.

- File Scan—You have the right to use DIR to see what files are in a directory.

- Modify—You have the right to rename and change files and directories as well as the right to change their attributes.

- Read—You have the right to read files and run programs.

- Supervisor—You have the right to play god on the LAN. Like I said, only the supervisor and perhaps one or two other people should have this right.

- Write—You have the right to write to files.

Security Tools and Other Enhancements

> He without benefit of scruples
> His fun and money soon quadruples.
>
> Odgen Nash (1902–1971)

Although the mainstream LAN operating systems provide a sophisticated degree of security, they are not always easy to set up properly and administer. For that reason, several companies market software that can enhance or simplify LAN security. Some will analyze your LAN security setup, looking for accounts with weak passwords, excessive access rights, and other potential security loopholes. **Looking for holes**

Many of the access control packages that I mentioned in Chapter 3 also come in LAN versions that permit you to administer and configure all of the access control packages in use from one workstation. COM&DIA's DiaLOCK BOOT and Security Integration's Stoplight 95 are two examples that come to mind.

Many, many access control packages on the market work in conjunction with NetWare's security. For example, Infinite Technologies' GuardIT! detects when a PC is logged on to the network but has been idle for a specified period of time, an indication that the employee has walked off and left the PC logged on. The package locks the keyboard until the proper NetWare password is entered.

Put Passwords on Autopilot

> Much as he is opposed to lawbreaking, he is not bigoted about it.
>
> Damon Runyon (1884–1946)

Password management is a key task for any LAN supervisor. It also happens to be time consuming. You can require employees to have passwords of a proscribed length and to change them often, but that doesn't mean they're using hacker-proof **Best practices** passwords. The only way you'll know for sure is to check from time to time. You can automate that process with products that generate passwords, oversee how often they are changed, and test them against a dictionary to make sure they are secure. Other products examine userID and password security, user account restrictions, and other security settings and compare them against a set of "best practices" to see whether yours are appropriate for your site. Baseline Software, which markets Password Coach, and Intrusion Detection, which markets Kane Security Analyst, make products like these.

Now a word from our sponsor. Not really, but I do want to take a second to plug Intrusion Detection's Kane Security Analyst. KSA is one of the best products around for assessing the security of a LAN running NetWare 3.x. Fire it up, and it will sniff out easily guess passwords, examine the access rights of users, and probe for several other security weaknesses. It costs $395 and is worth every penny. KSA was developed by Robert Kane, someone to whom I have turned repeatedly for help in trying to figure out what makes NetWare tick. I figure that I owe him one at this point.

Password generator   You can considerably enhance password protection on your LAN with two-factor authentication using a password generator. As I mentioned in Chapter 3, these devices randomly generate a new password once a minute or every time they're used, and then discarded.

To access a protected network, authorized users simply enter their personal identification number (PIN) and a unique code that is generated and displayed on the password generator. Assuming the information is correct, the system authenticates the user's identity and allows access to those network resources for which that user is authorized. Unauthorized intruders never get past the front door. Enigma Logic and Security Dynamics, among others, make password generators. This level of security comes at a steep price, however, because it requires a separate server. Expect to pay $7000 or more.

Intrusion Detection

> I's wicked I is.
>
> Harriet Beecher Stowe
> *Uncle Tom's Cabin*

Waiting until an employee or outsider has picked your pockets to find out that your LAN is not secure is plain dumb. That's obvious to people with common sense, but not enough LAN administrators fit in that group. It always surprises me that so many companies don't bother setting up security controls until something bad has happened. It doesn't have to be that way, of course.

One of the fundamental principles of computer security is auditing, that is, keeping an eye on the activities of the people who log in to (or attempt to log in to) your system. If users know that there is an audit trail of their activities, they're less likely to circumvent security controls, at least not with their own account.

If you read about protecting desktop and laptop computers in Chapter 3, you already got a look at some of the benefits of auditing. It's one of the few ways that you have of spotting an attempted security breach before the actual break-in occurs.

NetWare's auditing feature is pretty rudimentary, and it takes considerable diligence to sort through the reams of paper that it generates in order to spot patterns that might signal an attempted security breach.

Several audit programs maintain a trail of all activity on the network, including the programs that have run and the files that were opened, changed, and so on. Unlike NetWare's own auditing command, these add-on auditors are capable of creating comprehensive, yet easy-to-read audit reports.

Blue Lance, On Technology, Intrusion Detection, and other companies market auditing software that can be used to track successful and failed attempts to access the LAN and any unauthorized changes to security configurations as well as to pinpoint other potential security violations.

Software Meter Maids

> When a fellow says it hain't the money but the principle o' the thing, it's th' money.
>
> Kin Hubbard
> *Hoss Sense and Nonsense*, 1926

If the software you use is not paid for, you're violating federal copyright laws. No ifs, buts, or maybes. In Chapter 8 I'll tell you why you shouldn't copy that floppy, but right now, I want to tell you about how to keep track of the software that is on your LAN to make sure that you are not violating the law.

Lots of companies want to stay within the bounds of copyright law and do the right thing. That's not always easy. There are all sorts of licensing agreements, and they vary from one manufacturer to another. Employees, who often don't know any better, routinely load software on their work machines that they purchased for home use in violation of the copyright agreement. Software on a LAN only magnifies the problem because software is easily copied and shared among many users, well beyond the bounds of the licensing agreement.

Doing the right thing

Software metering tools scour your LAN for illegal software and to make sure that the software that is being used is in compliance with the prevailing licensing agreements.

There's an additional benefit of software metering, and that is to track what legimate software is being used and who is using it. The advantage is that your company may be able to save considerable amounts of money on the way it purchases software licenses.

Suppose your company buys all ten of its employees a copy of a program that costs $300 apiece, for a total cost of $3000. Using monitoring software, you discover that only five employees at a time are using the program. In that case, you could buy a concurrent license for five employees and pay $350 or so per copy for a total cost of $1750 (a savings of $1250).

Wait, there's more. Software metering tools can also be used to compile detailed information about the software you use. That sort of information would come in handy in the event of a disaster that forces you to duplicate your LAN offsite, or worse, replace it from the ground up.

Viruses on the LANscape

Viruses on LANs pose a particularly worrisome problem. If one workstation is infected and passes files along to another workstation or to the server, all of the workstations on the LAN can become infected in a matter of minutes. I have seen more than one instance where a virus outbreak on a LAN on one coast traveled to a LAN belonging to the same company on the opposite coast.

It's not that networked PCs' works are inherently more susceptible to viruses than standalone PCs. PCs in a carefully tended network, with reasonably tight controls over user access control rights and file and directory attributes, can ward off many of the ways in which viruses enter LANs and spread.

If all of the programs that employees use are on the network and are locked to prevent anyone from altering them, that would help minimize the spread of viruses (it would also do a lot to hinder productivity, which is an equally valid concern).

On the other hand, if the LAN has lax security, a virus could spread like kudzu vines. In some cases, you may even have to shut down the entire LAN until the virus is removed. (Talk about hindering user productivity!)

Guarding against viruses requires protecting individual workstations as well **First** as the server. The first line of defense is antivirus software that resides on each PC, as a scanner to detect known viruses, as a terminate-and-stay-resident (TSR) program or integrity checker to detect unknown viruses, or as some combination of those options. Some manufacturers offer PC and server protection in a single package; others sell off-the-shelf PC products and server products that work in concert.

The second line of defense is a server-based product that scans files on the **Second** server in real time, on demand, or according to a daily, weekly, or monthly scheduled determined by the administrator.

The third line of defense is a centralized administration program that enables **Third** the administrator to easily distribute software and updates to each workstation. These programs typically alert the adminsitrator if a virus is detected on a PC or on the server, and they check each PC to ensure that the antivirus software's protection features have not been disabled. They also allow the administrator to decide whether to immediately remove a virus or isolate it so it cannot do further harm.

Cheyenne Software, Command Software Systems, Intel, McAfee Associates, Symantec's Peter Norton Product Group, and several other companies market antivirus software for LANs.

The Rest of the LANscape

> When women go wrong, men go right after them.
>
> Mae West (1892–1980)

Several LAN tools such as LAN analyzers that are used for troubleshooting were designed for legitimate purposes, but in the wrong hands, these same tools can be used to "sniff" passwords, change access rights, and cause other mischief. Several freebie utilities such as Netcrack, a hacking program, cracks passwords by brute force, are readily available to members of the computer underground and are especially intended to breach LAN security. LAN administrators may find it tempting to use these free and inexpensive tools to monitor the activities on their networks, but they run the risk that they may be used against them.

If you're a LAN administrator, you must sweep your LAN periodically to find out whether these sorts of programs have been installed without your go-ahead.

Back Up, Back Up

> Toots Shor's restaurant is so crowded nobody goes there anymore.
>
> Yogi Berra

Backing up the data on a LAN is the single most important thing that you can do at the end of each day and at the end of each week (or month, if you're not as paranoid as you should be). I cover backing up in Chapter 7, but here I just want to mention some backup software designed for LAN backup.

Backing up a LAN is a lot easier than walking around and backing up a bunch of standalone PCs and Macs. In fact, I'm told by a backup maven I know that backing up individual PCs and Macs costs three times as much as doing a centralized backup off a LAN. I don't know if that's true, but it certainly seems plausible, what with the time and effort that is involved.

LAN backup   If you're going to back up data on a LAN, you will need two items. First, get a 4 or 8 millimeter tape drive, capable of stockpiling gigabytes of data at a single shot. Second, get LAN-happy network backup software capable of backing up both the LAN server and individual workstations. Lots of companies including Arcada Software, Cheyenne Software, and Palindrome, sell backup software for networks. Prices range from $150 to $2000.

Tips to Achieving LAN Security

Start slow and taper off.

Walt Stack

Activate your LAN's security features and train your employees to be on the lookout for suspicious activity, and the security battle is close to being won. Here is a list of steps you should take as surveyor of the LANscape:

1. Set up access to the LAN on a need-to-know basis. Name-brand LANs have solid security controls, enough to defeat all but the most dedicated or knowl-edgeable attacker. Your job is to make sure they are turned on and configured properly.

2. Use call-back modems and other access control mechanisms if you need to allow remote access to your LAN. Also set limits on when outsiders can access the LAN and for how long. If employees are going to dial out only, configure modems to prohibit dial-in access.

3. Allow only licensed software on the LAN, and keep accurate records of vendor information and version and license numbers. Store the configuration reports in a safe place in case the software has to be reinstalled.

4. Train employees not to leave their workstation logged in while they are away.

5. Use all of the common-sense techniques in this chapter and Chapter 3 when creating and using passwords: Require a minimum length password, use ran-domly generated passwords, set an expiration date for each password, and so on.

6. Install antivirus software on your workstation and server. Train employees to be on the lookout for virus activity and to scan all diskettes before using them.

7. Use encryption to protect sensitive data, including passwords, sent over networks.

8. Monitor the activity on your LAN for signs of suspicious activity that could signal an attempt to circumvent security controls.

9. Spell out what is ethical behavior—and what is not—in a comprehensive security policy since employees are not born with an innate sense of computer rights and wrongs. That policy should also detail what punitive measures may follow a security violation.

10. House your server in a secure room under lock and key. Anyone with access to the server itself can compromise security.

11. Don't overlook the prospect that someone may tap into cabling in order to attack the LAN. Copper cables are particularly vulnerable to this type of eavesdropping. Fiber cable is more difficult to attack, but it too is not secure. Bury or shield exposed cables where possible.

12. Enhance LAN security with add-on products. For example, you can prevent users from booting from a floppy, disable FORMAT and other dicey commands, and automatically shut down a workstation if it remains idle for more than a few minutes.

13. Some sensitive systems can be protected by removing the floppy disk drive, which would inhibit employees from loading or offloading programs and valuable data. That's not an option that a lot of companies are willing to exploit, however. Employees may have legitimate reasons to offload data— for example, to take work home.

ENTERING THE E-MAIL DIMENSION

> I talk to myself because I like dealing with a better class of people.
>
> Jackie Mason

After setting up their LANs, many companies immediately install electronic mail. It's a terrific productivity tool, of course. Employees can exchange ideas, collaborate on projects, and perform many other tasks that their jobs require no matter where they are and at nearly any time they feel like it.

Electronic mail also is adding a whole new security dimension to office work. Employees are using e-mail systems to harass fellow employees by sending them sexually charged or vulgar messages. Some employees have signed on using another employee's userID and password and then sent the boss nasty notes or other messages that are intended to cause trouble in the office. (Remember what I said in Chapter 3 about sharing passwords? Here's a good reason to keep yours to yourself if you're still not convinced it's a good idea!)

E-mail harassment

The problem of e-mail harassment has become so acute that many states have enacted or are preparing to enact laws to restrict this kind of antisocial behavior. Connecticut, for example, has enacted a law that now prohibits anyone from sending harassing or threatening messages via electronic mail. The legislation broadened a state law that covers harassing or threatening telephone calls and mail to include computer networks.

Some employees use e-mail systems for running their own businesses on the side. They use the system to contact prospective clients and even send company information to outsiders. Employees at Charles Schwab & Co. in San Francisco used the e-mail system to buy and sell cocaine.

Many employees believe they have a right to use a company's e-mail system for private correspondence. They think that sending an e-mail is akin to sending a letter in a sealed envelope, and that tearing open that electronic envelope is unethical. Well, they're wrong, but only if you tell them.

The key defense that you have as an employer is to establish a policy that emphasizes that the system belongs to the company and that it should be used solely for company business. Any violation of that policy puts the employee's job in jeopardy.

Although you may want to permit some amount of personal use, your e-mail policy should still set guidelines on how the system is to be used. In Chapter 8, I've included lots of guidelines that you can use to create your e-mail and other computer security policies and to raise employee awareness about security-related issues.

E-mail Security Tips

> Keep your eyes open and your mouth shut.
>
> John Steinbeck
> *Sweet Thursday,* 1954

I can guarantee that no matter what you say and no matter who you say it to, your message will be read. There's the risk that the message will go to the wrong person, someone will intercept it, or the LAN supervisor will read it. Using e-mail for anything other than routine office communication is like playing Russian roulette with six bullets in the gun. It's a game that you just can't win. Here are a few more tips:

1. Don't let your e-mail pile up. Get rid of messages that are no longer relevant. If you receive messages that you want to keep, offload them from the server to your hard drive or to a floppy disk.

2. E-mail systems often keep copies of messages you create as well as those that you delete. Make sure that you regularly delete the mail in your "out" box. And, just because you trash an e-mail message does not mean that it's actually gone for good. You may need to go into the "trash" and delete those messages, too.

3. If you have employees who work at customer sites, you must decide whether you'll permit them to have their e-mail forwarded to an outside firm where it might be read by employees at the other company. A lot of popular e-mail packages have a "forward" feature that can be used to forward e-mail from one site to another. It's too easy for sensitive information to fall into the wrong hands that way. If you want to give employees this option, determine what classes of information can be sent and set guidelines. For example, it might be permissible to forward "public" information but not "secret" information.

4. Proprietary information should be encrypted before it is transmitted. Chapter 5 has all of the details on just how to go about doing that.

5. Harold wants to add another e-mail tip based on personal experience. He says that before replying to an e-mail message, check to see who is the originator of the message. Lots of people use mail lists, Harold points out, so that the same message goes to a group of people. If you respond to a mail list on most systems, your message will go to everybody on the list and not just the person to whom you are replying. About a year ago, Harold tells me, he made some unkind remarks about a colleague, thinking that those remarks would go to only one person. Instead the message went to 11,000 people on the mail list! Harold says his face still turns red when he thinks about it.

STREAMLINED SIGN-ON

> Everything has been figured out except how to live.
>
> Jean-Paul Sartre (1905–1980)

In some companies, employees may have as many as four or five pairs of userIDs and passwords. They may have two to get into two different LANs, one for the mainframe and one to access a remote system at a branch office.

Aside from the fact that having to remember several pairs of log-in sequences hinders productivity, it also poses a security risk. A user who has to remember that her network log-in is "DAISY," but her WordPerfect Office password is "FLOWER," and her Microsoft Access password is "GARDEN" tends to find ways to circumvent password security or at least minimize its use. For example, she may opt for easy-to-remember (and thus easy-to-guess) passwords. Or she may use the same password to log in to all of the systems to which she has access rights.

**One userID,
one password**   If you're one of those employees, you're probably asking yourself why can't I have one set of IDs and passwords that will get me into all four or five systems? You can, if you opt for single sign-on (SSO). SSO is not something that a lot of small companies are using in a big way, so I'll hit the high points and move on.

The Single Sign-On Solution

> I'll try anything once.
>
> Alice Roosevelt Longworth (1884–1980), on giving birth at age 41

With single sign-on, the user logs into a system as he or she normally would without having to enter additional pairs of IDs and passwords to access other systems. The initial ID and log-on pair are checked against a database containing all of the other ID/password combinations that the user regularly uses.

Assuming the initial pair is cleared through the database, SSO automatically passes and synchronizes IDs and passwords to other systems and networks. It includes a template file function that can copy and customize the software's log-on exec file. The function automatically synchronizes network platforms to the SSO, so if a user changes his or her password, the software will update all other relevant passwords for use across the network.

Either/or   SSO functionality may be provided as a module in an integrated package or as a standalone product in a line of related security packages. Several companies market SSO software, including IBM, ICL, Fischer International Systems, and Mergent International.

The Benefits of SSO

> Egotist. A person . . . more interested in himself than in me.
>
> Ambrose Bierce (1842–1914)

There are several benefits of deploying single sign-on software. It frees you from having to remember many pairs of IDs and passwords. Consequently you're more productive and less likely to scribble your password on a scrap of paper that could find its way into the wrong hands.

Easier living   Single sign-on technology can also make life easier for system administrators, many of whom are looking to seamlessly link together different platforms and resources. SSO can help simplify password management because the technology allows an administrator or information security officer to determine the number of passwords required for each user. Some employees, managers, for example, could be given one password for access to all company environments and applications; other employees could be given one or two passwords for the select environments and applications they are authorized to access. Instead of spending valuable time trying to access environments and applications, users can perform their intended jobs and administrators can spend less time managing forgotten passwords.

For the greatest benefit, single sign-on technology must meet a number of basic requirements. First, it must be implemented as part of an overall security plan. Second, it must allow for customization to multiple security levels. Third, it must encourage increased user productivity and efficiency without impeding paths to data.

Single Sign-on Pitfalls and Loopholes

> The trouble with the rat race is that even if you win, you're still a rat.
>
> Lily Tomlin

Deploying SSO in an organization means having to resolve several potentially critical security issues, however. SSO could conceivably lead to vastly weaker security if end users do not take adequate precautions in choosing a difficult password and safeguarding its privacy. In that regard, using SSO is no different than any other password management procedure. Should a system attacker or user who is bent on exceeding his or her authorized access capture log-in IDs and passwords supported by SSO, he or she will be free to roam across more systems than might have otherwise been possible. This single point of failure may be the single biggest risk in implementing SSO.

Although some administrators praise SSO for the combination of access and security it provides, others say that SSO engenders a false sense of security. SSO software gives the appearance of a security solution, but actually it only implements the single sign-on part without enhancing security at all. In short, many SSO products are fundamentally insecure beyond the password management aspect. Products decode an encrypted file on the local PC to gain access to the various IDs and passwords needed to access the network's different resources. All of these products put a userID and password on the network in the clear. A determined intruder, using a sniffer program or other readily available hacking tools, has as much opportunity as ever to capture passwords and penetrate high-privilege accounts. **Faint praise**

Obtaining the sign-on or passwords from the different systems, each running different security packages, and coordinating and propagating password changes to the single sign-on system is complicated when the procedures are not automated. Thus administrators who buy into SSO thinking that it will save time and money could find themselves more wrapped up in password paperwork than ever before.

SSO also can lead to other technical and administrative nightmares, such as a network-wide collapse. If the security server goes down, SSO can also trigger a widespread lockout of applications. **Nightmares**

Another drawback to single sign-on is that currently no standard interface exists between security products nor is there a single API standard. Products developed by one vendor may talk to each other, but there may be little to no communication among products from different vendors. As a result, system administrators and information security officers seeking to deploy SSO must cobble together an SSO solution using pieces acquired from a variety of vendors. Invariably these pieces do not fit together seamlessly, creating security loopholes that did not exist previously.

Diversity hurts
In the end, the installed base of platforms and LANs may be so diverse that the SSO solution will not function properly. Some administrators may have to settle for partial sign-on capabilities rather than a complete single sign-on solution.

Ironically, SSO may elevate the security barrier but at the cost of productivity. Users may require extra training, for example. Authorized users may find themselves locked out of the system after traveling to another company location.

Until more elegant and secure single sign-on solutions reach the market, LAN administrators looking to cut the ID/password glut must balance simplicity of access against the critical need for security very carefully.

Remember This About SSO

> All the world is queer but me and thee, dear; and sometimes I think thee is a little queer.
>
> Attributed to a Quaker addressing his wife

SSO relies on the use of reusable passwords, a process that is inherently unsound. Because so much more is at risk when a password in an SSO solution is compromised, administrators should consider using an SSO package that works with smart cards, one-time password generators, or similar technologies.

1. Should you endorse the idea of single sign-on, keep in mind that there are no widely accepted security standards and no SSO provider has been able to implement single sign-on across a variety of LAN operating systems.

2. Single sign-on software should require mandatory encryption of reusable passwords and scripts to prevent any attempts to capture passwords using a sniffer or other hacking tools—not all products do.

3. Proper security is not achieved with a single solution and SSO must be part of an overall, sound security policy that encompasses a wide variety of solutions ranging from firewalls to remote access control security systems. Also, you should verify that the SSO software allows for a diversity of platforms—from dumb terminals to workstations—as well as a diversity of network communications.

4. Implementing and administering SSO should be the responsibility of network administrators and security officers, thereby adding another security level by controlling who manages the customization of environment access.

THIS WAY TO THE I-WAY

> I'm astounded by people who want to "know" the universe when it's hard enough to find your way around Chinatown.
>
> Woody Allen

The Internet, InfoBahn, I-way—call it what you like—is where everyone wants to be these days. The Internet is a huge matrix of computer networks, spread all over the planet (and beyond if you listen to the cyberspace zealots). In the last ten years, the Internet has grown from 50 to more than 10,000 networks. In 1988, the National Science Foundation estimated that there were over half a million Internet users. Today, the NSF organization estimates that 20 million people around the world use the Internet. (I've seen other estimates as high as 30 million people.)

The Internet was originally set up to support a multidisciplinary community of computer scientists, physicists, electrical engineers, and many other researchers. These researchers used the Internet for a variety of functions such as electronic mail, file transfer, and remote access to computer data banks and supercomputers. In recent years, thousands of companies have discovered the I-way, hoping to find new ways of doing business in cyberspace.

Not much thought has been given to I-way security, at least not until business decided to get involved. Now, everyone is concerned about I-way security, but thus far it's been a lot of talk and not much action.

There virtually are no codes of conduct beyond some vague notion of "netiquette." There is no policing of inappropriate networking behavior, and nearly anyone in the U.S., Europe, and Japan can hop onto the I-way without getting a license first.

The Computer Emergency Response Team, or CERT, a government-funded Internet security watchdog organization, calculates that the number of security breaches has risen from 180 incidents in 1990 to 2241 incidents in 1994.

Computer swat team

The rapid increase in commercial traffic is also making it more difficult to track and stop breaches. Although there is yet little hard evidence of companies with Internet links having suffered significant losses as a result of security breaches, you have to figure that it is only a matter of time. For the most part, these attacks have been aimed at universities, research centers, and other noncommercial sites. Obviously such attacks have financial implications associated with them, but they are still difficult to quantify.

Still, it is easy to envision what some of the potential consequences of a security breach via the Internet might be on a commercial organization. Given the enormous reliance most organizations now place on information systems technology, unauthorized tampering with those systems or the theft of the information they contain could have a serious financial impact.

Internet Security B&E

> There are 350 varieties of shark, not counting loan and pool.
>
> L. M. Boyd

Most direct connections to the Internet are made through a machine running UNIX. UNIX is not for the faint of heart. Heck, even people who claim to be UNIX gurus can't seem to configure their machines properly. If you're planning to set up your own connection to the Internet, you're going to need a lot more information than I can give you in this chapter.

I'll tell you right up front that if you run a small company, you would be better off setting up your employees with Internet connections through America Online, Delphi, Prodigy, or any of the many I-way service providers that are popping up like mushrooms after a rain. Let the service providers worry about security; they've got a lot more experience and resources than any small company that I know of.

After I wrote this paragraph, Harold came along and pointed out that AOL, Delphi, and Prodigy will not transmit encrypted messages. "They automatically refuse to send a message in which one line is encrypted," Harold says. Well, that was news to me, so I checked, and Harold is right. Still, if you want to give your employees Internet access, I maintain that using a commercial service is a secure way to go about it. Just don't use e-mail to send sensitive information or set up an account that can be used by only certain employees to send and receive encrypted e-mail. A growing number of companies are providing specialized Internet services aimed at small firms, so check around before you take the plunge.

If you decide to go it alone, you're going to need protection in the form of a firewall, a system that sits between your in-house system and the rest of the world.

Outsider Security Woes

> As Miss America, my goal is to bring peace to the entire world and then get my own apartment.
>
> Jay Leno

According to CERT, some of the top techniques that hackers use to break into computers connected to the Internet are:

- Password attacks either by means of sniffers or Trojan horses.

- IP spoofing.

- E-mail attacks of various types aimed at sendmail, the mail handler in UNIX.

Sniffing Out Passwords

> Losers walking around with money in their pockets are always danger-
> ous, not to be trusted. Some horse always reaches out and grabs them.
>
> Bill Barich
> *Laughing in the Hills,* 1980

Here's the scenario: A hacker breaks into a machine and installs a packet sniffer, a **Secret files**
program that is designed to monitor the network traffic that goes through the
machine. The sniffer is particularly interested in capturing the log-ons and passwords
that the machine's users enter before connecting to another machine. The sniffer
grabs the first dozen or so characters entered during these sessions—which contain
the log-ons and passwords—and stores them in a hidden file. Later the hacker
retrieves the secret file and uses the log-ons and passwords to break into other
computers. This attack is by far the most common, CERT says. It's difficult to spot,
in part because sniffer programs are tiny in comparison to most. In one episode,
the system's administrators were unaware that a sniffer had been installed until it
had captured so many log-ons and passwords that the machine's hard drive
became so full that it crashed the machine.

> **To defeat this attack, system administrators can shut off telnet, FTP, and other
> services that require users to first authenticate themselves. That means they
> will not be able to download files, which might not be such a bad thing. They
> can still send and receive e-mail, read newsgroups, and search the World-
> Wide Web, among other I-way activities that don't require authentication.**

IP Spoofing

> You call this a script? Give me a couple of $5000-a-week writers and I'll
> write it myself!
>
> Joseph Pasternak
> quoted in Max Wilk, *The Wit and Wisdom of Hollywood,* 1971

Data travels in "packets" over the Internet. They are called IPs (information
packets). Each packet is contained in an electronic envelope and, like any envelope, has "from" and "to" addresses. If my machine regularly connects to your
machine, we set up a trusted system that basically says: "I know you're a good

guy, and you know I'm a good guy, so we don't have to continually check each other out every time we want to send messages back and forth."

Hackers can take advantage of this trusting relationship in order to break into one of our machines. They create packets with, let's say, my address and send them off to your machine. Your machine thinks that I sent the packets, when in fact they're fake, and allows the connection.

Machine modifier

Once inside your machine, the interlopers can modify your machine so that they can nab the log-ons and passwords of the users on your machine. They can also install a back door, a secret entryway into the machine that they can use later. What makes this attack so sneaky is that the hackers can beat systems that require people on the system to use password generators before connecting to other machines. The hackers are able to hijack the connection after authentication takes place.

Warning Signs

CERT has published some warning signs that indicate that you may be a spoofing victim. If you monitor packets using network-monitoring software such as netlog, look for a packet on your external interface that has both its source and destination IP addresses in your local domain. If you find one, you are currently under attack.

Look at your logs

Another way to detect IP spoofing, CERT says, is to compare the process accounting logs between systems on your internal network. If the IP spoofing attack has succeeded on one of your systems, you may get a log entry on the victim machine showing a remote access, but on the apparent source machine, there will be no corresponding entry for initiating that remote access.

When the intruder attaches to an existing terminal or log-in connection, users may detect unusual activity such as commands appearing on their terminal that they did not type or a blank window that will no longer respond to their commands. CERT says that you should encourage your users to inform you of any such activity. In addition, pay particular attention to connections that have been idle for a long time.

I-way E-mail

> I never said, "I want to be alone." I only said, "I want to be *left* alone." There is all the difference.
>
> Greta Garbo
> quoted in John Bainbridge, *Garbo,* 1955

One of the most compelling reasons that people want a connection to the I-way is to send and receive e-mail. If you have a direct connection to the Internet, using a UNIX machine, you'll be using sendmail, the electronic mail handler in UNIX.

System administrators often rig sendmail to suit their own needs, blindly unaware of the security implications. What Ellis Island was to generations of immigrants, sendmail is to UNIX. It's how you get into the system. A number of loopholes have been exposed in sendmail in recent years. For example, a savvy user can exploit the debug option to get root access or use a loophole in the error message header option to read any file on the system. If that's what you're planning to use, make sure that you have a current release with all of the known fixes.

Ellis Island for UNIX

These are not the only ways in which security is compromised, of course. Some hackers have resorted to using "attack scanners," software that is designed to probe a machine for security weaknesses. These attack scanners such as the Security Analysis Tool for Auditing Networks (SATAN) in particular, were designed to be used as security tools. The idea is that you try the scanner against your own site and then close whatever loopholes are exposed.

Great Walls of Fire

> It matters not whether you win or lose; what matters is whether
> *I* win or lose.
>
> Darin Weinberg

Okay, you got your sendmail holes, you got your IP spoofing, you got your password sniffing, and you got all of your other security problems. The heck with it, you still wanna get on the I-way. So what's an eager lad or lass to do?

Set up a firewall, that's what. You'll hear the word "firewall" used a lot these days, although not everyone agrees exactly what a firewall is. It's main purposes are to insulate an internal network from the Internet and to act as a gatekeeper, overseeing the flow of data in and out of the company. It's not a cureall for everything that ails I-way security, but it's a start. You can do it yourself, if you're a technical whiz. Better yet, if you have the money, recruit a firm that specializes in firewall technology to build one for you.

Here's how a firewall works. The White Knight rides up to the castle and yells out "Hail to the King," or something equally friendly, and the watchguards lower the drawbridge. The knight reaches the other side of the drawbridge and the guards raise the gate. But then the guards make the White Knight get off his horse and take off his armor so that they can get a close look at him. For good measure, they also rummage through his bags for anything that looks out of place.

Gate to the castle

The firewall does all of these: raises and lowers the drawbridge, raises and lowers the gates, and posts guards at the door to give every visitor a close looksee. Just how they do that and how well they do that varies.

The most common firewalls are packet-filtering routers, application-level gateways, and circuit-level gateways. Think of them as good, better, and best. It probably goes without saying that better costs more than good but not as much as best.

Three common ones

Packet-Filtering Routers

> Leigh spends so much time with her hair because she wants the boys to attract her.
>
> Jessie S. Alexander, age 7

A lot of companies already have a router or two (or more) that facilitates connections between their LANs or between their in-house networks and the Internet. That's one of the reasons that packet-filtering routers are so popular. You have the basic box. All you need is to program the instructions on how it is supposed to handle Internet connections coming in and going out of the company.

You can set up the router to either permit all connections to pass unless expressly denied or prevent all connections from passing unless expressly denied. The first policy is less restrictive because it permits users to access services that may not be denied but are still not desirable (maybe it's a new service that you have thought about blocking, for example). The second policy is safer, but it is more difficult to pull off.

Put it on a table   Programming the router to cover all of the possible variations is a feat in itself. You may want some of your users to be able to access all I-way services; you may want other users to be able to access only some I-way services; and you may want still other users not to be able to access any I-way services but still to be able to receive e-mail from the outside. There are lots of variations, and it is easy to become confused about who is allowed to do what. All of these permissions and restrictions should be detailed in a policy. Then the policy should be used to set up the router's filtering tables.

That's easier said than done, as you can imagine. It requires considerable understanding of Internet protocols, for one thing. It's also easy to overlook some of the possible variations and leave plenty of holes through which intruders can slip, for another.

 A particularly savvy hacker can still get into the router, no matter how many pathways you shut down. Since the function of a router is to route packets, it does not provide any auditing or monitoring of unauthorized activity or attempts to subvert security measures.

All in all, a packet-filtering router is not going to give you top-shelf security, but using a router may be all that you need. It depends, in part, on what you have to lose. On the plus side, it's the least expensive option.

Application-Level Firewalls

> Mystics always hope that science will some day overtake them.
>
> Booth Tarkington
> *Looking Forward*, 1926

A packet-filtering router is the equivalent of a jack of all trades. In comparison, an application-level firewall is a specialist. It's a firewall from day one, not some box that was designed for one purpose and used for another. It oversees the security of individual applications such as electronic mail and file-transferring programs. When users dial in, they are first authenticated by the application-level firewall, and once they have gotten the go-ahead, they are passed to the specific application they are using.

It's a one-stop shopping deal where you get everything in one package at a stiff price ($30,000 to $60,000). If you've got that kind of dough to spare and your security needs merit it, Advanced Network & Services, Digital Equipment, Raptor Systems, or Trusted Information Systems, among other companies, would be more than happy to sell or lease you one.

Circuit-Level Firewalls

> Think twice before you speak and then say it to yourself.
>
> Elbert Hubbard
> *The Philistine*, published from 1897–1915

A circuit-level gateway performs all of the packet filtering that a router does and a bit more. The primary enhancement is the use of identification and authentication before an insider can access your in-house network. That I&A can be based on remote users using a password generator, for example.

If you want to know more about firewalls, pick up *Firewalls and Internet Security: Repelling the Wily Hacker* by Steven M. Bellovin and William R. Cheswick (Addison-Wesley Publishing, 1994). You'll get a complete rundown on the typical I-way security holes and what to do about them. The book was written for professionals, but if you insist on filling your head with technical stuff, then this is the book for you. By the way, Addison-Wesley isn't paying me to recommend one of their books, but if they want to put a little something extra in my royalty check, I won't quibble!

I-way Safety Patrol

> The world is a madhouse, so it's only right that it is patrolled by armed idiots.
>
> Brendan Behan (1923–1964)

What steps should you take to keep the techno-bandits from car-jacking your computer on the I-way?

1. Set up a firewall between your private networks and those outside such as the Internet.
2. Plug a filter into the firewall to prevent protocol spoofing.
3. Use encryption to scramble messages so that snoops can't read them.
4. Use one-time passwords to foil packet sniffing.
5. Train employees to protect passwords and confidential data.

Insider I-way Security Woes

> May you have employees.
>
> Yiddish curse

So much for the outside attackers. What about those wacky employees? They can compromise your system in lots of ways—sometimes accidentally, sometimes on purpose. Here are some examples.

Putting your company on the I-way and permitting your employees to send and receive e-mail, downloading files, cruising the World Wide Web—all of that adds new twists to the security game. Suppose one of your employees takes offense at something someone said in an e-mail message or a newsgroup and then decides to transmit 89 harassing, racist, or otherwise offensive messages to the supposed offender?

Watch those viruses
If employees can download files, there's nothing to stop them from downloading viruses at the same time. With I-way connections, it becomes even more critical that you ensure that each workstation as well as your LAN is running antivirus software.

There are all sorts of alt.sex newsgroups and other sites that appeal to a wide range of sexual taste, ranging from bisexual to bizarre. Many of these sites feature pictures and audio clips of graphic sexual nature. You're looking to get slapped with a sexual harassment suit the minute the first employee uses a company computer to download one of these files.

Hacker employees
Hackers use the Internet all of the time to carry out their activities. Ever thought that one of those hackers might be one of your employees? Also, many

companies are linking to the Internet so that they can maintain regular contact with suppliers and customers. Often, one company will have access to another company's database in order to check for product availability, place orders, and so on. There's not much that anyone can do if one of your employees decides to exceed his authorization and start rifling through someone else's system, using the equipment and connection that you paid for.

Last, cruising the Internet can be a massive productivity killer and time waster.   **Killing time**
Not all of the information is accurate, readily accessible, or business related.

You can place limits on your employees' activities, but if you close down too many I-way avenues, you should be rethinking why you even wanted to get connected in the first place.

No Way to Use the I-way

> When the cat and the mouse agree, the grocer is ruined.
>
> Persian proverb

A lot of companies plugging into the I-way need to consider drawing up or revising their computer security policies. Gordon & Glickson, one of a growing number of law firms that specialize in high-tech law (they're in Chicago), offers these suggestions:

- Teach Internet etiquette to avoid claims of defamation and sexual harassment and enforce a ban on sending any offensive messages to anyone.

- Implement confidential authorization codes or passwords with customers, suppliers, and others you do business with as well as with employees who have authorization to conduct business on the organization's behalf.

- Track transmissions to internal accounts and the amount of time spent connected to those accounts.

- Institute a policy that prohibits or limits employees' surfing the I-way and accessing bulletin board systems and chat channels.

- Warn employees that electronic mail may be monitored.

- Tell employees that information they download must be only for internal use to avoid potential liabilities for copyright infringement.

- Update software agreements to cover employees working at home or at other remote locations on company business.

- Put in writing that the consequences of unauthorized I-way use and the sharing of confidential codes and passwords may be grounds for termination or other punitive measures.

More About Electronic Mail

> You can get more with a kind word and a gun than you can with a kind word alone.
>
> Johnny Carson

When you send a friend a postcard, it gets handled by a variety of postal employees. As the postcard makes its way from the mail box to your friend, anyone along the way is able to read it.

Sending an e-mail message over the Internet is just liking mailing a postcard. The message travels from your machine through several machines before it arrives at your friend's machine. The administrators of those machines, or anyone with an inclination to intercept e-mail messages, can read your e-mail.

Most postal clerks don't bother reading postcards—they're too many and the really interesting ones are few and far between. That may be also true of the people who administer I-way computers that are used to transmit e-mail messages. Who knows for sure?

Sure bet   One thing is certain, some messages are okay to send on a postcard or in e-mail; others aren't. You know better than I which of your messages you don't want other people to read. Personally, I never e-mail my credit card numbers or nasty notes about the people I work with. If I were sending a book editor a proposal for an exciting new project, I would not e-mail it in cleartext.

If you don't want anyone else to read your e-mail, encrypt it before you send it. In Chapter 5 I give you a look at Pretty Good Privacy. It's free, it's easy to get a copy, and it works.

The Virus Is in the Mail

> The best cure for hypochondria is to forget about your body and get interested in somebody else's.
>
> Goodman Ace (1899–1982)

Virus hoax   Have you heard about the Good Times virus? Apparently someone got the bright idea that it would be neat to send subscribers of one of the online services an e-mail message warning them not to read any e-mail message with "Good Times" in the subject header. Opening such an e-mail message would trigger an insidious virus, warned the e-mailer. The rumor spread widely in only a matter of weeks. Even my father-in-law, who knows nothing about security, came to me with an official-looking document that he had received at work via fax, supposedly from some federal government agency warning businesses like his about the imminent danger of the Good Times virus. Although I told him that the virus was a hoax, I know he still doesn't believe me.

For the record, there is no Good Times virus, and there never was. Opening an e-mail message will not trigger a virus. If you read Chapter 2 you already know that a virus needs a program to latch onto before it can execute. Because e-mail messages are text files, not programs, there is nothing for a virus to use as a launch pad.

No Times like these

You should know, however, that a virus (or any kind of computer code, for that matter) can be attached to an e-mail message and sent to you. If you open the e-mail message and then open the code attached to it, you might get tagged by a virus.

A Word About the World Wide Web

> Thanks to the Interstate Highway System, it is now possible to travel coast to coast without seeing anything.
>
> Charles Kuralt

If you want to know where the action is on the I-way these days, get on the World Wide Web (WWW). In only a short time, it has become fabulously popular, partly because it's easy to get around. The best way to describe it is to compare it to a huge shopping mall, with thousands of stores, restaurants, movie theaters, amusement arcades, and other attractions.

Everyone who has set up shop on the WWW has a display window called a home page, with text, photographic images, and other graphics. Click on a highlighted bit of text on one home page and you are transported to yet another page.

Thousands of companies are scrambling to set up shop on the WWW to show off their wares. They're gambling that Web cruisers like you and me will buy goods and services at the click of a mouse button instead of hopping in our cars and driving over to a real mall. Maybe you're already thinking about joining this latest gold rush by setting up your own Web site. Hold that thought for just a minute.

Showoffs

Woes of the World

> Technology is a way of organizing the universe so that man doesn't have to experience it.
>
> Max Frisch

Setting up a World Wide Web site with the idea of allowing anyone in the world to dial into your personal or company computer network is not something you should consider doing without a good night's sleep.

Popular Web server software such as the National Center for Supercomputing Applications (NCSA) is being regularly hammered on by hackers and others in search of security loopholes. One such loophole permitted hackers to take over NCSA UNIX Web servers, find password files and other critical files, and execute programs. NCSA has issued a patch for this loophole, but it would be foolish to think that the fix has been universally applied. One terribly bright virus expert I know predicts that we'll see the launching of viruses designed specifically to attack PCs and servers running as WWW browsers and servers.

The safest and cheapest way for you or your company to get on the Web is to contract with an Internet service provider and use their servers instead of your own. If you opt to set up your own site, make sure that the server is outside of your security perimeter. In other words, make sure that it is not connected to the company's internal network.

Most Web servers are UNIX boxes, and as I mentioned earlier, UNIX is not easy to secure, even for UNIX gurus. From day one, UNIX was set up to be accessed and used by remote users. Over the years, hackers and others have probed UNIX's defenses and have exposed numerous loopholes that were originally intended to facilitate remote access.

Hole in the firewall   Web software may also permit users to circumvent firewall security. If the firewall is configured to prevent outsiders from using File Transfer Protocol, it might not request an FTP request that has been converted to HTTP (HyperText Transfer Protocol) by a Web server placed in front of the firewall.

Mac Web servers are not as vulnerable to hacking as their UNIX counterparts, by the way. The Mac's operating system was not designed with remote access in mind and, by default, is more difficult for hackers to exploit.

Also, Mac applications are somewhat self-contained in that they do not interact greatly with each other. They're generally easier to set up and administer than UNIX applications, reducing the prospect that a security door will be left open.

Who's Zoomin' Who?

> You know it's not a good wax museum when there are wicks coming out of people's heads.
>
> Rick Reynolds

When you're looking in on a World Wide Web page, how do you know that the page isn't looking in on you? That's not as far-fetched as you might think. When you access America Online, Prodigy, and other services, for example, all sorts of fancy graphics are sent to your machine, whether you ask for them or not. If an online service can write to your machine, what's to prevent it from reading what is stored on it?

Several programs take a look at the system configuration, perhaps during the installation and set up or as part of warranty information gathering. Symantec's Central Point, for example, included an electronic registration form for its PC Tools for Windows that scanned the owner's machine to find out how the machine was configured before sending that information along with the registration off to Central Point. The only way that owners were even aware that this was happening was that some customers discovered text files on their machines that had been created by the registration program. Central Point says that the scanning was unintentional and put a halt to it after owners complained.

Be careful when you plug into a Web site. Another company might want to get a closer look at you than you realize. If your hard drive spins up unexpectedly, someone might be scoping your system.

There's been a lot of talk about electronic commerce on the WWW. Not much is going to happen until consumers can be confident that when they order products and use their credit cards to pay for them, no one is going to snag their card number and rack up expensive purchases. Until you hear from me personally, don't send anyone your credit card data either on the WWW or in an e-mail message.

DIALING FOR DOLLARS

Telephone, *n.* An invention of the devil which abrogates some of the advantages of making a disagreeable person keep his distance.

Ambrose Bierce
The Devil's Dictionary, 1906

So what do telephones have to do with computer security, you ask? The phone systems that most companies use are in fact special-purpose computers. Unfortunately, not every company realizes that, so they wind up paying a lot more attention to computer security and leave protecting the phone system to someone else. That's been a huge and costly mistake for companies whose phone systems have been hit by hackers or phreaks—people who specialize in attacking telephone systems.

In what's left of this chapter, I'm going to tell you about telephone and fax scams, some of it computer related and some of it not. For good measure, I'm even going to tell you why using a baby monitor is a bad idea.

Privately Speaking

> Gossip is news running ahead of itself in a red satin dress.
>
> Liz Smith
> *American Way* magazine, Sept. 3, 1985

Dial-tone bandits break into company telephone systems to rip off long-distance calling services and to use voice mail systems as meeting places to conduct illegal business. Hackers want into these systems because they're looking for a free ride to other computer systems. Also, clever hackers can use long-distance calling services to mask their trails, making it exceedingly difficult to nab them.

If your telephone company's system is abused, you—not the telephone company or the company that installed the system—are liable for the loss. I have interviewed dozens of business managers in recent years who have had their phone systems hacked and then found out that, adding insult to injury, they had to pick up the tab. It's not unusual for the bills to run $100,000 or more. And it only takes but a couple of weeks to ring up a wallet-thumping bill.

Bill in a box   My friend Bill Cook, a former assistant U.S. attorney who once spearheaded a cybercrimes squad for the Justice Department and is now a Chicago attorney specializing in high-technology law, is fond of saying that often the first time the victim finds out that his or her long-distance telephone calling account has been compromised is when the phone bill arrives in a box shipped via UPS rather than the usual skinny envelope in the day's mail.

If all of these companies have one thing in common it is that they and their long-distance telephone carrier invariably wind up going head to head, sometimes in court, to square away the charges. The legal fees are costly, it's time consuming, and a lot of business is lost in the interval. Everybody loses.

Two Ways to Do It

> In order to make a man or a boy covet a thing, it is only necessary to make the thing difficult to attain.
>
> Mark Twain
> *The Adventures of Tom Sawyer*, 1876

Dial-tone bandits favor two main doorways into a company-operated telephone system, remote ports and voice mail systems.

Remote Ports

Nearly all of the sophisticated customer-owned telephone systems have remote access maintenance ports. These are little more than electronic back doors that permit the telephone seller and maintenance technicians to access the telephone system via long distance. Typically the technicians use the remote access ports to upgrade the telephone system's software and to perform repairs. However, thieves can sometimes enter the system using passwords they have discerned either by guessing or by using default passwords that the telephone system user neglected to change after the system was installed.

Once inside the system, the dial-tone thieves can make unlimited long-distance telephone calls. Often, the calls are made over a period of several days—even weeks. It's not until the telephone bill arrives that the theft is discovered.

Voice Mail Systems

The telephone thieves typically penetrate voice mail systems by figuring out easy-to-guess passwords used by employees. Once inside the voice mail system, the thieves can obtain a dial tone and call anywhere in the world. They also use the voice mail system as an electronic meeting place where they can conduct illegal business.

A few years ago, I covered a case where phreaks took over a real estate company's voice mail system for several weeks. They used voice mail boxes to swap stolen credit and calling card numbers and to leave tips on how to break into other systems. The phreaks, as many as 50, jammed the voice mail system with their activity so that legitimate callers could not get through and leave messages. When the realtor attempted to lock out the intruders, they brought the system down. Later they demanded that the realtor give them access to the voice mail system or they would repeatedly shut it down. The realtor called the U.S. Secret Service, who placed monitoring devices on the incoming calls, traced them back, and arrested several people, including the ring leader, a 35-year-old mother of two children.

Telltale Telephone Troubles

> Indeed, you won the elections, but I won the count.
>
> Anastasio Somoza Debayle (1925–1980)

One way to keep hackers, phreaks, and other rogues out is to regularly scrutinize your telephone bills for signs of suspicious activities. Here are some warning signs that may indicate fraudulent telephone behavior:

- Unexpected increase in telephone use
- Unusual use of the telephone during off-hours and weekends
- Calls to unusual locations or numbers
- Unexpected increase in international calls

- Long delays in making calls or while being put on hold
- Repeated crank or obscene calls
- Callers repeatedly hanging up
- Callers making odd requests
- Unexplained 900 number calls
- Unusually high credit card call activity

Beware Copier Repairpersons

> You can lead a horticulture but you can't make her think.
>
> Dorothy Parker
> quoted in *You Might as Well Live* by John Keats, 1970

There's one other telephone-related scam that you should know about, although it's not usually carried out by hackers and phreaks but rather by copier and other repairpeople. Here's how the scam works: Your copier (or some other device) needs service, so you call a repairperson. He or she shows up, looks the machine over and says that he needs to call the office to check on the availability of a part or to ask a technical question or some other seemingly innocuous reason. Instead, the repairperson places a 900 call to a business with which he or she has an ongoing relationship. 900 number services charge you for the call, and the costs can sometimes be rather high. The cost is charged to your telephone, and even if it's noticed, there may be not much to do but pay it. Meanwhile, the repairperson is long gone when the bill comes in and no one ever thinks to put two and two together.

Freaking out the Phreaks

> Progress robs us of past delights.
>
> Sam J. Ervin, Jr.
> *Humor of a Country Lawyer*, 1983

Protecting a voice mail system is not much different from protecting any other computer system:

- Use secure passwords. They are a key first line of defense.
- Change the default passwords that are used to set up and maintain the system.
- Disable unnecessary features of the phone system such as the ability to transfer to another extension or to make outside calls from voice mail. (Have employees use a calling card instead.)

- Keep a sharp watch on telephone calling activity and closely monitor your monthly statement.
- Take advantage of the security-related services—from AT&T, Sprint and other companies—that are aimed at keeping phreaks out of your PBX and voice mail as well as alerting you when telephone use falls outside of normal activity.

Cellular Telephone Trickery

> Is this the party to whom I'm speaking?
>
> Lily Tomlin, as Ernestine the operator

Cellular telephones are everywhere these days. Motorists gab on the phone on the way to work; salespeople stand on busy street corners working out the latest deal; and entrepreneurs use them to check their voice mail at the home office. Cellular technology also is the up and coming way to transfer files and faxes from laptops in the field to corporate information systems.

What many cell phone users don't realize is that cell phones may be one of the least secure communications systems ever devised. Using a cell phone is not much different than yodeling to convey your private affairs from one mountaintop to another.

Cellular Snooping

> All phone calls are obscene.
>
> Karen Elizabeth Gordon

Armed with a scanner radio, costing no more than $99, even a casual snoop can eavesdrop on conversations. In fact, listening in on cellular telephone calls has become so commonplace that law bar associations in at least five states have cautioned their members that talking on a cell phone is likely to jeopardize the dictates of attorney-client confidentiality.

In September 1994, while O.J.' s defense team and prosecutors were battling over procedures used to gather evidence against the Juice, famed attorney and member of the dream defense team, Alan Dershowitz, is overheard on a cell phone discussing details of the case while he's kicking back at his summer home on Martha's Vineyard. Luckily for Dershowitz, the listeners happen to be public-spirited citizens employed by a Chilmark ambulance company who decide to call Dershowitz and tell him that he ought to be more careful about what he says on his cell phone.

Ambulance chaser gets caught

Cell Phonies

> If you rub up against money long enough, some of it may rub off on you.
>
> Damon Runyon
> "A Very Honorable Guy," *Furthermore*, 1938

Listen to cellular telephone calls for more than a few minutes and you'll hear business people using cellular telephones to dial into their companies' voice mail and computer systems. You'll also be violating the Electronics Privacy Communications Act, which prohibits eavesdropping on cell calls, although that doesn't seem to stop anyone.

Those touchtone beeps that you'll hear can be recorded and decoded using a device called DTMF (short for dual-tone multi-frequency) decoder. Using this tone grabber, crooks are able to decipher telephone numbers, voice mail box access numbers, and better yet (for the crooks) credit card and long-distance telephone dialing card numbers. Tone grabbers cost about $100.

Organized crime has gotten hip to the information society just like everyone else. High-tech criminals already are adept at intercepting voice and data signals transmitted over satellites as well as using these systems to arrange illicit deals and to mask their activities. Drug dealers also intercept telephone calls in hopes of getting numbers that they can use to make free long-distance telephone calls to such places as Columbia, Pakistan, and Thailand to set up buys.

Cellular Phone Cloning

> I saw the sequel of the movie *Clones*, and you know what? It was the same movie!
>
> Jim Samuels

Cell phone crooks are also interested in cloning your cell phone. Why? Because to the cell phone system, all phones look alike. It doesn't matter one whit who has the phone, only that the cell system can identify it and bill someone for using the phone service. The way the phone is identified is through each phone's unique Mobile Identification Number and Electronic Serial Number (MIN/ESN).

Cell phone cloners capture a paying customer's MIN/ESN as they are transmitted over the air and program these numbers into another phone. Cell phone cloners lurk where there is a lot of cellular telephone calling activity. For example, they'll perch themselves outside of a long tunnel. Invariably, motorists who are ready to use their cell phones will wait until they clear the tunnel before picking up the cell phone.

The crooks sell cloned phones for about $300 a month, often with a guarantee of replacing the phone if the service is cut off within a month's time. There are all sorts of buyers for the phones, ranging from drug dealers to unscrupulous business professionals who want to make calls on someone else's dime.

Cell phone carriers are working on shutting down cell phone cloning. In some areas of the nation, customers are required to enter four-digit PINs before using their phones. The carriers also have set up teams to monitor cell call activity for signs of unusual behavior.

Clone Defense Tactics

> You don't need a lot of bureaucrats looking over your shoulder and telling you how to run your life or how to run your business. We are a people who declared our independence 200 years ago, and we are not about to lose it now to paper shufflers and computers.
>
> Gerald R. Ford, in a speech in Chicago, Aug. 25, 1975

You're not going to be saddled with the bill if someone clones your phone, but that doesn't mean you shouldn't take steps to protect yourself. Personally, I'd do anything to keep from having to explain to some telephone representative why that $10,000 phone bill is not really mine. Here's what you do:

1. Keep an eye on your bill. As soon as you spot something that doesn't jibe, contact your carrier. I have a friend whose company paid the bills for a clone phone for more than a year simply because no one bothered to double-check the bill to see if it made sense.

2. If you use valet parking, lock the phone. Someone can punch up the MIN on the phone and retrieve the ESN off the phone itself.

3. Be wary about where you use the phone. If you use it in an area where there is a high concentration of activity such as a convention hall, there's a good chance that eavesdroppers are lurking nearby.

4. If you're victimized, notify your cell carrier and have the phone reprogrammed immediately.

What's to Come

The problem of telephone eavesdropping—at least in the short term—will certainly get worse. Cell phone use is growing rapidly, along with a host of other new services based on cellular technology.

However, a lot of cell phone companies are converting their systems from analog to digital (the difference is like going from LP record player to compact disc). Once the signals are transmitted in digital form, they can be readily scrambled so that intercepting them will do little good. You have to figure, however, that eavesdropping technology will keep pace. The bottom line is to be smart about when and where you use your cell phone.

Cordless Phones and Baby Monitors, Too

> Speak clearly, if you speak at all;
> Carve every word before you let it fall . . .
> And when you stick on conversation's burrs,
> Don't strew your pathway with those
> dreadful *urs*.
>
> Oliver Wendell Holmes, Sr.
> *A Rhymed Lesson,* 1846

While I'm rolling along on the subject of telephone snooping, let me also fill you in about cordless telephone listening. That same scanner that can pick up cell phone calls can also pick up conversations on cordless telephones.

A basic scanner can pick up phone conversations in a one-mile radius. It can easily cover twice that distance if the eavesdropper lives in a suburban neighborhood and is using an antenna tailored to pick up cordless phone frequencies.

None of this requires high-tech gear, by the way. Even a dirt-cheap (under $50) scanner picks up the frequencies used by cordless telephones. An antenna designed to pluck cordless phone calls out of the air costs about $5 (it's only about 15 feet of copper wire in a T with a plug at the bottom of the T that goes into the scanner).

Manufacturers of recent vintage cordless telephones would have you believe that their phones are more secure that ordinary cordless phones. They point out that their phones operate at higher frequencies (in the 900-megahertz range) and that they scramble conversations. That helps, but it still is not foolproof. In fact, I know of at least one scanner that has built-in circuitry that is designed to unscramble these supposedly indecipherable conversations.

I own a cordless phone called the Tropez, marketed by VTech Communications. It digitizes your conversations and encrypts them so that even if they are intercepted, all you hear is a whooshing noise. They sell for between $150 and $300, not much more than what any good quality 900-megahertz cordless phone would cost.

Oh, yeah, what about those baby monitors? You have kids? Maybe you have a baby monitor in your infant's bedroom to help you keep an ear on things? Basically you've just bugged your entire house.

Those scanners that can pick up cellular and cordless telephone calls also can easily tune into the same frequencies used by baby monitors. Even normal conversations in other parts of the house are readily picked up by the baby monitor receiver and transmitted over the air. Remember that the next time you decide to get into a loud argument with your spouse!

You Call, They Sell

> Don't get the idea that I'm knocking the American system.
>
> Al Capone (1899–1947)

Call-sell operators will pilfer a credit card calling number either by listening to telephone calls or, better still, by using the low-tech approach of shoulder surfing—actually peering over your shoulder—as you make a call from a phone booth in an airport, bus terminal, or similarly busy place.

Later, while standing at a phone booth with your long-distance credit card calling number in hand, they'll sell long-distance calls of nearly unlimited duration to passersby at $10 apiece. Most of the calls go to places like Columbia, Pakistan, and Turkey. That's why they call them call-sell operators, don't ya know.

Phone Fraud Fighters

1. Don't discuss confidential or sensitive matters on a cellular or cordless telephone call.

2. Be wary about when and where you use your cellular telephone.

3. When using a pay phone to make a credit card call, block the view of anyone who might be looking over your shoulder.

4. Regularly check your phone bill for accuracy.

5. If you use a baby monitor, keep in mind that someone may be listening.

Only a Facsimile of Security

> A stitch in time would have confused Einstein.
>
> Unknown

In only a few years, fax machines have gone from high-tech communications systems to something that you get when you buy a modem, whether you want it or not. The American Facsimile Association says there are 30 million fax machines in use; half of them are standalone machines and half of them are in PCs.

Just the fax, ma'am

Using a fax machine to transmit sensitive information is seldom a good idea. The most common way that faxes get out of hand is as a result of misdialing the telephone. Assuming the fax reaches its destination, it will sit on the fax machine

Not a good idea

long enough for an entire company to have the opportunity to read it. Fax messages are easily intercepted, using a computer designed especially for that purpose, although it's not likely that your neighbor or even a competitor will have one.

If you worry about fax security, take a look at some of the new fax machines that have built-in security features. Some sport a key lock to prevent unauthorized use or demand a password in exchange for the right to transmit. If you use polling to receive faxes during off-hours, some fax machines can be set to only receive faxes from predefined senders or at predefined times.

Gotta encrypt, got it?

Fax mailbox services, which require entry of a PIN number for access, are valuable for protecting faxes until the proper individual is ready to receive them. However, only encryption—scrambling—can render voice and fax transmissions completely secure from theft, redirection, and alteration.

A growing number of software companies such as PrivaSoft and InfoImaging Technologies market software that will scramble a fax so that it is indecipherable before sending it. The only way it can be decoded on the other end is with a special software key. Software like this sells from $60 to $200.

5 Secret Messages and Digital Hancocks

In 1940, the British government set up the Maud Committee, made up of the most esteemed physicists of the day, to advise the government on how to go about building an atomic bomb. The committee got its name as a result of a telegram that Niels Bohr, the famous Danish physicist, managed to send to his colleagues and friends in England soon after the Germans occupied Denmark. In the telegram, Bohr assured his contacts that he was safe, and he ended his message by asking one of his colleagues to "Please inform Cockcroft and Maud Ray, Kent." The message was thought to have been written in a secret code and was decoded to read, in part, "make uranium day and night." Later, it was learned that Maud Ray had been Bohr's English governess!

Encoding messages to keep secrets from spies goes back to at least the time of Julius Caesar, and as you can see, has not always met with great success. Today it is perhaps the single most important security tool that you have to protect personal and private information from snoops.

ENCRYPTION AND DIGITAL ENVELOPES

> Trust in Allah, but tie your camel.
>
> Arab proverb

If you're on vacation and you decide to drop Granny back home a note, you scribble "Wish you were here" on the back of a postcard and drop it in a mail box. If someone at the post office reads it, you don't care much. Suppose you want to send Granny a letter asking for your inheritance a bit early because you need to pay off some gambling debts. You would seal the letter in an envelope before mailing it, right? That's pretty personal stuff that only Granny and you should know about.

You should apply the same sort of thinking to your electronic mail. Sending an e-mail message is like writing on the back of a postcard, giving a great number

Digital envelopes

of people the opportunity to read it. If you want to send someone a message of a private or personal nature, you should encrypt it, which is sort of like putting your message in a digital envelope.

Encryption is the process of scrambling a message so that only the people you want to read the message are able to do so. The military and banks are the most active users of encryption, for pretty obvious reasons. Both have a lot to lose if someone were to intercept important messages such as "We attack at dawn" and "Transfer a zillion dollars to my Swiss bank account."

Encryption also is quite useful for protecting private or confidential information stored on your desktop or notebook computer. Even if someone circumvents security controls and manages to get a peek at your files, he or she will be unable to read them.

Encryption devices can be either hardware- or software-based or a combination of both. Generally speaking, the process of encrypting and decryption is faster with hardware than software, which is an issue if you do a lot of it over networks. Even so, in the past decade, software crypto applications have become quite common.

Make mine munitions   Encryption products are classified as munitions by the State Department, and you need an export license to sell them overseas. The U.S. government has long been reluctant to grant export licenses for really good crypto products. The National Security Agency—the government's supersecret spy agency—must approve the export licenses and they're only willing to do that for crypto products they can crack. Hey, no point in making their job more difficult, right?

The makers of crypto products have been trying to get the government to lighten up on crypto export restrictions. One argument in their favor is that there's no way that the Internet will ever be made more secure for commerce until the trade restrictions are lifted and crypto freely used. Also, many of the restricted products are already widely available overseas because many European companies market crypto products. Restricting exports only stymies competition and gives the edge to the other guys, U.S. makers say. I buy it, but the government does not—not at this point anyway. I'm telling you all of this just in case you have the urge to start shipping crypto products overseas. Don't be surprised if the feds come knocking on your door.

Scrambled Messages

Here is a crash course in encryption. Some of this cryptic stuff can get pretty, well, cryptic, so I'm only going to hit the highlights. If you want to know more, go to the library, frequent Usenet groups such as alt.security.pgp, and read the FAQs (Frequently Asked Questions).

Crypto experts define encryption as the process of taking "plaintext" and scrambling it into "ciphertext." Decryption is just the opposite—transforming ciphertext back into plaintext. Zounds, what a concept! **Plain as text**

Plaintext is just what it sounds like—plain English, or any other language for that matter—and ciphertext looks like gibberish. Plaintext also sometimes is called "cleartext" because it is sent in the clear.

Plaintext is scrambled into ciphertext by either transposing or changing the order of the plaintext characters or by substituting cipher characters or symbols for plaintext characters. A formula, or algorithm, is used to scramble the message, usually by translating the messages into a series of numbers.

Somewhere along the way, crypto experts decided to specify precisely how plaintext characters should be transposed or how the plaintext characters should be arranged. They came up with a key, a number that is used with the algorithm, for specifying what goes where.

The Secret Is in the Keys

> All that we see or seem
> Is but a dream within a dream
>
> Edgar Allan Poe
> "A Dream Within a Dream," 1827

Two basic types of crypto schemes are in use in publicly-available products: symmetric and asymmetric. With symmetric crypto, one key is used to scramble and unscramble messages. With asymmetric crypto, two keys are used, one to scramble and one to unscramble messages. If one key is kept private and the other made publicly available, the scheme is called public-key cryptography. Today most advanced encryption schemes are asymmetric.

This is how encryption works in its simplest form. Let's say you and I are bookies and we want to swap messages that only you and I can read. First, we meet at some out-of-the-way dive down by the waterfront to decide on the algorithm that we'll use to unscramble our messages. Our algorithm may be something like changing the letters to their corresponding numbers so that ABC is 123. If we were any smarter, we might be trying to earn a living as bookkeepers instead of bookies. Later I scramble a message—something like, "The Lemon Drop Kid says to bet $10 on Fireplug to show in the fifth"—using both the algorithm and the key so that it appears to be unreadable gibberish. I send you the message, let's say by electronic mail. You use the same key that I used to scramble the message to unscramble it and read it. **Bookies do simple crypto**

Now, let's suppose some rival bookie has managed to find out what our key is and has been eavesdropping on our electronic mail. Because he knows the key that I used to scramble the message, he can read the message just as you can. The rat fink calls the cops, and we wind up in the slammer for bookmaking. So much for security, eh? How does the fink know the key? Perhaps he overheard us talking from the booth behind us at that waterfront joint; perhaps either you or I were careless and left the key in a place where the fink could find it; or perhaps the key we came up with was too simple and was cracked. In any case, what happened was that we did not manage our secret key very well. This whole process of getting together in a bar or talking over the telephone, deciding on a key, and keeping the key safe from prying eyes is called key management. Poor key management equals poor to no security. That's one of the big problems with one-key crypto systems.

One for You, One for Everybody Else

> Nihil peccat nisi quod nihil peccat.
> (His only fault is that he has no faults.)

> Latin proverb

In the public eye Well, if the one private key idea is not so hot, there's gotta be something better, right? There is, and it's called public-key cryptography.

Here's how it works. Each person gets two keys, a public key for scrambling messages and a private key for unscrambling them. Everybody and his mother uses your public key to scramble messages before sending them to you. Once the messages are encrypted, only you—the person with the corresponding private key—can read them. Not even the person who wrote the message can read it once it has been encrypted with your public key.

Back at the ranch, you have a private key that you keep to yourself, at least you do if you're smart. The private key is used to unscramble messages that have been scrambled using your public key.

One key, two keys The keys used in single and public-key (PK) crypto are generated by the encryption program. Most often, you have the option of deciding how long your key will be. The longer it is, the more secure it is.

PK crypto was invented in 1976 by two really bright guys named Whitfield Diffie and Martin Hellman as a way to solve the problem of managing keys. The private key doesn't have to be shared with anyone, a big improvement over single-secret-key crypto systems. Better yet, you and I no longer have to meet in seedy bars on the waterfront to decide on a key and can instead spend more time drinking grog and getting in fights with sailors.

DIGITAL JOHN HANCOCKS

> There, I guess King George will be able to read that.
>
> John Hancock, after signing the Declaration of Independence,
> July 4, 1776

There's another good thing about public-key crypto. It can be used to create a digital signature, one that will probably even hold up in court. Let's say you decide to send me and everyone else in our gang of bookies a message—something like "At dawn, we ride with the breaking wind." You use your private key to scramble the message. At the same time, you create a digital signature, one that is based on a calculation with the private key and the message itself, only a piece of the message—a unique sequence of characters—is encrypted with the private key. This unique sequence is the equivalent of a "digital fingerprint" and that's what's sent as the signature along with the original message. The reason it's done that way is that it's faster than sending the entire message twice.

Breaking wind

Anyway, everyone in the gang can read the message but since you're the only one to have the private key, we know that only you could have sent the message. Later, if the cops bust us and arrest us for conspiracy, we can all point to you and say, "He's the one to come up with the stinkin' idea in the first place!" You can't deny sending the message or claim someone impersonated you because the message has your unique digital signature.

Public Servers for Keys

If you're using a public-key scheme, you want as many people as possible to be able to find out what your public key is so they can exchange encoded messages with you. The best way to do that is to register your public key with a certifying authority called a public-key server. The certifying authority will send you a certificate to verify that this key is actually yours. The certificate also keeps someone from masquerading as you. There are several (thousands) of these public-key servers, although they change from time to time. In any case, all you need to do is send your key to one server and it will, in turn, send your key to the others. You can get a list of current key servers by reading the FAQ on alt.security.pgp.

I'll bet you're wondering how you can find someone else's public key at this point. The easiest thing to do is ask him or her (usually via e-mail) for the key. You can also check one of the public-key servers.

You should store your private key in a safe place so that it can't be used by someone other than yourself. The best way is to encrypt the key itself, assign a password to it, and store it on a disk. As a further precaution, lock the disk in a cabinet or some other secure storage unit.

If you lose your private key or forget the password assigned to it, you're flat out of luck. You won't be able to encode or decode messages. You'll need to generate a new key and let everyone know not to use the old public key to scramble messages they intend to send to you because you won't be able to read them.

The Best of Both Worlds

Although PK crypto offers industrial-strength security, that does not mean that private or secret-key crypto has gone off to the great compactor in the sky, or wherever old crypto systems go when they're no longer useful.

PK crypto's scrambling and unscrambling are slow in comparison to secret-key crypto, and that's a big concern for anyone who has to send and receive long messages.

One solution has been to combine the best of public-key and secret-key crypto systems, marrying the security of public-key with the speed of secret-key. The public-key system is used to encrypt a secret key that is, in turn, used to scramble the message. Remember I said a while ago that PK crypto was originally devised to make it possible for you and me to securely exchange keys, and it is still good for that.

Okay, that's a rundown on secret-key and public-key crypto systems. Now, we'll take a look at some of the most popular systems in use.

Data Encryption Standard

> They talk about conscription as being a democratic institution. Yes, so is a cemetery.
>
> Meyer London, in a speech in the House of Representatives,
> April 25, 1917

DES is the Data Encryption Standard, an encryption scheme developed by IBM and officially endorsed by the U.S. government. It's been the number-one crypto standard since 1977. DES has never been cracked, although many people have tried and some are reportedly closing in on the elusive solution.

DES is a one-key (symmetric) system, just like the one you and I came up with in the bar. The same key is used to scramble and unscramble messages. And, just like our encryption scheme, the key is susceptible to being intercepted and used to unscramble our supposedly secret communiqués.

One way you and I can better protect ourselves, if we use DES, is to change the keys often. We can also come up with a more secure way than meeting in a waterfront gin joint to decide on what key to use.

If we were really paranoid, we could encrypt our message three times, each time using a different key. The technique is called triple encryption. Why three times? The result is that we've effectively doubled the size of our DES key, making it nearly impossible for anyone to crack. Obviously triple encryption takes three times as long as single encryption, which is bound to be a problem if you send a lot of messages.

Changing the DES key all of the time is not practical if you're using DES just to scramble files stored on your PCs. You would have to unscramble and then rescramble all of your files every time you decided to change the key. If you have lots of files, that's going to get tired real fast. The better approach is to store all of the different keys in a single file and encrypt the file with a master key. Every so often, you change the master key.

One of the problems with DES is that it can't be exported. The federal government classifies many encryption schemes as munitions, mainly because they don't want our enemies (and our friends, for that matter) to be able to keep their secrets from our nation's foreign intelligence snoops. That's the theory anyway. The truth is that DES is widely available overseas. The export restriction is only relevant if you happen to be setting up shop overseas or plan to bring your secret decoder ring that uses DES when you go on vacation to EuroDisney in France next year.

Although DES has not been cracked, some crypto experts think that it's only a matter of time. Theoretically one could construct a supercomputer to crack DES using what's called a brute force attack. Worrying about DES being cracked is not something that should keep many people awake at night. If you use it to encrypt files on your hard disk or if DES is used as part of a password protection scheme, there's not much to worry about. **Sleep peacefully**

You don't need to be James Bond to use DES, by the way. Quite a few commercial and shareware computer security programs use DES encryption.

RSA

> Our whole way of life today is dedicated to the removal of risk. Cradle to grave we are supported, insulated, and ioslated from the risks of life—and if we fall, our government stands ready with Band-aids of every size.
>
> Shirley Temple Black, in a speech quoted in *The Sinking of the Lollipop*, 1968

If one key is good, two must be better, right? Well, yes and no. RSA Data Security markets a public-key crypto scheme called RSA, which is rapidly becoming a popular alternative to DES. The company is named after Ron Rivest, Adi Shamir, and Leonard Adleman—three MIT profs who came up with the algorithm used in RSA in 1977.

RSA does two things that DES can't. First, it gives you and me a way to come up with a key to scramble our messages. Second, it creates one of those digital John Hancocks that I mentioned earlier.

The irony (well, a small irony) is that RSA uses DES for part of the encryption job. Messages are encrypted using the DES key, and RSA is used to encrypt the DES key. Both keys are sent in what RSA calls an "RSA digital envelope."

The obvious question is: Why not just use RSA and forget about DES? Well, you could. It's just that DES is faster than RSA, so you might not want to use it by itself for long messages. RSA readily admits that DES, when used in software, is generally at least 100 times as fast as RSA and 1000 to 10,000 times as fast in hardware. The company says that, although it will probably narrow the gap, RSA will never match the performance of DES.

RSA for networks

RSA is best used when several people are at work. One of its strong suits is that you and I can swap keys across a network with little fear that someone will crack the keys' codes if they succeed in intercepting them and unscramble our messages.

Let's say we're still busy with our bookmaking, and I want to send you a message. Here's how it would work using RSA. First, I encrypt the message with DES using a key chosen at random. Next, I use your public key to scramble the DES key. The two keys and the message go into a RSA digital envelope and are sent to you over a network. You unscramble the DES key using your private key and then use the DES key to unscramble the message. Pretty neat, huh?

RSA's strong suit is that it is based on the difficulty of factoring prime numbers, a concept that only guys like Pythagoras and other mathematicians can understand. This little bit of explanation comes from an RSA press release:

```
Prime numbers are those numbers that are divisible by only them-
selves and 1. Any non-prime number can be always represented as
the product of its prime factors. For example, the number 113549
can be represented as the product of its prime factors 271 and
419. Finding the prime factors of a given number is known as
factoring it. The larger the number, the harder it is to factor.
The largest number to be factored thus far is a 128-digit number.
Each RSA user has a unique key of around 150 digits so, even if you
were able to factor the number, you would have a single user's key.
```

If you understand all of that, I'm impressed.

RSA is widely used in many products, but it's not something that you can buy and use off the shelf as a standalone public-key crypto product. The company has been very aggressive in signing licensing agreements with several of the major computer industry companies. For example, RSA is used in products made by Apple, IBM, Lotus, Microsoft, and Novell. Although it's not an official standard, it's heading that way. If you use a product that features encryption, it is is helpful to know what kind it is, not only for peace of mind, but also for compatibility with other programs.

RSA also makes a product called RSA Secure, which sells for about $99. The company claims it is the fastest and most secure software-based hard disk encryption on the market. It uses RSA's RC4, a secret-key encryption scheme that RSA says is 10 or more times as fast as DES in software. The length of the key can be varied—so you can use short keys for not-so-important stuff and long keys for really important stuff.

Pretty Good Privacy

> I have never liked working. To me a job is an invasion of privacy.
>
> Danny McGoorty (1901–1970)

There's a public-key encryption program called Pretty Good Privacy that's fast becoming the crypto package of choice for many DOS, Apple, and other computer users. Aside from the fact that it features industrial-strength protection, it's also free. The program was developed by a public-spirited citizen by the name of Phil Zimmerman who thinks that everyone should have the right to privacy. In fact, Zimmerman calls PGP "guerrilla freeware."

PGP is more than pretty good—it's very good. It's so good, in fact, that the U.S. government would rather that you didn't use it. (Ah, but you can, and as long as you don't ship it overseas, it's as legal as the day is long.) PGP uses the International Data Encryption Algorithm and RSA algorithms.

Pretty doggone good

IDEA, invented in 1991, is being touted as a possible successor to DES. The key is twice as long as that of DES, and even longer than that of triple DES. Yet IDEA is similar enough to DES that it could be used as a plug-in replacement for DES.

There are DOS, Apple Macintosh, Commodore Amiga, Atari ST, UNIX, and other versions of PGP. PGP also comes in two DOS flavors: PGP, which is free but not licensed, and MIT PGP, which also is free but licensed for noncommercial use in the U.S. only. It is not compatible with earlier versions. There is, however, a modified version called PGP with UI in the version number (UI stands for "unofficial international") that has not been approved by Zimmerman. There's also a version called ViaCrypt, which is licensed for commercial use in the U.S. and Canada.

My friend Harold, the famous security expert, doesn't think much of PGP. He worries that it hasn't been thoroughly tested, for one thing. He also worries that someone may get the idea of hacking PGP to put in a hidden loophole and then posting that version in as many places as possible. These are certainly legitimate concerns, but as long as you're not swapping messages with the Central Intelligence Agency, you don't have much to worry about—yet.

Get it online   You can get the program from a wide variety of sites, including commercial online services such as America Online and Prodigy as well as by anonymous file transfer protocol and bulletin board systems.

If you're Internet savvy and you have a program like archie, you can search archie servers to find out where the file is stored and then download it. Search for "prog pgp26a.zip" for the PC version and "pgp2.6" for the Macintosh version.

PC users can telenet and Mac users can Fetch the PGP program from several sites offering anonymous FTP. While you're getting your copy of PGP, also get "PGP Guide for PC" if you're a PC user or "How to MacPGP" if you're a Mac user. Both freebie guides provide handy info on how PGP works and how to set yourself up. If you're a Windows user, also get pgpwin.zip, a freeware Windows front end for PGP. There's also a shareware version called winpgp.zip that costs $45, but I'm not sure why you would want it, given that the freebie version does the job quite adequately.

If you're unable to run FTP, but you have e-mail access, you can get PGP sent to you. To find out how to do it, send an e-mail message to:

```
To: ftpmail@decwrl.dec.com
From: yourname@internet.site.com
Subject:
```

Leave the Subject: line blank. In the body of the message, type Help. In a couple of hours or less, you'll get instructions on how to use the service.

Setting Up PGP

Okay, here's a quickie course on setting up PGP. For the most part, the process is the same whether you're using a PC or Mac version. I'm not going to go into the steps of actually using PGP. The documents that come with PGP do a very good job of that as do the guides I mentioned earlier. And if you're using pgpwin for a Windows front end or the Mac, it's pretty intuitive. However, there are a few things that you should know about the setup that the documentation really doesn't cover.

Everything in Its Place Create a directory or folder for PGP. Unzip or unstuff PGP if you haven't done it already and store the files in your PGP directory or folder.

If you're a PC user, you'll also need to use the SET command twice in your AUTOEXEC.BAT. The first is to SET the pathname for the directory where you unzipped PGP. To do that, type SET PGPPATH=C:\PGP. Next, SET the time zone for your system. You do that by typing SET TZ= and your time zone as indicated in the PGP documents. For example, if you're on the East Coast, you would type SET TZ=EST5EDT.

Generate Keys Start PGP. First you need to generate your private and public keys. If you're looking at a graphical user interface, poke around until you find something that says "Generate keys" and click on it. If you're in DOS, type pgp-kg. After that, follow the instructions that appear on screen.

PGP gives you a choice of four key sizes: 384, 512, 1024, or a user-selected number of bits. The larger the key, the more secure is the RSA portion of the encryption. Select 1024. It takes longer to generate a key of that size, but key size will not impact the speed at which you can encrypt and decrypt messages.

Enter User Name Next, you'll be asked to enter a user name. Type your name followed by your e-mail address in angle brackets, just like the onscreen example.

Create a Pass Phrase Next, you'll be asked to enter a "pass phrase." PGP encrypts your secret key with this pass phrase to ensure that only you can use it. That and your secret key are what will protect your from the Vandals, Visigoths, and other barbaric hordes, so you'll need a pretty good pass phrase. Your pass phrase has to be long enough that it is not easily guessed, yet memorable enough that you're not tempted to write it down. It should also be a mix of numbers and upper- and lowercase characters. As PGP's docs will tell you, if you make your pass phrase a single word, it can be easily guessed by having a computer try all the words in the dictionary until it finds your password. That's why a pass phrase is so much better than a password. A more sophisticated attacker may have his computer scan a book of famous quotations to find your pass phrase. An easy-to-remember but hard-to-guess pass phrase can be easily constructed by some creatively nonsensical sayings or very obscure literary quotes. Your phrase should probably be a minimum of 8 characters (more is even better). Here is an example of a pass phrase: i8an8BAll4diNner@meLs.

Mix 'em up

> As much as I try to invent pass phrases and passwords that are easy to remember, yet secure, there's just no way that I can remember them all. Inevitably I have to write them down someplace. That's risky, I know, but I'm not a computer.

The other reason that you might want to write down your pass phrase is that if you forget it, there's no way for you to unscramble your files, a thought that is more worrisome to me than the thought of a Bulgarian spymaster breaking into my database of secret sauce recipes. In any case, an attacker would need both the pass phrase and the secret key to unscramble my messages. It's not likely that he will be able to steal the key and figure out my industrial-strength pass phrase, too.

If you choose to write down your pass phrase, store the piece of paper away from the computer. If you really have cause to worry or are just paranoid, you could also store your secret key on a backup disk and the pass phrase on another disk and scramble these two using yet another pass phrase.

Enter Random Keystrokes Next, you'll be asked to enter a bunch of random keystrokes. PGP times the keystrokes and from these gets random numbers that it uses to create the keys. You'll hear a beep when you've typed enough. After the beep, PGP starts generating the keys. Depending on the speed of your machine, it should take about a minute or two to make the keys. That's it. You're set.

Keyrings Are for Keys

> O'er the land of the free, and the home of the brave?
>
> Francis Scott Key
> "The Star Spangled Banner"

Your keys are stored on keyrings. (What a concept!) There's a private keyring and a public keyring. The private keyring has your private key on it. The only thing protecting the key is your pass phrase, so you can see why it was so important to choose something that would take the Oracle at Delphi to divine.

Public keyrings   The public keyring is where you'll keep your public key, which is probably obvious, but I get paid to point out things like that just in case you don't think it's obvious. Public keys also are stored on a public keyring in a key server. To add yours to the keyring, send a mail message to:

```
To: pgp-public-keys@pgp.mit.edu
From: yourname@your.iway.address
Subject: ADD
```

Use your public key for the body of the message.

You'll also have a public keyring of your own, containing the public keys of the public as well as the keys of friends, colleagues, and others with whom you communicate.

You can retrieve the PGP key of a single user or of all the users on the server as well as perform other key-related tricks using the same setup. PGP's docs will fill you in about using INDEX, GET, and other commands.

You'll probably want to maintain a short keyring consisting of the public keys of people with whom you frequently communicate and a long keyring of "everybody else in the world." The reason is that PGP must search through the keyring to find the right one. If the keyring is short, encrypting and decrypting are relatively fast. If the keyring is long, the process is long, excruciatingly so.

Deleted But Not Gone

Once you've scrambled your message, you need to get rid of the original plaintext message and any temp files that might have been created by your word processor.

> **Deleting the file is not likely to do the trick, however. Any number of recovery utilities on the market can be used to retrieve your supposedly trashed files.**

The way to prevent deleted files from being resurrected like Lazarus is to overwrite the plaintext file. PGP does this using the PGP -w (wipe) option. There are also several utilities that can be used to permanently shred a file. After that only the National Security Agency or its equivalent can get those files back.

If someone steals your keyring or pass phrase, you need to create a key revocation certificate and send that to one of the public servers. Basically what the certificate does is alert everyone that the public key can no longer be trusted. The problem is that if you lose either the secret key or the pass phrase, you can't create the certificate.

> **There's an out to this Catch-22, however. First, create a key revocation certificate at the same time that you generate your key pair. Then extract the revoked key to another ASCII file using the -kxa option again. Delete the revoked key from your public keyring using the -kr option and put your nonrevoked version back in the ring using the -ka option. Next, save the revocation certificate on a floppy, and store the secret key on a backup disk. Finally, put the two disks in a safe place (safe, as in a safe or bank deposit box).**

More Digital John Hancocks

PGP, like RSA, is a public-key crypto program. Also like RSA, it can be used to create digital John Hancocks. PGP also can be used to attach a digital signature to a message without encrypting it. You would use that feature if you wanted to post a message that anyone could read, but you want to assure them that the message actually came from you. The digital signature prevents anyone from changing the message, at least not in such a way that the change would not be spotted.

For example, giving the command PGP -sat <filename> only signs a message, it does not encrypt it. Even though the output looks as though it is encrypted, it really isn't. Anybody in the world would be able to recover the original text.

ViaCrypt

A commercial version of PGP is available called ViaCrypt PGP, which is marketed by ViaCrypt for about $100. Zimmerman, PGP's author, licensed the company to sell the program, and it is virtually identical to the PGP 2.3 version. So why spend 100 somoleans for something you can get free any time of the day? The commercial version has fewer bugs than PGP, for one thing. For another, the company also has gotten licenses from RSA and other companies whose technologies are used in PGP. In addition, it is currently available only for MS-DOS and UNIX. ViaCrypt developed its PGP in-house after acquiring a license for the algorithm from PKPartners. Also, ViaCrypt incorporates a few bug fixes. The private-key crypto algorithm is IDEA, for which ViaCrypt has obtained a license.

Other Crypto Schemes

There are other crypto schemes such as Kerboros and RIPEM. They're not in as widespread use as DES, RSA, and PGP, but I'll give you a quick rundown on three: RIPEM, Kerberos, and Clipper.

RIPEM

The public key-program called RIPEM can be used to securely send messages across the Internet. RIPEM features encryption and digital signatures, using RSA and DES algorithms. It is based, in part, on Privacy-Enhanced Mail, an emerging standard for sending Internet e-mail. There are shareware versions for Mac, MS-DOS, and UNIX machines.

Kerberos

Kerberos, named after the fearsome three-headed watchdog in Greek mythology that guards the gates of Hades, also happens to be the name of an encryption scheme that enables computer users to use the applications on UNIX networks. Kerberos is a secret-key network authentication system developed at MIT in 1979, and it uses DES for encryption and authentication.

Kerberos server   A Kerberos system uses a designated Kerberos server to handle key management and other tasks. The server has a database containing the secret keys of all users, generates session keys for users, and authenticates the identity of a user who wants to use certain network services.

When you first log in to a networked computer, you enter your log-in ID and password. Your log-in ID goes out to a Kerboros database that contains the IDs and passwords of everyone authorized to use the system and compares that to your password. Your password remains at the workstation, where there is little chance of it being intercepted.

If you want to use applications that are on the network, you must first authenticate yourself (that is, prove you are who you say you are, a notion that Freud would have had a lot of fun with). To do that, you request a "ticket" from a computer called the key distribution center. The KDC confirms your identity and issues the ticket, which is only good for a certain period of time. You send the ticket along with an "authenticator" that serves to validate the ticket to the application. The application examines both ticket and authenticator and lets you in.

Clipper Chip

The Clipper Chip is not really a crypto standard that you have the option of using, but you may have read about it in newspapers or heard it discussed on television and radio news shows. The Clipper Chip triggered quite a bit of controversy in 1993 when the federal government proposed it as a national standard for encryption. Under the proposal, the chip would be used in telephones to encrypt conversations so that anyone listening would not be able to understand what was being said. There also was some talk about using it to scramble data. So far so good.

The Clipper Chip proposal went one step further and also proposed that law enforcers should have a way to decrypt conversations for court-approved wiretaps. The key that would be used to unscramble the conversations would be held by a trustworthy third person who would release the keys only when presented with a wiretap warrant. As an additional safeguard, the key would be split in two and each half would be given to different holding agencies. **Good for wiretappers**

The Clipper Chip met with vociferous opposition from a variety of groups, particularly civil libertarians and others concerned about individual privacy. Wait a minute, you say. Isn't the Clipper Chip intended to protect privacy? Who could be opposed to that? The problem is that the technology was developed by the National Security Agency (NSA), the federal government's supersecret spy agency, and virtually no one trusts them to stay within the bounds of the law.

The reasoning is that the NSA probably knows how to unscramble conversations without having to get the keys. If everyone used Clipper to protect confidential conversations, the reasoning goes, the NSA would have a ready-made backdoor through which it could eavesdrop. Also, the NSA is unwilling to let anyone get a good look at the formula to scramble conversations, so it is uncertain just how secure the Clipper Chip really is. It does not seem that Clipper will ever come to pass, but you never know. **Forewarned is forearmed**

Hard Disk Encryption

If you're mainly interested in protecting files stored on your hard drive from nosy colleagues and other assorted snoops, there are several shareware and freeware ecryption products that implement DES, IDEA, or some other known-to-be-secure crypto scheme. You can get shareware programs from many bulletin board systems as well as dozens of sites on the Internet. All it takes is a modem to download them. At the end of the book, I'll include a list of sites where you can get programs.

Enigma One program I happen to like is called Enigma, and it comes in Mac and Windows versions. There is a freebie version with a limited version of DES that still provides enough security to keep all but the most dedicated zealots out of your affairs. The shareware version, which costs about $20, features full-strength DES and is not likely to be cracked by anyone but the National Security Agency and former KGB master spies.

Curve Encrypt, a freeware program for the Macintosh, features the IDEA crypto scheme. IDEA is even more secure than DES, although it has not undergone the same level of scrutiny. The author of IDEA claims that it would take a billion times the age of the universe to try every single possible key. I don't know if that's true, but I do know it would take the average snoop more time than it would be worth to crack it.

Encrypting a file is a snap. Select "encrypt file" or something along those lines, select the file to encrypt, enter a pass phrase, and you're done. To decrypt, the process is the reverse. Everything in life should be so uncomplicated. The only drawback is that if you forget your pass phrase, you're out of luck. That doesn't mean much if all you're doing is encrypting an occasional steamy love letter, but if it's a large file representing many hours of hard labor, it's the end of the world. Inevitably what's going to happen is that you're going to use the same pass phrase for all files or you're going to write the phrases down—neither approach is particularly safe.

These and a number of other shareware, freeware, and commercial products will also do a "DoD wipe" that will overwrite files with characters so that the original plaintext file can no longer be recovered with a utility. DoD is short for Department of Defense, by the way.

Products That Use Encryption as a Feature

Products that use DES, RSA, or some of the other mainstream encryption schemes are pretty secure. Even if they can be cracked, it's not likely that your office mate, neighbor, or spouse will be the one to do it. If nothing else, it would take time and money—probably more than it would pay back. However, products that use top-shelf crypto also command higher prices, and thus you may be tempted to use something that is not quite as secure or a product that claims to be "just as good as the best one on the market"—but really isn't.

Not all companies want to pay licensing fees to use a particular algorithm (many times they're patented), so they come up with one of their own.

Keep in mind that if you buy one product that uses encryption based on a proprietary algorithm, you may be buying yourself little more than a false sense of security. There's no way of knowing just how good it really is. In any case, if someone really wants to know how a particular algorithm works, they can figure it out using software that they can get at any Egghead software shop.

Reputable sellers of encryption products want their algorithms to be closely scrutinized to ensure that they are indeed secure. Not only does that mean the product will stand up under repeated attacks, it's also good business. The algorithm for DES, one of the most widely used encryption standards today, has been hammered on for more than 20 years. In that time, some of the brightest crypto experts have tried unsuccessfully to crack it. **It's good business**

All that said, encryption products that use proprietary encryption schemes are often good enough to stymie casual spies. If all you want to do is protect a few files on a hard drive, they may be perfectly adequate. It's a tradeoff between what you can afford to pay and what you can afford to lose.

A growing number of products such as word processors and databases feature encryption to protect passwords and files. These applications use watered-down crypto schemes that, for the most part, are easily circumvented. Either they use poorly implemented crypto or weak algorithms, or they can be circumvented by someone using a cracking program.

For example, AccessData in Orem, Utah, sells a software program that will unscramble WordPerfect, Lotus 1-2-3, QuattroPro, Microsoft Excel, and Paradox files. It costs $185, which might not be much to someone who is really interested in seeing what's on your machine. The company will send you a free demo disk that will decrypt passwords that are 10 or fewer characters (most are, I'd bet). By the way, the product was originally developed to help computer users get back into their systems and recover files after they had lost their passwords.

6 Natural and Unnatural Disasters

Years ago, before I learned the benefit of backing up, I was sitting at my Apple IIe computer busily creating a spreadsheet with which I planned to track the family budget. I spent hours setting up the categories, making sure the formulas worked, filling in cells with financial data, and so on. After I got everything set up several hours later, I saved the spreadsheet on a floppy, took it out of the machine, and laid it on my desk. As I reached around to the back of the machine to turn it off, I stood up slightly and when I did, my head banged into a shelf on the wall behind the machine and right above the desk. The shelf was flimsily mounted on one of those metal bracket systems and I whacked it hard enough that the shelf and all of the books on it tumbled down, pulling the mounting bracket away from the wall. A fine mist of drywall powder settled on my computer and the hard-earned disk lying on the desk.

I frantically blew the dust off the disk and stuck it into the drive. "Jeez, I hope this thing still works," I said. Of course it didn't work. What's more, the disk drive never worked reliably after that either and eventually had to be replaced. Was I stupid or what?

The point is that whatever will go wrong, will go wrong. Sometimes it's things that you might anticipate, such as a hurricane blowing into town. Other times, it's things that you would never consider, like a shelf full of books tumbling on your head. In this chapter, I'm going to talk about some of the ways in which you can minimize the impact of both natural and unnatural disasters. You'll find quite a bag of tricks here, from disaster recovery to ergonomics. In Chapter 7, I'll tell you all about backing up—the ultimate protection against all manner of disaster—and recovery utilities that will help you wrest your data from the black hole where all data goes when it dies.

Murphy's Law

WELL-LAID PLANS OF MICE AND MEN

> A man gazing on the stars is proverbially at the mercy of the
> puddles on the road.
>
>   Alexander Smith (1830–1867)
>   *Dreamthorp, Men of Letters,* 1863

There are all sorts of calamities—natural and otherwise—that can cripple your computer (or computers, if you run a business) and send your information sailing off to parts unknown. There are hurricanes, floods, fire, and other so-called acts of God, and then there are what I call the unnatural acts such as power outages, chemical spills that cause the evacuation of one's neighborhood or business district, and the bathtub overflow that causes water to pour down through the ceiling.

My friend Harold, the security genius, says I should not forget to mention the data-destroying potential of smoke. There's smoke from a fire, of course, but he also says that you shouldn't overlook smoke from, say, a BBQ grill near a basement office window where the computer happens to be.

If you rely on your computer system for your livelihood or to operate a business, you must protect yourself against the day that trouble comes your way. Trouble finds everyone sooner or later, so you might as well expect it and get ready.

Most big companies are ready for disasters, with their sophisticated contingency planning specialists and a whole slew of fail-safe backup equipment and procedures. Large organizations call this sort of looking for trouble disaster recovery planning, contingency planning, or business resumption planning. Take your pick.

 Not enough small and midsize companies have given disaster recovery much thought, unfortunately. The truth is that the small fry have the most to lose because they usually don't have the resources to weather the really bad storms.

On the other hand, with proper disaster recovery techniques, small companies, which are usually more flexible and adaptable than large companies can use their size to their advantage during times of adversity.

Hope for the best   The big idea is that if a hurricane blows through or some other calamity strikes, there's not much you're going to do about it except hunker down and hope for the best. Businesses are most concerned with what happens after the damage is done. Their plans are all aimed at getting the business back on its feet.

Even if all you use your PC or Mac for is to store recipes, compute home finances, and perform other routine tasks, you should prepare for the worse. That doesn't mean you need to draw up the same sort of comprehensive disaster recovery plan that a business would use since that would be overkill. Still, you can do a lot to insulate yourself from trouble and recover from evil happenings. For example, there are uninterruptible power supplies to keep systems running long enough to save your work and safely shut down the system, surge suppressors to guard against massive circuit-cooking jolts of power, tape and other backup systems, diagnostics tools to troubleshoot problems, and recovery utilities to retrieve lost data and restore sanity to your life.

THINGS THAT GO BUMP DAY AND NIGHT

> The mistakes are all there waiting to be made.
>
> Savielly Grigorievitch Tarakower (1887–1956), Chessmaster, on the game's opening position

Right now, I'm going to cover some of the disaster recovery procedures that self-employed professionals and small business operators ought to consider. Even if you don't fit in that category, you'll find plenty of tips and suggestions for protecting yourself from disaster.

Small companies have some advantages that large companies don't have when recovering from a disaster. Unlike, say, a commodities trading firm, which can lose millions in mere minutes, small companies often have a cushion of a few days to get back into action.

Also, small companies can often be back in business by simply picking up a few PCs and setting up shop in the boss's garage or in a hotel conference room.

The first thing small (big ones, too) companies need to do is anticipate all of the things that can possibly go wrong and plan for them. The main troublemakers, outside of malcontented employees, that any company has to worry about are power outages and viruses. That's according to a survey by a company that specializes in disaster recovery planning, by the way. Some of the other natural and unnatural disasters any company needs to worry about include:

- Floods or other water-related catastrophes
- Hurricanes
- Earthquakes
- Fire
- Lightning strikes
- Sabotage

Not all of these disasters are going to be bothersome to every business. People who live in San Francisco worry about earthquakes; people who live in Boston worry more about freezing rain bringing down power lines. You probably already have a good idea of what sorts of misfortune you are likely to encounter in your piece of the world.

Fear the unknown   There are also unforeseen disasters that may result from, say, a fire sprinkler system being set off by a prankster or an overturned tanker truck carrying a toxic chemical on a nearby highway forcing an evacuation of the area in which your business is located.

The key is not worry too much about all of the things that can go wrong but simply accept that there are a variety of disasters that are likely to have a serious impact on the business's ability to operate. It doesn't matter that the water pouring into your home or business came from a flood, a broken water main, or an overflowing bathtub—water is water, right?

Once you've figured out all of the things that can go wrong, you'll have a good idea of what you need to protect. You'll also have an idea of what the impact will be on your business operations. If you know the business is not likely to recover from a hurricane within a week or so, you'll also know what you stand to lose in business in that time. On the other hand, a power outage may last only a few hours, and a generator may be all you need to keep the doors open.

I Hear a Train A-Comin'

Nothing is impossible for the man who doesn't have to do it himself.

A. H. Weiler

Okay, so let's say you agree that you're sitting in the middle of the railroad tracks and somewhere down the line, the disaster train is heading your way. The question you need to answer at this point is "What business resources must I protect first? Is it the computer I use for order processing or is it my entire local area network? What about my telephone system? Is it my fax machine and copier?

Don't forget your most critical resource of all: you and your employees, if you have any. Will you be able to set up shop somewhere else if the building is suddenly uninhabitable? If there is a serious disaster that affects the region, perhaps a hurricane or a nor'easter, you and your employees may not be able to count on coming into work. Obviously you and they also have families and homes to think of under those circumstances.

Running Hot and Cold

> Hell is paved with Good Samaritans.
>
> William M. Holden

Large companies subscribe to disaster recovery services that provide hot sites—   **Sites insight**
fully equipped facilities with computer gear already up and running at a moment's
notice. The service companies provide computers, networks, telephones, and fax
machines—in short, nearly everything a normal business operation would require.
Companies that use these services pay a monthly subscription fee and then
additional fees if they actually use the service. Needless to say, the costs of using a
hot site can easily run into thousands of dollars a day. The costs are worth it for
many companies, however. They can count on being up and running in only a day
or so in most instances.

Some disaster recovery companies also set up cold sites. These sites are not
operational but have computers, networking connections, and other useful stuff
that can be set up and ready to go in a matter of hours if the trouble express barrels
into town.

**Here's a good use for your old equipment: If you upgrade your equipment
every few years like many people do, pack up your old equipment and store it
someplace where it will be reasonably safe from cat burglars, wire-munching
rats, and other dangers. What you have here is the makings of your own cold
site. If your primary system or systems bite the dust, unpack your old stuff and
go to work. (You might not be working as fast as you would like, but it beats
shutting the doors while the other system is being put back together.) Of
course, this is only going to work if your old stuff was made in this century.**

Most small companies cannot afford the pricey luxury of subscribing to a
disaster recovery service that provides hot or cold sites, but you could seek out
firms in your area that may be willing to agree to a reciprocal arrangement. The
trick is finding a company or environment that is reasonably compatible with the
one you have. If you're an all Mac shop, make an agreement with another
company that also runs a lot of Macs. You could also investigate the possibility of
establishing a relationship with one of those fully functional office facilities that
many businesses use when first starting up.

Other Considerations

> An optimist sees opportunity in every calamity.
> A pessimist sees calamity in every opportunity.
>
> Anonymous

You can't expect that your power and telephone service will be available immediately following a disaster. You need to figure out in advance what you are going to do until power and telephone service are restored. Also, you must consider that your building may not be inhabitable for some time, if ever, following a serious problem. Thus you must first determine what business operations are the most vital and take steps to protect them.

As an example, if you determine that your telephone system is the most vital piece of equipment because you spend much of your time on the telephone selling, it would be a reasonable precaution to buy a cellular telephone. If your client database is what's most important, you want to make sure that you have up-to-date backups stored in a safe place as well as a computer system on which to run them.

If your business is adversely affected and your equipment is destroyed, you may not have the funds immediately available to repurchase the equipment you'll need. But wait a minute, what about insurance? You do have insurance, right? Yeah, but trying to get most insurance companies to fork over the dough quickly is about as easy as moving a herd of elephants across the Alps in the middle of winter.

You can save yourself considerable heartache if you have a proper inventory of all of your equipment in hand before you sit down with your insurance agent. Inventory everything of consequence to the business—that includes computers, printers, modems and other peripherals, fax machines, copiers, and so on. Don't overlook those often pricey add-cards and other upgrades to PCs.

The inventory list should include the manufacturer's name, model, serial number, and a brief description of the product. Also, gather up receipts, sales slips, and other supporting evidence. As an added precaution, video tape everything in sight, including the equipment. (Get close-ups of identifying marks such as model and serial numbers.)

Keep up to date   You also need to have supporting materials for software, although if you've taken the precaution of backing up the software you use and storing the duplicates in a safe place, you may not need to file a claim for those. Doing all of this from scratch is a downright pain. If you manage to do it, however, remember from then on to keep the inventory up to date by writing down each new acquisition.

If you have a network, keeping track of hardware and software is a lot easier if you use an inventory program like one of those that I mentioned in Chapter 4. Not only is it a good way to keep track of the hardware and software on your network, but if you're ever called upon to provide licensing data for software you use, you'll have the backup information that you'll need. These programs are capable of generating reports that can be used to support insurance claims and can also be used as shopping lists should you need to buy equipment.

Gather up all of this supporting material and store it in a safe place off site, preferably in a fireproof lock box, safe-deposit box, or similar place.

Write It Down, or It Ain't a Plan

> The cost of living is going up and the chance of living is going down.
>
> Flip Wilson
> *On Being Funny,* by Eric Lax, 1975

All of this information goes into a written disaster recovery plan. A notebook should suffice. Detail what steps you'll take to get the business back on its feet. If the job seems overly burdensome, there are companies that provide software to draw up a recovery plan. Three programs that come to mind are Chi/Cor Information Management's Vue-It ($995), the Institute of Internal Auditors' Automated Systems for Contigency Planning and Disaster Recovery ($200), and Kingswell Partnership's DC/DREP Distributed Communications Disaster Recovery Plan ($995). All you have to do is fill in the blanks.

The disaster recovery plan should include:

- An itemized list of computer and other business resources that are to be protected

- The minimum equipment that will be required to set up shop again

- Contact information and procedures for notifying employees, customers, and suppliers in the event of an emergency

- Location of the off-site meeting place, along with directions on how to get to it

- Procedures for obtaining backup tapes and restoring the system, with details of precisely who will do this, when it will be done (in what sequence), how it will be done, and what will be required to do the job

This plan should go into a disaster recovery tool kit, which should be kept in the office, near the door so that someone can grab it on the way out.

You also need to test your plan from time to time to make sure that it works. It's akin to a fire drill. You don't want to wait until there's a fire before you figure out how you're going to get out in one piece. You also need to see if the time that you have allotted to getting back on your feet is realistic. Testing the plan involves checking to see that your backup media is current and that it, in fact, actually works. If the backups are encrypted, who knows the key?

Damage control mode   When disaster strikes, go into your damage control mode and start implementing your plan. Also, pick up a camera or a camcorder and document the amount of damage. And, since you'll be spending money by the truckload, immediately implement a program of capturing costs incurred, from temporary roof repairs to extra security. Accounting for expenses in the beginning will make it infinitely easier to process insurance and federal assistance claims down the road.

Get Employees Involved With the Program

> The best way out of difficulty is through it.
>
> Anonymous

One of the key changes many organizations are making to their disaster recovery plans is to ask their employees to become more involved in disaster planning and to be better prepared for contingencies. With the increased distribution of information throughout many organizations, each employee is being asked to take greater responsibility for the information at their desktops. To involve your employees in your disaster recovery plan, consider the following issues:

- If employees are suddenly asked to immediately leave the building, they should take their personal files and Rolodexes with them. They may need to contact relatives, fellow employees, customers, and others.

- Employee phone lists, supplier contacts, outstanding orders—anything and everything critical to maintaining the company, on disk or on paper—must be identified and accessible. A lot of vital information resides outside networks on the hard drives of individual employees.

- Make sure that your staff knows what to do in an emergency. Ask key managers to keep backup copies of the disaster plan at home; keep another copy in a bank's safe-deposit box or another secure place off site.

- Explain to your employees that not everyone can be involved in a disaster recovery operation. Initially only key employees should be involved; others later as needed. If resources are already stretched thin, bringing on more people will hinder the recovery effort.

People Come First

When people speak about disaster recovery planning, they are usually referring to the steps an organization takes to make sure that its information systems are up and running as soon as possible following a fire, hurricane, or some other calamity. One important piece of that planning that is sometimes overlooked is making sure that people—employees and their families—are also taken care of when adversity strikes.

The American Red Cross has compiled a list of essential items to have on hand in the event of a natural disaster. You might want to consider assembling the same items for yourself and your employees:

The essentials

1. Bottled water (at least three gallons per household member)

2. Canned or precooked food for three to seven days

3. Battery-operated radio

4. At least one flashlight next to your bed

5. Heavy shoes for each family member

6. Extra batteries

7. Well-stocked first aid kit

8. Fire extinguisher

9. Automobile survival kit with items such as an emergency blanket and flashlight

Water Everywhere and Time to Think

> Winter lingered so long in the lap of Spring, that it occasioned a great deal of talk.
>
> Attributed to Bill Nye

In the spring, my thoughts turn to floods. Flood victims who discover that their computer hard disk drives, floppy diskettes, tape backups or removable media have sustained water damage are most apt to think they have no recourse. Not so fast.

Several data recovery companies put out products, such as OnTrack Data Recovery, Lazarus Data Recovery, and Total Recall, that are able to retrieve data from hard and floppy disks. They're equipped with dust-free clean rooms and use specially formulated cleaning solutions to raise your data from the dead. Here are some tips (recommended by OnTrack) if you suddenly find yourself wading in trouble:

Wading out of trouble

1. Think positively. Data can often be recovered from what may seem like impossible circumstances.

2. If a hard disk drive is waterlogged, don't try to operate it.

3. If a hard or floppy disk is waterlogged, don't take it apart in an attempt to dry it out. Also, don't try to heat it or freeze dry it.

4. Don't try shaking the hard drive in hopes of getting the water out.

5. If a floppy disk has been submerged in water, don't try to retrieve the data using a recovery utility.

6. Time is of the essence. If the drive or storage media is visibly water damaged, don't wait for it to dry on its own. Send it to a data recovery company to take care of it.

Some Additional Common-Sense Safeguards

> Avoid running at all times.
>
> Satchel Paige (1906?–1982)

Whoever coined the old expression that "an ounce of prevention is worth a pound of cure" was probably an early computer user. To help ward off trouble before it strikes your computer, here are some tips:

1. Don't eat or drink around your computer, or anyone else's for that matter. Accidents happen more often that we like to think.

2. Regularly check and tighten your PC's cables and electrical connections. Replace any that are worn, frayed, or cracked. If you're one of those hardy souls who has ventured to open your computer's case, check to make sure that boards are properly seated and that nothing has shaken loose. Always unplug the computer before opening it!

3. When installing new software, plug-in cards, and the like, make one change at a time rather than all at once. That way, if something goes wrong, there will be fewer variables involved in diagnosing the problem.

4. Be prepared for trouble. Create an emergency disk containing the files and setup information needed to boot your computer. You also should have handy disks containing programs designed to pinpoint trouble such as a virus or a balky hard disk drive and to backup and restore tape. Several utilities on the market from companies such as Peter Norton and Central Point can be used to help you out of a jam.

YOU'VE GOT THE POWER, MAYBE

Providence protects children and idiots. I know because I have tested it.

Mark Twain (1835–1910)

You can get an awful lot of work done between backups, a lifetime really, if you think about it. You can also lose an awful lot of data between backups. One of the most likely ways that's going to happen is that you're going to have a power problem.

Power Problems

There are basically five power-related problems that can leap up unexpectedly and kill your data: blackouts, sags or brownouts, spikes, surges, and noise.

Blackouts

Blackouts are pretty easy to understand. There's a complete power loss. A car bangs into a utility pole and knocks it down; ice cakes a power line, causing it to snap; an overzealous backhoe operator rips up the line—you get the picture, I'm sure. The consequence is that whatever you're working on gets tossed into the electronic ether, and there's no way you've ever going to see it again because it was in RAM. Sometimes your hard drive's file allocation table is trashed along with data or the computer won't reboot when the power comes back.

Oh, gee, no juice

Sags or Brownouts

Sags, or brownouts, are blackouts that never quite make it. It's one of the most common power problems, according to one study by Bell Labs. The problem is often caused by too many people chasing after too few kilowatts, like on a summer day when everyone is cranking up the air conditioner at the same time. "Loretta, it's gosh darn hot in here, turn up the AC will ya?" When demand exceeds supply, your local utility cuts voltage levels back and that, in turn, is what causes a sag, or brownout. What happens on your end is that your PC starts gasping for power. "Scotty, more power, blast it!" "But Captain, I cannae give you ana more!" Systems crash, data is trashed. Repeated sags can shorten the life of electrical motors, like the one in your hard disk drive.

Too few kilowatts

Spikes

Spikes are nasty. They're like a tsunami of power blasting its way down the power pipe into your home or office. Boom—when it strikes, sayonara baby. Not only is

Power tsunami

all of that hard work of yours zapped, but your computer and hard drive—maybe your telephone and fax, too—are fried. Spikes are caused often by a lightning strike or the power surging back on after being turned off as a result of a storm, car accident, or similar problem.

Surges

Wimpier   Surges are like spikes, but wimpier. You might get them when you or someone in your family has been using one of those Suck-all Hurricane Force 9 vacuum cleaners and you turn the machine off, sending the extra voltage coursing through the wiring. They don't cause that much of a problem, although over time they may send your PC off to an earlier-than-expected death.

Noise

Electrobabble   Noise is noise—weird electrobabble on the line—caused by the motor in your Jacuzzi, ham radio equipment, satellite dish rotator motors, and all of the other toys that are necessary to one's well being. If the problem is severe, it may cause some programs to do a cha-cha when they are supposed to be waltzing.

Different parts of the country are susceptible to different power-related problems. In the Northeast, where I live, I worry about brownouts in the summer and blackouts in the winter.

Three Ways to Deal With Power

> Your chances of getting hit by lightning go up if you stand under a tree, shake your fist at the sky, and say, "Storms suck!"
>
> Johnny Carson

Don't wait for a power-related problem to strike before you decide you need to take precautionary measures. There are basically three types of equipment designed to deal with power problems:

1. If spikes, surges, and noise bother you most, you probably need a *surge suppressor*.

2. If sags are a drag, a *voltage regulator* will smooth out the power flow.

3. If spikes, surges, sags, blackouts, and noise tend to gang up on you, you need the big stick—an *uninterruptible power supply*.

Rein in Surges and Spikes

A moment's insight is sometimes worth a life's experience.

Oliver Wendell Holmes, Sr.
The Professor at the Breakfast Table, 1860

Some years ago, I was the smug owner of an Atari 1200XL home computer with a 5.25-inch floppy disk drive. An Atari PC doesn't sound like much of anything today, but back then it was a pretty fancy system and it was expensive. I had just embarked on my sideline freelance writing business, and I expected to get a return on my investment many times.

One day, not long after getting the computer, I was busily working on an assignment and the power went out without warning. I lost the document that was in the computer's memory, but fortunately I had saved my work to a disk only moments before. "I should be in pretty good shape when the power comes back on," I told myself. What I didn't think to do was flick the power switch off or unplug the machine and disk drive. **Off, not on**

A couple of hours later, the power came on and the surge zapped both the computer and disk drive, frying both of them beyond repair (fixing them would have cost almost as much as I paid for them new). I was literally out of business in a matter of minutes. A costly mistake, all because I didn't know enough to buy a $30 surge protector.

Surge suppressors sell for between $5 to $200, although the average probably is about $50. They're inexpensive enough that I have them on all of the electrical equipment that I really care about, like my laser printer, multimedia loudspeakers and other computer adds, fax machine, and hi-fi and video equipment. **Cheap protection everyone should have**

I use surge protectors made by Panamex, one of the name-brand companies in the business. I paid about $60 for the fanciest model I have with six plugs. I can't guarantee that it will work if lightning comes barreling down the line, but so far, so good. I also have an uninterruptible power supply for my computer, which I'll tell you about in a minute or two.

A surge suppressor won't stop massive energy spikes, but it can help contain the potential damage. If a thunderstorm rolls into town, finish whatever it is that you're working on and Save As (not Save, Save As). If the power shuts down while you're saving, kiss that file goodbye, but you'll still have the original file safely tucked away on your hard drive. You'll lose whatever work you did since the last Save, but it shouldn't be much if you're a regular saver. For good measure, unplug your computer and peripherals until the storm passes.

Surge suppressors are useful not only for protecting computer gear but also for telephones, printers, fax machines, and other sensitive equipment.

An inexpensive or poorly made suppressor may provide little more than a false sense of security. In fact, it may even cause noise that can damage circuitry. Once it's been used to stop a power surge, it no longer works and you may not have an indication that it has been rendered ineffective.

Here is what you'll need to know when you shop for a surge suppressor:

- One of the most important specifications you should look for is the reaction time. Obviously, the faster, the better. You'll want a suppressor that has a reaction time of less than a nanosecond (that's a billionth of a second).

- The amount of energy the device dissipates is expressed in joules. Good-quality units are rated at 450 or more joules. At the other end of the scale, poor-quality units may be rated at as little as 120 joules.

- Most top-quality surge protectors are equipped with either a catastrophic or thermal fuse. The first shuts off power to the equipment if the voltage is too high; the second shuts off power if the temperature of the device exceeds 140 degrees.

- If you're interested in protecting only certain pieces of equipment, say, a fax machine, look for a modular surge protector. These are devices designed for a specific purpose and can be economical because you are not paying for features that you may not need.

- The better surge protectors also are equipped with indicator lights to alert you if a device plugged into it is not grounded or otherwise improperly installed as well as to indicate that the suppressor has been fried by a surge and should be replaced.

- Make sure that the suppressor has been tested and approved by Underwriter's Laboratories. How can you tell? Look for "UL1449 approved," which should be stamped on the surge suppressor. That means it has been approved to handle 330 volts.

Watch out for devices marked "UL1449" but not the "approved" on the package. That's an indication that the device has not actually been tested.

Several makers of surge protectors such as American Power Conversion, Deltec, Panamax, and Tripp Lite provide insurance with their products. Basically they guarantee to replace whatever equipment was damaged or pay several thousands of dollars in the event that their products should fail. Nothing beats a company putting its money where its marketing mouth happens to be!

Well Conditioned and Regulated

> Power is the great aphrodisiac.
>
> Henry Kissinger
> *New York Times,* January 19, 1971

Off-the-shelf PCs and Macs have built-in power supplies that are designed to filter out noise and cope with variations in the power supply. But if you live in an area where the line voltage varies greatly, fluctuating either too low or too high from a safe level, what you may need is a power conditioner and voltage regulator (one box does both tasks and acts as a surge suppressor). The box automatically corrects for brownouts by boosting voltage and prevents overvoltages by stepping down the voltage to levels that are safer. Obviously, if the power should fail entirely, a power conditioner/voltage regulator is not going to do squat to save your data.

These boxes also are able to withstand surges and, in fact, may be more effective than simple surge suppressors in combating surges and electromagnetic interference. A power conditioner/voltage regulator for a single PC setup sells for about $150 to $200. A unit that is designed to accommodate several systems sells for about $250 to $300. American Power Conversion, Deltec, Square D, and Tripp Lite, among several other companies, market them.

Never Ending Power

> The computer is down. I hope it's something serious.
>
> Stanton Delaplane
> *San Francisco Chronicle,* July 11, 1984

The uninterruptible power supply (UPS) is to power protection what Goliath was to the Philistines—it's what you bring in when you want to do some heavy lifting.

Not only will a UPS (a decent one, anyway) protect you against surges, spikes, sags, and noise, it will also provide power—enough of it so that you can save your data and safely shut down the system. In fact, the day before I wrapped up this book, a storm packing 70-mile-per-hour winds knocked down power lines nearby, causing a blackout. My UPS politely beeped once or twice to let me know that it was running on batteries, alerting me to save my work and shut down. Until that happened, I didn't even realize that the power in the rest of the house had gone out.

A UPS delivers power to a system when the usual electrical supply has been cut off. The basic UPS has a battery and a battery charger as well as circuitry that converts AC power to DC to charge the battery and then back again to power the system. The juice flows from the wall, through the battery, and into the system. When the power goes off, the battery kicks in immediately and the system doesn't miss a beat. This UPS is a Line-Interactive UPS because the UPS's circuitry interacts with the AC power to boost or replace power and to perform other tasks.

Standby   There is a variety of the UPS called a Standby UPS or Standby Power System that does not feed the juice through a battery. Instead, power is fed through a surge suppressor and other protective circuitry while at the same time the unit is siphoning off power that is used to charge a battery. If the power suddenly shuts off, a power-sensing circuit detects the loss, flips a switch, and kicks the battery into action. The time that takes is milliseconds, which is fast enough to keep the system on its feet. On the plus side, a Standby UPS costs a lot less than a UPS—about half as much, in fact.

 The risk is that because the power is not continuous and requires a transfer time, this box may not provide adequate protection when you're trying to protect a mission-critical network.

The runtime—the amount of time that the UPS will provide power—varies between 5 and 30 minutes, depending on the load and size of the unit's batteries. Line-Interactive UPSs typically feature longer runtimes than Standby UPSs.

Not a lot of bucks   All in all, both types provide a terrific amount of protection for not a lot of bucks. Several companies market UPSs of both types, including American Power Conversion, Best Power Technology, Deltec, Minuteman, Oneac, Tripp Lite, and Upsonic. How many bucks, you ask? If you want to protect the typical computer systems, expect to pay about $120 to $350 for a Standby UPS and about $300 to $450 for a Line-Interactive UPS. To protect a small network with a single server, figure on spending $500 to $700 for a Standby UPS and $550 to $1300 for a Line-Interactive UPS.

I use an American Power Conversion Back-UPS Pro 650, a Line-Interactive UPS with enough capacity to handle a heavily configured PC or Mac. It's got a 5-minute runtime on a full load, which is plenty. The UPS has never been sorely tested by any power problems that I'm aware of, but if it or any of my equipment that's plugged into it is fried by electricity, I'm covered for up to $25,000 worth of damage. You can pick one up for about $280.

 Most people can do quite well with only 5 minutes of runtime while operating with a full load. That's plenty of time to save your work and power down the system. You may need more time if you're running a business, especially if you're protecting a network whose operating system needs plenty of time to make a graceful exit.

You should shut off the UPS before the battery is drained because these batteries are damaged when they're completely spent. Fortunately, most UPSs will alert you before that happens. They also you to periodically test the battery to see if its performance is up to par. Batteries routinely require 4–5 hours to recharge.

You'll need to replace the UPS's batteries every 3 to 6 years. Just how often you'll change the batteries depends in part on how often you let the battery run down.

When trying to make up your mind between two different products, check the cost of replacement batteries. Harold says that he recently received a solicitation from a UPS vendor who wanted to sell him a UPS for $89. The problem, says Harold, is that you must replace the battery once a year at a cost of $70!

Some UPS makers also include software with their UPSs that is useful in helping you perform tasks such as monitoring power to the system, performing diagnostics, scheduling tests of the UPS's performance, automatically shutting down the system during an extended power failure, and rebooting it when power returns.

Figuring out what size UPS you need takes a minute with a calculator:

1. List all the equipment that you want to protect.

2. Calculate the voltage and amperage (VA) rating of your equipment. Look on the back of the equipment or in the owner's manual to find out how much power the device consumes. The power requirements may be expressed as a VA rating, amps, or watts. If it's amps, multiply by 120 to convert into VA. If it's watts, multiply by 1.4 to find the VA. Add up all of the VA ratings.

3. Choose a UPS that features a VA capacity that is equal to the total VA that you have just calculated. If you're planning to expand your system, buy a unit with a higher capacity than you need at the moment. Also, larger units tend to have larger batteries and thus are capable of operating for longer stretches without AC power than smaller units. There's no point in buying far more than you need, however. Somewhere down the line, you'll have to replace the batteries and there won't be any payback for the expense.

If you have a typical system, your VA might be as follows:

Device	VA
Desktop Pentium PC	250
14" VGA Monitor	80
External CD-ROM	60
External Modem	30
Total VA	420

When determining the capacity of the UPS that you'll need, in many instances, you can omit figuring in your laser printer. Keep in mind that your main objective is to prevent the loss of data, and you're not going to lose data if your printer goes down. Also, laser printers periodically draw significant amounts of power and may overload the UPS unless it's one of those jumbo models. Instead, protect the laser with a good-quality surge protector.

LET'S GET PHYSICAL

> We must believe in luck. For how else can we explain the success of those we don't like?
>
> Jean Cocteau (1889–1963)

In July 1992, a construction crew punched a hole into the bottom of the Chicago River (that's in Chicago), sending water cascading into a system of tunnels underneath the famed Loop district. The power to many buildings downtown had to be shut off for several days while the hole was plugged and the tunnels pumped of brackish water and dead fish. Without power, many companies also were shut down for several days; the lucky ones were able to find alternative sites from which they could set up business.

When workers were evacuating the buildings, enterprising gangs of thieves used the confusion to enter the buildings and steal computers and other vital business equipment. Not many disaster recovery planners would have foreseen that possibility!

High-tech thievery Thieves made off with $882 million worth of personal computers last year, according to Safeware, The Insurance Agency Inc., based in Columbus, Ohio. That's just the hardware; the figure does not include the value of the information stored in those PCs or the time it took to replace the lost information. Putting a number on the value of information is about as easy as trying to pin down a blob of Jell-o with a nail, but one study I've seen by the American Bar Association puts the value of information lost as a result of computer equipment theft at about $1 billion a year. No one really knows. Suffice it to say that it's a lot.

One thing is certain—computer theft is on the increase, partly because more thieves are beginning to recognize that information can often be worth more than the actual PC hardware and software.

Batten Down the Hatches

You can take several precautions to prevent a thief from stealing your computer equipment, or at least make it so difficult and time consuming that it may be better for the thief to find an easier mark. The obvious precaution would be to wire your home or office with a good-quality burglar alarm system. There are many ways to do this, but you'll have to see an alarm specialist for the details. That involves a lot more than we've got time for here.

The quick and cheap solution is to put a solid lock on your office door and then use it every time you leave. An industrial-strength deadbolt lock will deter most thieves, especially if it's easier for the thief to go next door and rob your neighbor.

Thieves tend to shy away from equipment that has been clearly etched with a name or social security number prominently on the case. If you don't want to mark up your precious goods (after all, you may want to sell the stuff at some time), put a label inside each piece of equipment. The label should indicate who the gear belongs to and, if it is recovered, how to get in contact with you.

If your business employs a network with a server, the server should be locked in a secure room where only authorized personnel can access it. Many companies use a broom closet for that purpose, but that's dumb. Closets are not really all that secure, for one, and the server needs proper ventilation, for another.

Remember that list of equipment with serial numbers, date of purchase, and other relevant information that I said you should compile? Not only is it necessary for your disaster recovery efforts, it will also prove handy if a thief makes off with your worldly goods.

Locked Up, Locked Down

>   Baseball is 90 percent mental. The other half is physical.
>
>   Yogi Berra, on baseball

A variety of relatively inexpensive devices that lock down PCs, portable computers, and related equipment are on the market. The most common of these antitheft devices is a locking device that attaches to the PC, monitor, and other equipment and a galvanized steel cable or plate that anchors the equipment to a desk, radiator, or other immovable object. The locking device attaches to the equipment either with a strong adhesive or by means of the screws in the PC or other equipment. Several vendors market these products, including Anchor Pad Products, Compu-Gard, PC Guardian Security Products, Qualtec Data Products, and Z-Lock Manufacturing. They sell for $25–$70.

More sophisticated security systems keep watch over computers by using your computer network or by means of a special fiber optic cable. When a PC is detached from the network or cable, the antitheft system sounds an alarm or transmits a status alert to the system administrator. Globus Systems and Computer Security Products make antitheft systems of this type.

Sound an alarm

Another approach that sounds an alarm when a PC is taken is based on affixing a sensor on or inside the equipment you want to protect. Antennas installed in the room or building exits detect these sensors when they pass by and trigger an alarm. SonicPro International and Sensormatics Electronics Corp. market these systems.

All of these devices work with varying degree of success. For example, a thief may simply opt to snip a cable, thus rendering it useless. Also, if the security system includes a locking device, but the key is stored where it can be easily found, the system will be of little use.

Some Other Approaches

If your equipment is stolen, notify the Stolen Computer Registry. The registry, which is maintained by the National Computer Exchange, a used PC brokerage firm based in New York City, maintains a database of serial numbers for stolen computer equipment. Registration is free, and you can dial in your serial number via modem to the registry's BBS (212/505-7526). Computer resellers and law enforcement and insurance agencies check the Registry when recovering stolen PCs and return the machines to their rightful owners.

Various access control programs will lock your hard disk and prevent an unauthorized person from easily reformatting the hard drive. Take a look at Chapter 3 on access control for more information about these programs.

COVER YOURSELF WITH INSURANCE

> And down in fathoms many went the captain and crew;
> Down went the owners—greedy men whom hope of gain allured;
> Oh dry the starting tear, for they were heavily insured.
>
> Sir William Schwenk Gilbert (1836–1911)
> *The Bab Ballads,* "Etiquette," stanza 1

Corporations have insurance with special riders to cover losses in the case of theft. But what about your own computers?

Some insurance companies, even if they cover home computers, don't automatically insure systems used as part of a home business. Special policy riders must be written to cover those machines.

If you use a computer at home, it's probably time to review your homeowner's or renter's insurance and assess your needs. Homeowner's replacement policies cover up to a specified amount of computer equipment. That may not be adequate to cover everything such as expensive laser printers and other peripherals. A specialized computer policy will cover you for losses that your homeowner's insurance won't, such as power surges and virus attacks. The yearly cost for a typical system—computer, monitor, and printer—is about $70 to $100 for about $5000 of coverage. Two national firms that provide this sort of coverage are Safeware at (800) 822-2345 and The Computer Insurance Agency at (800) 722-0385.

If you live in a high-crime area and want to enhance your existing policy, look to the Federal Crime Insurance Program (FCIP) for a specialized policy. FCIP can be reached at (800) 638-8780.

FCIP, underwritten by the federal government, provides secondary coverage at a subsidized rate and ignores non–crime-related losses like fire and liability. If your primary policy doesn't cover your burglary losses completely, FCIP will, up to an additional $10,000. FCIP is available in California, Florida, Illinois, Kansas, Maryland, New Jersey, New York, Pennsylvania, Puerto Rico, the Virgin Islands, and Washington, D.C. Some states have similar programs. To find out more, call FCIP or your state's insurance commission.

Protect yourself even further by taking photographs or videos of all of your equipment as well as all of your other household items.

Keep an inventory of equipment to make it easier to determine just how much insurance you need and to give to an agent when shopping for insurance. A simple database program with fields for serial number, purchase price and date, manufacturer, and model number will simplify recordkeeping. Print a report and keep it in a safe place; the inventory won't do you much good if it's stolen along with the computer.

THE AGONY, NOT ECSTASY OF USING PCS

> Every tiny step forward in the world was formerly made at the cost of mental and physical torture.
>
> Friedrich Nietzsche (1844–1900)
> *On the Genealogy of Morals*, First Essay, Aphorism 9 (1887)

While you're taking care of all of this computer security business, who's looking out for number one? If you think about it, making sure that your computer doesn't do you in is the ultimate form of computer security. After all, if you aren't well taken care of, your computer won't be either. You need to be careful out there, Bunky.

Putting in too many hours without a break at your keyboard may result in aching wrists or other repetitive-motion disorders. There also are emissions from computer monitors to worry about, and health experts have been looking closely at that problem in recent months.

Believe it or not, there's little evidence that directly links health woes with computer use. Even though no scientific studies have shown that typing at a computer keyboard causes injuries, no one can argue that a properly set up computer and sensible work habits are not useful in promoting general workplace comfort and health.

Ergonomics 101

> I do most of my work sitting down; that's where I shine.
>
> Attributed to Robert Benchley

Over the more than fifteen years that I have been pounding a computer keyboard, virtually every day for hours at a stretch, I have been plagued by back pains, blurry vision, headaches, and a mild (fortunately) case of carpal tunnel syndrome. These days, I have few computer-using, health-related problems because I have taken a lot of steps to cover my butt, back, and every other part of me. I'm not an ergonomics expert, but I can tell you how my workstation is set up and what I do to minimize potential problems. I've also talked to real ergo experts to find out what they suggest that computer users can do to take care of themselves. If you're having trouble with your wrists, back, eyes, or any other part, go see a doctor. Go now. I'll wait until you get back.

Okay, what are the primary considerations? Your chair, the height of your desk, and the height of your computer's monitor. These three things work together like Tinker, Evers, and that other guy in the famous baseball poem.

Number one, go get yourself a decent chair, if you don't have one. Decent, in this case, means a chair that can be adjusted every which way to support your back and your butt. I look for a chair for which I can:

- Adjust both the height and angle of the back rest.
- Adjust the height of the arm rests.
- Adjust the height of the seat.

I'm told by one ergo expert that it doesn't make that much difference (to your back, that is) if you lean forward or back. I've found that it helps to angle the seat as straight up as I can get it. Other people like to angle it slightly forward, along with the chair seat so that they lean forward a wee bit. The accepted range is something like an 85- to 120-degree angle between the seat and chair back. Choose whichever is most comfortable for you, at least to start, and see how that works out. For goodness sakes, don't slouch! That will do serious damage to your back, as your mother has already told you innumerable times. **Back or forward**

The chair has to have adjustable arm rests, and don't let anyone tell you otherwise. I wouldn't look twice at one of those so-called "secretary's chairs" or "computer workstation operator's chairs." The arm rests are important for the very reason that they support your arms and keep them level with the keyboard. The height of the arm rests should not be set so high that resting your arms drives your shoulders up.

Last, the height of the chair must be adjustable so that you can set it at a height that supports your thighs and keeps your feet comfortably on the floor. The seat of the chair should be generous and comfortable. **Generous seat**

A couple of other chair goodies include wheels (five or six, not four, for greater stability) and well-finished knobs and levers that operate smoothly and are easy to reach.

Decent chairs cost an arm and a leg. At the very least, you're looking at $200–$400; many ergonomically designed chairs go for far more than that, especially when you start throwing in such niceties as leather from a golden calf, titanium ball bearings, and arm rests that were designed by NASA for its space program. A simple rule is to spend whatever it takes, relative to how much time you plan to sit in it. Remember, we're talking about your health here—since when can you put a price tag on that? That said, I bought a chair meeting all of my requirements in a store specializing in selling nothing but chairs on a close-out sale for $220. It has been worth every cent and then some. **Arms and legs**

I used to work for a newspaper that provided all of its reporters with chairs that couldn't have cost more than $15 apiece. I mean, these chairs were really pathetic: no adjustable arm or back rests and a seat that only a bicyclist could love. Meanwhile, the boss-editors were sitting in the lap of luxury with these super-deluxe, ergonomic beauties that had more controls than the flight deck of the Concorde.

If you work for a company like that and have a chair that's not up to the job, there are a few things that you can do. You can use specially designed back rests and seat cushions to add support where needed, for example. You can use a foot rest if the chair can't be adjusted to a comfortable height.

The Details Are in the Desk

> It ain't enough to get the breaks. You gotta know how to use 'em.
>
> Huey P. Long

To figure out the optimum height for your desk, sit in your chair and place your arms on the arm rests—your arms should form an L or 90-degree angle. (If they don't, adjust the arm rest.) Your desk should be a couple of inches below your forearms and elbows. With your keyboard in place, the top of the keys and arm rests should be about level, so your hands are positioned immediately above the keyboard.

Okay, so what if the desk height is where it should be? Many desks have adjustable legs that screw up and down to allow you to adjust the height. Failing that you can add spacers or even cut the legs. (Well, if it's your desk, you might want to consider it.) You might be able to adjust the height of the chair a bit. (Remember, you want your thighs to be supported and your feet even on the floor.)

Keep Your Eye on Your Monitor

> History will be kind to me for I intend to write it.
>
> Winston Churchill (1874–1965)

How good are your eyes? The best height for a computer monitor is about eye level or slightly lower. I say "about" because it also depends somewhat on just how far away the monitor is. If the monitor is 3 or more feet away, it should be at eye level; closer than that, it can be slightly below eye level, but not by much. The idea is to reduce strain on your neck and back and to minimize having to raise and lower your head repeatedly while using the keyboard.

Just how far away the monitor should be depends on a variety of factors such as your eyesight, the screen size, and the sort of work that you do. If you do a lot of word processing, you probably want to be a bit closer than someone who spends time creating graphics. You're probably going to find yourself at a distance of 18 to 28 inches. One ergo expert I know suggests that the farther away you can sit, the better, because images will appear crisper. I'm not sure I agree with that, but I mention it in case you want to give it a try.

I've found that one of the most certain ways to end each day at the computer with a headache and blurry vision is to stare through the glare of light that is reflected on the screen. Position the computer workstation away from a window to reduce glare caused by daylight. If overhead lights are the problem, replace the bulbs with 40- or 60-watts bulbs. You can also try tilting the monitor forward slightly.

If you work in an office that has overhead fluorescent light panels, replace the lens (the plastic covering the fluorescent tubes) with an egg crate louver, a type of lens that directs the light straight down to minimize glare.

One of the best solutions is to install an antiglare filter over the monitor, even if your monitor already has an antiglare coated screen. These filters work very well to knock out light. They sell for $20–$80, not a lot to pay to avoid unnecessary eye strain, don't you think?

Some scientists are becoming increasingly concerned about the amount of radiation emitted by some computer monitors. These computer monitors are being blamed for causing such maladies as headaches, fatigue, skin or eye irritation, and respiratory problems. Again, more work needs to be done to establish a clear link between computer monitor emissions and health woes. Many of today's monitors meet the Swedish government's MPR-II limits on extremely low frequency and very low frequency radiation. If yours does not, consider purchasing a screen filter designed to minimize electric (not magnetic) radiation. The drawback is that most of these screen filters reduce picture clarity. Screen filters that reduce glare as well as dust-sucking static and electric radiation sell for about $80 to $150.

Monitoring health

Last, keep your monitor screen clean. After my kids use my Mac, the screen is dotted with sticky little fingerprints because they delight in pointing things out to each other (in between the pointing out, their fingers are either in a mouth or some other orifice).

You should know that commercial glass cleaner can ruin your monitor's screen by removing the antiglare coating, and flammable glass cleaners can be hazardous if there's static electricity. It's safest to use distilled water or a cleaner recommended by the computer monitor's maker.

Tickling the Keys

> Early to rise and early to bed makes a male healthy and wealthy and dead.
>
> James Thurber
> "The Shrike and the Chipmunks," *Fables for Our Time*, 1940

Once you've got your chair adjusted so that your back is comfortable and your feet are solidly on the floor and your desk and monitor are at their proper heights, you're almost ready to get down to work. Keep your wrists straight, elbows at your side, forming at least a 90-degree angle with your forearms and upper arms. Gently curve your fingers toward the keys and start typing. Try to minimize wrist motion when typing because that could lead to unhealthy results.

Rested wrists   Some people have found wrist rests aid in supporting the wrists while at the same time minimizing overly zealous wrist and hand movement. Personally, I don't use one because I think it's too confining.

A number of companies now market ergonomic keyboards, which are designed to keep your hands in a natural position. The keys or even the entire keyboard may be angled. They offer a variety of adjustments, all of which are intended to keep your wrists straight. Some feature touch-sensitive keys, again to help minimize stress on hands and wrists.

Too many uninterrupted hours at the keyboard could lead to the modern plague that has become known as RSI, short for repetitive strain injury. RSI is a set of ailments including headaches, neck aches, eye strain, carpal tunnel syndrome, fatigue, and stress caused by repetitive activities. Some of these injuries can be so severe that users become disabled. The most famous repetitive-motion disorder is carpal tunnel syndrome, and it is caused by continuous stress on the median nerve, which passes through a narrow channel in the underside of the wrist called the carpal tunnel. Damage to this nerve leads to tingling, numbness, and pain, and the wrist may eventually require surgery.

 What to do about RSI? Take regular breaks from the keyboard. Get up, stretch, and walk around. Stare off into space to take your eyes off the keyboard. Take care of yourself. If you start to experience chronic back or wrist pain, blurred vision, or other health problems, go see a doctor ASAP.

7 Lose It? Get It Back!

An expert is one who knows more and more about less and less.

Nicholas Murray Butler

After losing countless hours' worth of work to every sort of problem imaginable, I decided that I'd wise up and start regularly backing up my most important work. This was in the days when even a small hard disk or tape drive sold for more than $700. I couldn't afford either one, so I resolved to back up to floppies. My routine was to make a copy of my working disk, thinking that these two disks—the one containing whatever project I was working on and a backup copy—would give me enough protection against whatever calamity came my way.

One memorable day, I sat down at my PC to resume working on a lengthy **Spin doctor** freelance article for a major national magazine (the first of what I hoped would be a number of lucrative assignments from them). I booted up my machine, put the word processing disk in drive A and the work disk in drive B. The word processor loaded, but when I tried to open the file on the disk in drive B, that disk started to spin and spin and spin, but the document wouldn't load.

"Gee that's funny," I said. "Must be something wrong with the disk." The only way I could think to get the disk out was to pop it out, even though it was still spinning. "I'll try the other disk," I said. I stuck my backup disk in and the same thing happened. Now, even a well-trained pigeon knows enough not to yank a disk out of a drive while the disk is spinning, but not me (well, not then anyway). I found out later that the problem was not the disks but the disk drive. However, it was too late. I already had trashed both copies of that all-important story and had to start over almost from scratch.

```
Lesson: Not even backups will protect you if you're just plain stupid.
```

THAT BACKUP RELIGION

> A reformer is a guy who rides through a sewer in a glass-bottomed boat.

> Attributed to Jimmy Walker, c. 1928

There are two kinds of PC users: those who have lost data and those who will lose data. Despite your best efforts to secure your critical data, sooner or later something will go wrong. Your hard drive will fail, a virus will eat your data, or one of your kids will decide to do you a favor and reformat your hard drive.

If you have backups, you can save yourself a lot of serious heartache (to say nothing of loads of time and dough). These backups can be anything from floppies that you keep in a box next to your computer to digital audio tapes that you store off site.

I got that backup religion
The main thing is that you gotta make backups (that's the Underground Guide to Computer Security Rule 2, by the way). Unfortunately not enough people take the time to back up, mainly because they think that losing data is something that happens to other people. I used to think that way, even after I lost some serious stuff, not once, twice, or even three but four times. What can I tell you? I'm slow on the uptake, but now I got that backup religion and I'm going to preach to you. In this chapter, I'm also going to give you some tips on how to yank your good stuff out of the data gap, that black hole where all data goes to die.

 Even the cleanest living computer user who diligently backs up once a day is going to lose data. That's a given. Why? Trouble will probably come knocking between backups. Sooner or later, you're going to fall into the data gap—that time between yesterday's backup and the backup you plan to make tonight.

WHY BACK UP?

> Business is a good game—lots of competition and a minimum of rules. You keep score with money.

> Nolan Bushnell, founder of Atari

Making backups regularly and storing them properly can be both tedious and time consuming. But, have you ever wondered just how tedious and time consuming it would be to replace all of your data if you did not have a backup to fall back on? To start, you would need to replace all of your programs and tailor them to your particular needs. What would that take—a few hours?

Next, you would have to replace your data. That may be impossible without backups, but let's assume that you could get the material from diskettes, personal files, and so on. What would that take—a day? Maybe. If all you're doing is storing recipes on your PC, a day might be enough, but if you're doing serious work, it would take you an average of one week to recreate data lost to a virus, hardware failure, or other mishap. That's according to a study of 800 PC users conducted by one of those fancy market research firms.

Meanwhile, the National Computer Security Association, a trade association based in Mechanicsburg, Penn., calculates that for a business the average cost of recreating 20 megabytes of sales and marketing data is $17,000. For accounting data, the financial whack amounts to $19,000; for engineering, it's a stunning $98,000. Add to that the very real costs of emotional stress, perhaps lost jobs and lost business, and the costs go through the roof. Suddenly, making backups hardly seems to be much of a bother, does it?

Ouch!

Deciding how often to back up involves finding a balance between how much time you have to devote to do it and how much security you want. Backing up once a month requires little effort, but it does not provide much security. Backing up every day is time consuming, but it provides a lot of security.

When writing this book, I saved whatever file I was working on to my hard drive at least every 10 minutes (sometimes more often than that). I also saved a copy of the file to a second hard drive that I use for backup once every half hour or so or after each time I made major changes. A few times during the day, I saved the file onto a removable media drive called a Zip drive that I also use for backup. One of these days, soon I hope, I'm going to buy a tape backup drive—the biggest sucker I can afford. Oh, I also wear suspenders *and* a belt.

Zippety doo dah!

TAPE ME UP, TAPE ME DOWN

> Don't let it end like this. Tell them I said something.
>
> Last words of Pancho Villa (1878–1923)

A wide variety of storage media can be used for backup: floppy disks, hard disks, cartridge disks, magneto-optical disks, tapes, recordable CD-ROMs, and a few other lesser known backer-uppers. All of them involve tradeoffs in price, performance, and storage capacity, but the one backup medium that most people opt for is QIC tape. It's reliable, the tapes are readily portable, and it's a cheap way to back up huge amounts of data.

QIC action

First let me give a rundown of the wonders of tape. After that, I'll fill you in on tape backup strategies. At the end of the chapter, I'll give you the pros and cons of the remaining backup options.

Quarter-Inch Cartridge Tape

> Technological progress is like an axe in the hands of a pathological criminal.
>
> Albert Einstein (1879–1955)

The QIC-80 (short for Quarter-Inch Cartridge) drive and minicartridge tape is the system of choice for everyone who gives a fig about backing up a desktop system. There are others, but the QIC-80 is the most popular for now.

QIC-80 drives cost as little as $100 for an internal model; a minicartridge tape costs about $20 and holds 120 megabytes of data (almost twice that amount when the data is compressed). Prices are falling fast, and you'll probably be able to find a QIC-80 drive close to the $100 mark before long. All in all, peace of mind comes at a better-than-fair price. Assuming that you have a standard PC, with less than say 200 MB of data on your hard disk drive, you'll be able to get all of your information onto a single tape.

That's important because you want to be able to back up your data without having to stand by waiting to swap tapes, which is about as much fun as sucking the dirt off rocks.

Now, what you want to do is slap one of those tapes into the machine and go off to do something really useful, like pound sand or count sheep, and then come back only after the job is done.

Tape drive makers like to exaggerate just how much data you can pack onto a minicartridge tape. Most will tell you that you can get up to 250 megs on a 120-meg tape. Whether that's true depends much more on what it is that you're backing up than anything else.

Text files compress more than graphics files, for example. Files that are already compressed won't scrunch up any more. When calculating just how many tapes you need, figure on getting 200 megs of information on a tape, just to be on the safe side.

I can hear you say, "Yo, Mikey, everybody I know including my kid sister has a PC with a 500-meg hard drive. What are guys like me gonna do while everyone else is pounding sand and counting sheep? Can't I back up my entire hard drive to a single tape, too?"

Not to worry. Higher capacity tapes and drives are moving into the market in a big way just for data dudes and dudettes like you. If you have one of those monster drives, say, 500 megabytes and up, there are other QIC-drive formats that will cover from 255 MB (uncompressed) to 4 GB. (That's gigabytes, or roughly the equivalent of all of the data in the world laid end to end from here to Timbuktu or something like that.) The price is right, too. Internal units are selling at $399 to $499; the tapes are selling for $25 to $40 apiece (buy more at a time and save a few bucks).

4- and 8-Millimeter Tapes

> Computers are useless. They can only give you answers.
>
> Pablo Picasso (1881–1973)

If you're looking to back up a really big hard drive or several PCs, you really don't want a QIC-80 drive. The storage capacity is inadequate, and the backup software that comes with these drives can't be used with networked PCs. You could go for one of the larger QIC formats, such as the QIC-3010, but I suggest 4-millimeter digital audio tape. There's also 8-millimeter tape and you can stow a bajillion bytes (all right, I exaggerate, you can store many gigabytes) on one tape, but only one company—Exabyte—is marketing 8-millimeter taps drives at the moment. The 8-millimeter tape format is suitable for backing up local area networks, with several workstations attached to it.

The 4- and 8-millimeter tape drives operate like that VCR you have at home to record soaps and play back movies rather than like standard tape machines. The recording and playback heads are mounted on a cylinder that whips around a million times a second, furiously packing data at an angle across the width of the tape onto a fast-moving, high-density tape. Trust me, if you can't picture it, it's a marvelous sight. In comparison, standard tapes run straight past a fixed set of recording and playback heads. It's all very ho hum, but very reliable. **That's really QIC**

Digital Audio Tape

> You can't unscramble scrambled eggs.
>
> American proverb

Digital audio tape (DAT) has been a flop with hi-fi enthusiasts but a hit with computer enthusiasts who must store gigabytes of data at a single shot. The tape is small enough to fit in the palm of your hand, yet can hold between 1.3 GB and 10 GB of data. A 4mm drive sells for about $750 to $1500, which ain't peanuts, but mucho worth it, especially for someone or a small business that is cranking out valuable data like sausages. The tapes come in three lengths—60, 90, and 120 meters—and sell for $10 to $23 apiece (less if you buy more). **That's DAT**

If you want to use the longest format, you need a drive that is DDS-2. They sell at the upper range for DAT machines, but you already knew that, huh? DDS is both a standard that permits you to swap tapes between drives made by different manufacturers and an indication that the drive is a higher grade of DAT machine for computer storage (as opposed to a hi-fi tape machine).

DAT machines are screamers in comparison to other tape backup machines. They suck data onto a tape at the rate of many megabytes per minute. But that's totally irrelevant if you're doing the backup when you're supposed to, which is while you're eating lunch or copping some zzzs.

The Secret Is in the Software

> Great moments in science: Einstein discovers that time is actually money.
>
> Gary Larson cartoon caption

Tape drives are sold with software designed to handle most backup chores. Not all software is created equal, obviously. In general, software bundled with a backup drive allows you to decide exactly what to back up and to pick a backup schedule that's right for you.

You can back up your entire hard disk, individual files and directories, or only files that have been modified within a specified time period or those that have certain file attributes. Once you have selected the files to back up, typical software gives you an estimate of backup time, although the accuracy of that can vary quite a bit from one package to another.

Put backing up into autopilot   Even the most basic backup software allows you to set a schedule for backing up. Again, if you choose the right capacity and type of drive, you'll be able to do a full backup with a single tape while you're doing something more interesting, like reading this book. The big idea is to put backing up into autopilot so you don't have to think about it.

Some programs also give you the option of running backups in the background. That's a feature you should reserve for quick backup jobs, however.

Although you can continue working with other applications in the foreground while the backup goes on in the background, the machine usually goes into snail mode. For the same reason, you should kill your screen saver when doing a full backup. The screen saver also causes the backup to run in the background, and again the machine slows to a crawl.

If you are hoping to do a backup during lunch, for example, you might find the job still in progress when you get back even though you have been sipping martinis for most of the afternoon with your homies.

Most backup software comes in DOS and Windows versions. If you're a Windows user, you most likely will want to use this version since it will make your life easier.

However, if you have a serious problem and need to restore a bunch of applications and files, you'll want to run the DOS version to save time. Otherwise, you'll have to reinstall DOS and then Windows before you can get down to the business of bringing your system back to life.

Even if you find that the bundled software pretty much does the job, don't overlook buying a more sophisticated backup program to make your life even easier or more secure. For example, if your backup software doesn't encrypt data using DES or something as robust, get one that does. It takes longer to create an encrypted backup, but assuming that you've scheduled the backup at an opportune time, it really doesn't matter how long it takes.

Good, better, best

Encryption provides an additional level of security that is well worth the extra time it takes to make the backup. If someone snatches your tapes or a mean-spirited employee decides to sell your info to ex-KGB agents, you're protected. Change the key regularly, and if you insist on writing it down, make sure that it's stored someplace safe. Try swallowing the piece of paper on which you've written the key, for example.

It's Incremental, My Dear Watson

> When you have eliminated the impossible, whatever remains, however improbable, must be the truth.
>
> Sir Arthur Conan Doyle (1859–1930)
> *The Sign of Four* (1890), Ch. 6

What should you back up? The short answer is "everything that you care about." Of course, you'll want to back up all of your data—word processing documents, databases, spreadsheets, and all of the good stuff.

A lot of experts will tell you not to bother backing up programs because you can use the backup disks that you made when you copied the originals. First, that assumes you even bothered to make backups of the original disks. If you haven't, shame on you. Go to your room right now and back up those disks. You'll be happy you did, trust me.

Okay, now about backing up those programs. I suggest that when you make your initial backups, back up your entire hard drive, including programs. If you're like me, you probably do a lot of tweaking and customizing of your programs. If something goes drastically wrong, you can restore the entire program without much fuss.

**But that does not mean you should keep on making backups of your pro-
grams. That would in fact be a waste of time. It could also be dangerous if your
programs become infected by a virus.**

A lot of programs are customized as you use them to suit your unique needs.
Back up such files as .CFG and .INI files in DOS or Windows and preference files
for Macintoshes. You should also back up CONFIG.SYS and AUTOEXEC.BAT
files in DOS. These files are modified when new software is loaded onto your
machine. If the new software does not operate as expected or you decide that you
don't want it, having the backup will be invaluable in getting your system back
into good shape.

There are probably other files like these. Check the manual that came with the
program to make sure that you have them all safely tucked away on a backup tape
as well as on a disk.

**Why a disk too? If you suspect that one of these files has been corrupted and
may be at the source of a mysterious crash or other problem, use the files
stored on the disk and not the files stored on your backup tape. Those files
may be corrupted, too, and you won't be able to figure out what the problem is.**

Dantz Development's DiskFit Direct ($50), DiskFit Pro ($75), and Retrospect
($150), and Symantec/Peter Norton Group's The Norton Desktop ($120) are good
choices for backing up desktops systems.

More Tape Thoughts

> Tell us your phobias and we will tell you what you're afraid of.
>
> Robert Benchley
> "Phobias," in *My Ten Years in a Quandary, and How They Grew,* 1936

**Bigger than
you need**   Even basic PCs are being sold these days with hard drives of 350 MB and up. If
you're investing in a tape backup drive for the first time, you might want to consider
that the next PC you buy probably will have a hard drive in the 500 to 1 GB range.
My advice is to buy a tape drive that is bigger than what your current needs dictate.

Depending on how much data you have and the backup tape system you're
using, backing up takes anywhere from 5 minutes to more than an hour. That
doesn't include tape formatting, which takes about an additional half hour.

**You can buy formatted tapes for about $5 more than the usual price. A
preformatted tape will save you about a half an hour of formatting yourself.
That may be worth it to you if you have a lot of tapes to format or if you (like
me) are an impatient sod.**

Don't forget to regularly back up the drive on a portable computer to the desktop system, floppies, or tape, whichever works best. File synchronization software makes the task all that much easier to back up from the portable to the desktop system.

I have to admit that I did something pretty stupid soon after I wrote this chapter and I came back here to tell you about it. I mentioned earlier that I bought a Zip removable disk drive to use for backup. The drive came with backup software called Personal Backup, which I set up without giving adequate thought. To make a long story short, I overwrote the latest version of a file with a version that had been created about six hours earlier. The net result is that I lost six hours' worth of extensive editing that I did on Chapter 3. Moral: Make sure that you understand how the backup software works before you really start to count on it.

Run an antivirus software scanner before doing a backup. If a file is infected and is backed up, say good-bye to your data.

Make a full backup before running defragmentation or compression programs. If an error occurs while the hard disk is organizing your programs and data, you risk losing everything on the drive.

After you have made your first set of backups, test restoring some data to **Try it out first** make certain the drive and software are working properly. If trouble comes around, you'll know what to do to get your data back into action. Periodically go back and test the drive and software to make sure everything works; tape cartridges have a way of misbehaving when you can least afford it.

Use your backup program's verification feature to ensure that the backup is written to disk or tape accurately. This slows down the backup process, but that's a small price to pay for reliability.

Tape is the best medium for short-term storage (a few years or so). Tape, like other forms of magnetic media, loses data under constant use. Once the data is gone, that's all she wrote. Tapes will give out sooner or later, but don't wait for that to happen. Retire the tapes that have been in rotation after about a year and use them to archive applications, data, or anything else that you don't need to access often.

Innies and Outties

> A verbal contract isn't worth the paper that it's written on.
>
> Samuel Goldwyn (1882–1974)

Internal QIC tape drives cost about $100 less than comparable externals, and **Internal** that's a nice piece of change. Internal models are generally the better choice if you have a need for speed (they tend to be faster than external units). Just make sure that your PC or Mac will accommodate the drive. A 3½-inch drive obviously won't fit in a 1-inch bay. On the other hand, you have to open the box to install it or remove it in the event that it craps out. Neither is hard to do, but if you don't know what you're doing, you'll probably have to hustle up someone to do it for you and then pay them as well.

External   If you lack a free drive bay or need to back up more than one computer with the same unit, you'll want an external model. The costliest external drives are parallel port units, which plug into printer ports, but that's what makes them easy to switch from machine to machine. These drives cost as much as $100 more, but it's worth it in my book for the convenience and versatility.

Personally I prefer an external drive of any kind—whether it's for tape, hard disk, or CD-ROM. Every few years, I put an ad in one of my local newspapers and sell my system so that I can upgrade to the next best thing. With technology's rapid march, old systems aren't worth much, and I don't expect to get much when I sell. However, have you ever checked to see what pricey internal add-ons like extra memory and tape drives add to the overall selling price of a system that you would like to unload? Nada mucho, baby. People who buy used systems don't always appreciate all of the fancy extras—they're mainly concerned about getting a good price. Ergo, I sell the basic system and keep the externals to use with my next system, or if I decide to unload them because they're getting long in the tooth, I sell them separately. It's more of a hassle, but I can always use the extra bucks.

IF THIS IS DAILY2, THEN IT MUST BE TUESDAY

> There is nothing perfectly secure but poverty.
>
> Henry Wadsworth Longfellow, in a letter, Nov. 13, 1872

If all you're concerned about is protecting the data on a single desktop computer, backing up is relatively straightforward. Here's what you do:

1. If you don't have them already, buy four backup tapes. Two of the backup tapes will be used for daily backups and two of the tapes will be used for weekly or monthly backups.

2. On day one, back up the entire system onto a single tape and label it Daily1.

3. On day two, backup the entire system onto another tape and label it Daily2.

If it's any easier to keep track of the tapes, label one tape Monday, Wednesday, and Friday and the other Tuesday and Thursday. (If you're thinking about labeling the tape Saturday and Sunday because you also work those days, you and I need to talk about your getting a life.)

Rotate the daily tapes, backing up at the end of each day, or first thing in the morning while you're reading your newspaper and slurping a cuppa joe. Use Daily1 one day and Daily2 the next. What could be more simple?

At the end of the week, whether you're doing weekly or monthly backups, do yet another full backup of the system on the third tape and label it Weekly1 or Monthly1. At the end of the second week, do another full backup of the system on the fourth tape and label it Weekly2 or Monthly2. Each week or month, rotate between those two tapes. Store the two tapes at a friend's house, bank deposit box, or other place that is convenient and reasonably secure.

Once you've done the full backups, you'll do incremental backups from then on. You're only going to back up stuff that has changed from one day to the next or one week to the next. This saves time—lots of time. Also, what's the sense of backing up the same old stuff if you already have a complete copy of it, right?

The daily and monthly backups are rotated to protect against the prospect that the backups become corrupted or the tape fails in some way. For added security for really valuable stuff, the files stored on daily and monthly backups should be encrypted, just in case they're lost or stolen.

In the ideal world, each night you would also take one of the daily backups home. But if you work out of your home, not even Houdini can pull off a trick like that. In that case, although you have backups, you really don't have complete security. If there's a fire, your backups are going to barbecue along with the rest of your system. Whaddya say? Does storing the backups off site seem to be a reasonable thing to do at this point? I hope so. It's the only way you're ever going to be truly covered.

A trick for Houdini

The alternative to storing tapes off site is to buy a media vault—basically a fireproof box. A box large enough to store your tapes sells for about $150 (larger, small-business-size boxes sell for $250 to $700). I also store important documents like birth records, passports, and home inventory lists and video-tapes of my family's worldly goods in my box.

These specially designed storage boxes are UL rated to maintain an interior temperature of no more than 110 degrees Fahrenheit and no more than 60 percent humidity in a building fire. And that's in the average building fire, which gets to 1200 or more degrees F. They'll even survive a flash fire or an explosion of up to 2000 degrees F, although I haven't tested that myself (one of these days, I hope). In general, the bigger boxes are able to withstand more heat and battering, say, in the event the box drops through a couple of floors in a building.

BACKUP STRATEGIES FOR HOME OFFICES AND SMALL COMPANIES

Put all of your eggs in one basket—and watch that basket.

Mark Twain
"Pudd'nhead Wilson's Calendar," *The Tragedy of Pudd'nhead Wilson*, 1894

If you run a small company, you should be thinking about weekly, rather than monthly, backups. It's four times the bother, but you've also got more to lose, like your business.

Here's a backup plan that offers both a high degree of security without expending an onerous amount of effort for it. You have two sets of three backup tapes: one set is used daily and the other is used weekly. The daily set is labeled Daily1, 2, and 3 (or anything else you want that is going to allow you to tell them apart). The weekly set is labeled Weekly1, 2, and 3.

Starting with the Daily set, do three full backups of all your PCs—one backup per tape per day. After that, you'll do incremental backups of all data that has changed from one day to the next. Rotate among the three tapes. The daily backups are kept on site during the day and one of the three is taken home by you or a valued employee each evening.

Take it to the bank   At the end of the first, second, and third weeks, do another full backup of all of your PCs, using a different tape each week. The backups are stored off site in a secure place like a safe-deposit box or with an off-site storage vendor who will look after the backups for a fee. Once a week, someone must fetch the weekly backup and do a full backup (overwriting the old data). You can also arrange for the off-site storage vendor, if you use one, to regularly pick up and drop off backups as needed.

Not everyone has the resolve or the level of paranoia necessary to keep up the task of making backups on a weekly basis. Only you know what your data is worth to you, but if you think you can live with only monthly backups, skip the weekly backups, do monthly backups, and go fishing instead.

Why two sets of three tapes or some other combination involving more tapes? If you're worried that two sets of three tapes does not provide enough of a cushion in case the tapes fail, by all means use four or any other number you like. Personally I feel comfortable enough with having only two sets, but I'm not working on secret reports that are going to make the Pentagon Papers look like a junior high school term paper when they're published. If you are, you might need more sets.

Backup Safety Net

> There is no human problem which could not be solved if people would simply do as I advise.
>
> Gore Vidal

Backing up a small business is much easier if the PCs are connected to a network. You don't have to schlep the tape drive from one machine to another, for instance. These days, probably every company—big and small—should network its PCs. Networks not only allow you to back up from one place, they also allow you to share other peripherals and data and do lots of other neat, businesslike activities. When doing backups on your network, don't overlook the probability that some data will be stored on the server and other data will be stored on individual workstations. All of it is equally valuable, of course.

More and more companies are asking employees to get involved in backing up vital information. They're instructing employees to store critical files on the server (which is regularly backed up) rather than on their desktop systems (which may never be backed up), for example.

Get employees involved

Some organizations permit their employees to take their disks home at night as an added precaution against theft and fire. Whether or not they should take the disks home, however, depends on the nature of the information, its importance to the organization, and other factors. If you decide to let employees take disks home, you need to give them guidance about how the information should be handled. Requiring that the disks be used for company business only, properly labeled, and scanned for viruses when returned to the office are some procedures that come immediately to mind.

Taking Care of Tape Chores

If you plan to designate someone to oversee the tape backup job, here are a few considerations:

1. Assign the job to a specific individual.
2. Set a backup schedule so that backups are done routinely.
3. Set standards for the tapes that are to be used and how they are to be labeled.
4. Specify where the tapes will be kept in the office.
5. Specify where tapes will be stored off site and who is responsible for shuttling them back and forth.

OTHER BACKUP OPTIONS

Flip Flops on Disks

> I've been on a calendar, but never on time.
>
> Marilyn Monroe
> *Look*, Jan. 16, 1962

If you have only a few data files that you work with regularly, you should be able to simply copy them to a couple of floppy disks at the end of each day. Floppies are cheap, which is about all you can say about them as a backup medium.

Backing up to floppies alone is not going to provide you with much protection if a tornado rips your house loose from its foundation and tosses it into the next county, however.

You'll also need to follow some of the procedures that any business might use and create a set of disks for daily and weekly or monthly backups. In the ideal world, those floppy disks should be stored off site in case something should happen to your home, or at least in a media vault if you insist on keeping them around the old homestead.

Built-In Floppy Copiers

> Imitation is the sincerest form of television.
>
> Fred Allen (1894–1956)

If you're a PC user, you have a set of backup utilities in DOS called either MSBACKUP (if you're using DOS 6) or BACKUP (if you're using an earlier version of DOS). I'm not going to go into a lot of the DOSnits and DOSgrits here. I assume that you know how to type stuff like C: COPY and C:MSBACKUP and all of those other DOSsie kind of things. (If you don't, observe The Underground Guide to Computer Security Rule 1: Read the manual.)

The DOS copy and backup utilities give you the option of backing up a single file, a subdirectory, or just certain files that have changed within a period that you define. If you're backing up a couple of files or a small subdirectory at a time, use COPY. It's easier.

To back up the entire drive, go to your local computer store and ask the nice man or lady there to sell you a jumbo box of floppies. Figure on one high-density disk per megabyte. Ergo, if you've got an 80 MB drive, get 80 disks. That assumes you've got a recent vintage PC. If you've got one of those older jobs that can't handle double-sided, high-density disks, get twice as many floppies (more or less).

> **Run BACKUP or MSBACKUP and stick a floppy into the drive. When it's full, you'll be instructed to replace it. Keep doing this until your arm falls off or the entire drive is backed up, whichever comes first.**

To restore your backups, run MSBACKUP again (or RESTORE, if you're using an earlier version of DOS). Keep sticking disks into the floppy drive until your other arm drops off or until all of your files have been restored.

Armed forces

If you're a Mac user, use the mouse to drag the files you want to back up over to the little picture of the floppy disk. To restore all of your files, repeat the process, this time in the other direction, with your remaining arm.

Symantec/Norton, Dantz Development, Chili Pepper Software, and a number of other companies publish software for PCs and Macs that will take over the backup-to-floppies (or any other medium, for that matter) chores. Also, you can speed up the process and save a ton of disks at the same time if you opt to compress files for backing up first. DOS 6.22—the latest version—has a utility called DoubleSpace that will do the trick. Mac users can use Aladdin's Stuffit deluxe ($75) or Stac Electronics' Stacker ($65) to compress files.

> **But really folks, who's got time to back up to floppies except for a guy who's got a gang of elves with time on their little hands? Go get yourself a tape drive or a second hard drive—even a small one. You'll save money and lots of time over the long run.**

Hard Facts About Floppy Disks

> Never face facts; if you do, you'll never get up in the morning.
>
> Marlo Thomas

You've put a lot of hard effort into that report you've been writing on your personal computer and naturally you want to make sure nothing happens to it. You grab a floppy disk, copy over the report, and slip the write-protect tab over to prevent the disk from being accidentally erased. You've covered all of the bases, right? Not so fast. Did you think to put a label on the disk? Where are you going to store the disk for safekeeping? Here are some tips about how to keep floppies working for you:

1. Store the disks away from heat and magnetic fields generated by magnets, motors, and the like. Don't spill anything on the disk (better yet, don't eat or

drink anywhere near your personal computer). Don't touch the recording surface of the disk—you've got oil on your fingers that could damage the disk.

2. Write-protect disks by either sliding the little tab in the corner of the disk to open the little window if it's a 3.5-inch disk or by covering the notch on a 5.25-inch disk with one of those sticky tabs that came with the box of disks. That will keep data from being accidentally erased as well as keep viruses from infecting the disk.

3. Put a label on the disk. That seems pretty obvious, but not enough people do it. A disk without a label is a disk that begs to be formatted or put aside where it is forgotten.

4. Not many people are using 5.25-inch floppy disks these days, but if you are, remember to write on the label first and then stick it on the disk. Don't write on a label that is already on the disk, unless you use a soft, felt-tip pen.

5. The label on the disk should provide some very specific information about who the disk belongs to, what's on it, perhaps a serial number to facilitate tracking it, and color coding if it contains particularly valuable information. If you routinely scan disks for viruses, mark that on the label so you'll know that it's been done. If the contents of the disk should always be encrypted, indicate that on the disk label, too.

6. When disks are used at your desk, keep them in a disk storage unit. Don't leave the disks lying on your desk when you leave for lunch or for the day. Lock them in your desk.

7. If you permit employees to take disks home, set some guidelines. Particularly valuable information should never be taken home on disks.

8. Disk that are taken home should be carried in a sturdy container to protect them from dirt, dust, or other harmful stuff. Don't let them wander around loose in your briefcase or tuck them into a shirt or coat pocket.

9. At home, use the same procedures that you would use at the office to protect valuable data. A properly labeled, write-protected disk, for example, will keep one of your kids from using the disk as a coaster (well, maybe).

Hard Charging Drives

> First secure an independent income, then practice virtue.
>
> Greek saying

The cost of hard drives has fallen so much that you might want to consider getting a second one to use for backup. Backing up from one hard disk to another is very fast and convenient, for one thing. A file synchronization program will ensure that the files are kept up to date, requiring little intervention on your part. If your primary drive fails, you can switch over to the second and keep right on working. You can buy an internal 500 MB hard drive for about $250 these days. That's a heck of a lot of storage for not a lot of money.

The risk is that while you have backup, you don't have complete security. If both hard drives are internal units, or even if one is internal and the other external, it's impractical to disconnect the drive and store it off site each day.

If someone wants to steal your data, nothing will prevent him or her from taking the second drive. Then there are all of the other things that can go wrong: fire, hurricane, and all of those nasty misfortunes that having a second drive will do nothing to offset.

Hard Drives on the Road

> There are worse things in life than death. Have you ever spent an evening with an insurance salesman?
>
> Woody Allen

A handful of companies like Mountain Gate, for instance, market removable hard drive systems that consist of an internal chassis and a drive cartridge that loads like a tape into a videocassette recorder. The chassis and cartridge are sold separately, and you have the option of buying hard disk cartridges that store anywhere from 170 MB to 1080 MB. It's an expensive way to go about backing up your system, however. You'll pay twice as much for one of these hard drives compared to a regular one.

Where the removable hard drive shines is as a security option when you're worried about someone stealing your data as opposed to it being trashed by a natural or unnatural disaster. Use the drive during the day, and then take the cartridge with you when you leave at the end of the day or store it in a vault or other secure place.

Go Twice as Far With Removable Media Drives

> Progress might have been all right once, but it has gone on too long.
>
> Attributed to Ogden Nash

If you need a removable media drive, say, to send large files to a service bureau for processing, you can put it to work as a backup system as well. Dollar for dollar, tape is far cheaper than most removable cartridges, but if you can put the removable drive to a second use, it's definitely worth considering. **Dollar for dollar**

There are two popular removable media options: SyQuest and Bernoulli. They're not compatible with each other. Get whichever one the other guy you are going to exchange information with uses.

Soul Searching with SyQuest

A SyQuest cartridge operates pretty much like a hard disk although it's a lot slower. Each cartridge contains an aluminum disk coated with magnetic material. A pair of reading and recording heads skim the surface of the disk, just like any other hard disk drive. Unlike a removable hard drive, though, the read/write head remains in the drive when the disk is ejected; only the platter is removed.

SyQuest drives come in a variety of formats between 44 MB and 270 MB. The drives sell for $250 to $525 or so. The most popular SyQuest formats are the 88 MB, 105 MB, 200 MB, and 270 MB, and they cost between $60 and $100. (There are quantity discounts, as well.)

At those prices, a SyQuest should not be number one on your hit parade purely as a backup medium. But if you're in the graphic arts industry, you might do well to stick with a SyQuest because it is what most service bureaus are set up to deal with.

Keep in mind that SyQuest drives are not as rugged as other storage media. If you try to remove the cartridge while the drive is still spinning or if the drive is jolted hard enough, the head could bang down onto the disk surface. This collision of head and disk can cause one to contemplate suicide. Data stored on the disk can be trashed, and you may be looking at a major repair bill to replace head and disk.

Bernoulli Takes Flight

Bernoulli removable cartridges also use a disk (actually two stacked disks) coated with a magnetic material; in this case, the disk is made of a plastic similar to the one used in floppy disks. There's a pair of read/write heads—one on each side of the disk stack.

The format gets it name from Daniel Bernoulli, the Swiss mathematician who first observed that air flows faster over the top curved surface of a tube than it does across the same tube's flat surface underneath. This, in turn, creates lift, and that's how airplanes fly. That's also how Bernoulli disks operate. They spin around and lift themselves into position. Enough of this technical mumbo jumbo— I just wanted to see if you were paying attention.

Bernoulli drives have been around for several years and you would think that by now they would be dirt cheap, but they're not.

The drives sell for between $300 and $575. Bernoulli disks come in 35 MB to 230 MB formats. The most popular are the 90 MB, 150 MB, and 230 MB formats. Those cost between $95 and $110 apiece (buy more and get a better price).

Like the SyQuest, a Bernoulli is not something I recommend that you buy purely for backup, but if you need a reliable and rugged medium to transport data as well as to back up, it's worth looking into.

Look Out Below, Prices Falling

Everything is in a state of flux, including the status quo.

Robert Byrne

The storage world is changing fast. Only a few weeks before writing this chapter, Iomega introduced a Bernoulli removable cartridge drive called the Zip drive, which is about the same size as the standard paperback bestseller. It costs about $200 and is capable of stowing 100 MB of data on a cartridge that is about the same size and dimensions as a stack of two 3.5-inch floppies. The company sells 100 MB Zip disks for about $20 apiece (less if you buy in quantities of three or more). They also claim to market a 25 MB version, although I have yet to actually see it in any store or mail order catalog.

I bought one. For a long time, I have been using a second external hard disk   **I've got Zip**
drive to back up on, and although that has been comforting, it hasn't been really all that secure. If my house burns down or someone steals my system, that second drive with all of my precious backups is going to go bye-bye. Not having the bucks to spend on a DAT drive, I bought the Zip. I can get all of my data, at least the stuff that I can't afford to lose, onto a single 100 MB. The drive comes with backup scheduling and other software; I haven't bothered to use the scheduling software since it takes only seconds to do an incremental backup of my important stuff. I keep one disk containing a week's worth of backups at a relative's house. I also have a daily backup that I take with me whenever I leave my house.

> **SyQuest says it is getting ready to introduce a removable cartridge drive capable of storing 135 MB on a small cartridge. Not only does it promise better storage capacity, it's twice as fast, yet costs the same as the Zip. In fact, it may already be on the market by the time you read this—it should be worth a close look as a low-cost backup option.**

Compaq and a couple of other companies are working on alternative storage systems that they say will pack 100 MB or better onto various types of floppies and cartridges. Compaq says it will have a system out soon that will also be compatible with ordinary 3.5-inch floppies. All of this is good news for consumers because the increased competition will push down prices and make backing up even cheaper.

The High-Bred Magneto-Optical Drive

> If I'd known I was going to live this long, I'd have taken better care of myself.
>
> Eubie Blake, who smoked since age six and refused to drink water

If you need to back up your files for long-term storage, a magneto-optical (MO) drive is your best bet. MO cartridges are reliable and capable of storing data for ten years or so without fear that your precious information will do a disappearing act. That's about twice as long as magnetic media, give or take a few years.

 The tape and disk drives use a magnetic field to record and retrieve data. Over time, data is lost as a result of wear and tear on the tape or the tape or disk comes in close contact with other electromagnetic fields. (Just about anything that generates an electromagnetic field, like motors and hi-fi speakers, can scramble data.) There are other reasons that your data stored on magnetic media might not stick around, but in any case, the upshot is you lose your precious stuff.

MO drives and cartridges are impervious to magnetic fields, wear and tear, and some of the other things that can scramble data. Data is stored on an MO with the help of a magnetic field too, but for added protection, the data is stored under a protective plastic coating. The data is retrieved by a laser, much in the same way that music is read on a compact disc (and you know how durable those are).

Here's how it works. A laser heats spots on the disc to 150 degrees Celsius, priming the magnetic particles so they can be imprinted with data. An electromagnetic head actually writes the data before the spot has time to cool. Each spot and the spaces between spots—and there are a gigazillion—represent a 0 or a 1. Do that enough times, and the MO is packed with all that good information. Data is retrieved by aiming the laser at a reflective layer directly underneath the MO cartridge's magnetic layer. By detecting the polarity of the once-hot spots, the laser is able to read whether it's a 0 or 1.

 The downside is that MO drives tend to be pricey, ranging between $800 and $2000. The most popular formats are the 3.5-inch 128 MB and 230 MB disks, which sell for $40 to $50. If you've got tons of data, buy the 5.25-inch 512 MB and 1.3 GB disks. They sell for about $100.

It's All in the Disc

CD-Recorders are another of those storage media that makes for a good backup system if you already have a need, say, to publish reference materials for a bunch of rocket scientists. Prices of the CD-Recorders are falling fast, but they're still pretty expensive. Philips, Pinnacle Micro, Ricoh, and Sony, among others, sell them for anywhere between $1600 and $5500; recordable disks sell for $15 to $25 apiece.

What makes them attractive for backing up is that you can pack a whopping 550 MB to 650 MB of data onto a disk. The disk is damn near indestructible, it's got a shelf life rivaling that of plutonium, it takes up hardly any space, and magnets bother it not at all. Mix the data around using brand-name encryption and you've got the ultimate backup medium.

Well, almost. You can't use a CD-R over and over again like a tape. Depending on how much data you want to sock away, the cost of disks is really going to add up.

In Case of Emergency

> At my lemonade stand I used to give the first glass away free and charge five dollars for the second glass. The refill contained the antidote.
>
> Emo Philips

If you step on a poisonous snake and the sucker plants his fangs firmly into your rear end, what should you do? Get out the snake bite kit, and right quick, of course. No snake bite kit? Kiss your bootie good-bye. What you need is the equivalent of a snake bite kit just in case your hard drive turns nasty on you. What's in the kit? A set of disks that can be used to get your PC back on its knobby knees and, failing that, to rescue your data from the jaws of doom.

If you're a PC user, make backups of all your DOS disks with all the save-your-butt goodies on them such as UNDELETE, UNFORMAT, MSD, and SCANDISK. Which of these handy utilities you'll have depends on what version of DOS you're running. Make up a few bootable disks and put those utilities on them so you can get back to the business of getting back to business.

Get back into business

Once that's done, slide the write-protect tab into place if you're using 3.5-inch floppies or stick a tab over the notch if you're using 5.25-inch floppies. Slap a label on the disk with a suitable message such as "Break glass in an emergency."

DIAGNOSTICS, RECOVERY, AND OTHER USEFUL UTILITIES

> Character is much easier kept than recovered.
>
> Thomas Paine
> *The American Crisis*, No. 13, April 19, 1783

Although you're one of those folks who treats your PC or Macintosh like a member of the family, it suddenly starts behaving erratically or, worse, conks out altogether. It's time to get out the diagnostic software and take the equivalent of an x-ray of your system. DOS 6.X and Windows 3.1 come with Microsoft Diagnostics, which is abbreviated MSD. Yeah, it should be MD but then again, MD means "make directory" in DOS. Anyway, here's what you do.

The first step is to use MSD to take an inventory of your system. The information will be useful later if you encounter a problem and are trying to figure out what went wrong or, heaven forbid, if you have to talk to a technical support person.

If you install software, a peripheral, or some other add-on device and you encounter problems, you can restore the system's "before" configuration to set it all right and then try to divine what the "after" configuration is actually supposed to look like.

Take a snapshot
The second step is to take a snapshot of your computer's current setup. To get a detailed report, type MSD /P MSD.RPT at the DOS prompt. To print a report, which I suggest you do, follow the earlier command with TYPE MSD.RPT > PRN. Use MSD to print a new report whenever you make a significant change to your system. You'll need to run MSD from DOS, however. Running it from within Windows will not give you the same level of detail.

If you're a Mac user, you already have a disk with some of the goodies you'll need—it's the Disk Tools disk that came with the rest of your MacOS disks when you bought the machine. Disk First Aid, on the Disk Tools disk, will repair damaged files and verify that your hard drive is up to snuff.

Dealing With Deletes

> If I had my live to life again, I'd make the same mistakes, only sooner.
>
> Tallulah Bankhead (1902–1968)

There you are, happily trashing old files willy nilly, when suddenly—the horror, the horror!—you toss out the Great American Novel that you have been so carefully crafting. Not to worry, Goober. Not to worry, that is, if you have DOS 5 or 6, which comes with a handy data resurrector called UNDELETE. To use it, type UNDELETE and the filename and you've saved yourself a lot of *touris*, which is Yiddish for "Your mother has been having trouble with her heart because you don't call her often enough."

Just because you've got UNDELETE doesn't mean you have a license to be careless. It's more like a learner's permit.

If you want to snatch back a file from data hell, do it right away. Later, you'll be constantly writing and rewriting data on top of the Great American Novel and it won't be possible to get it back no matter how many lambs you sacrifice. Mac users aren't so fortunate. They don't have anything like UNDELETE in the MacOS. Tough bupskies, because even Mac users make mistakes on occasion.

A bunch of companies market data recovery, disk diagnostics, and repair utilities. For my money, you can't beat Symantec's Norton Utilities for both PC and Mac platforms. The latest version, at least when I was writing this, is Norton Utilities 8.0 for DOS and Windows (about $115) and Norton Utilities for Macintosh 3.1 (about $99). I wouldn't leave home without either one and neither should you.

One for the money

NU 8.0 has a bunch of tools for troubleshooting and repairing PCs running Windows. There's INI Tracker, for example, which recovers damaged DOS and Windows configuration and system files. It also records and tracks vital setup files allowing users to identify and undo changes made by other programs. You can even UNFORMAT a hard disk if you accidently formatted it.

Get Files Lost, for Good

Sometimes you don't want to get a file back. In fact, you want it to get lost, forever. Most of all, you don't want some snoop pulling it off your hard drive when you're not looking.

> **To wipe out that file for good, you need something like Norton Utilities' WipeInfo or ASD Software's FileGuard, which will not only delete the file but overwrite it with gibberish. The shareware programs, Shredder from Jeff Prosise for the PC and Burn from Michael Watson and Paul Jensen for the Mac, will do the same thing. I'm not sure what the shareware fee is, but I'm sure that it is next to nothing, like most shareware.**

Symantec also markets Norton Desktop 3.0, a set of essential Windows utilities. It includes antivirus protection, backup, unerase, disk diagnostics, file defragmentation, and other good stuff. It sells for about $117.

I'm not going to spout off anymore about Norton for fear that you'll think I'm getting a kickback. (I'm not, I have been a devoted fan since the early days when I was regularly deleting files that I meant to save for all time and then getting them back with Norton.) Head on down to your local software store or thumb through some mail order catalogs and decide for yourself.

Last and Least, Uninstallers

> Cleaning your house while your kids are still growing
> Is like shoveling the walk before it stops snowing.
>
> Phyllis Diller
> *Phyllis Diller's Housekeeping Hints,* 1966

Windows wash   Windows programs, it has been rumored, make using a PC easier. But have you ever tried getting rid of a Windows program on the day that you decide you no longer need it or when something better comes along? There are files scattered all over your hard drive, and there's little to show the difference between the file you want to get rid of and the one that will send your PC crashing to its knees when it's gone.

It even does windows   What you need is an uninstaller, a handy little program that seeks and destroys those useless little things that you no longer want on your system. MicroHelp's UnInstaller does Windows better than most programs of this type. And it cost a mere $39, which is mighty fine in my checkbook. It cleans up unwanted fonts, duplicate files, and pieces of old code that have been lying around taking up space and looking to cause trouble.

Mac users have the same problem, but they have an even better option for getting rid of data detritus because it's free: Clean Sweep. This dandy freebie will get rid of duplicate files, dangling preference files, and a bunch of other stuff. There's one small fly in the old ointment, however. Clean Sweep is only available from the ZiffNet/Mac service on Compuserve, Applelink, and eWorld.

8 Taking Care of Business

I once worked for a company where the owner instructed the LAN supervisor to give me access to the directories of everyone who reported to me (about a dozen people). My boss wanted me to have this access, he said, because he wanted me to make sure that the employees were not using the company's LAN improperly. I'm not sure what he meant by that, but I suppose he meant for me to make sure that employees were not running gambling operations, dealing cocaine, or moonlighting for competitive businesses at his expense.

Believe it or not, the boss is not the bad guy here. He's not even being unethical, if you really want to know the truth. It's his company, and he owns the system. All that goes on in his business *is* his business, and he has a right (an obligation, too) to protect his company's assets against abuse by the employees.

I never got around to checking what the employees were up to. The boss never bothered to tell the employees that this monitoring was taking place, nor did he ever tell anyone what sorts of activities would and would not be permitted. In the absence of a written policy, I believe this sort of monitoring is flat out wrong. If nothing else, the boss and I could have found ourselves on the receiving end of a lawsuit if the spying had been discovered. There are at least a few instances of employees suing their employers for surreptitiously monitoring their activities on the job.

If you run a business, you must have a clearly stated policy covering precisely **Precise policy** how information, computers, and related resources are to be used by the employees. If that policy includes monitoring employees, you should tell them in writing. If you have set ideas about what the employees ought not to do with the company's computer resources, they should be spelled out in a policy, too. Finally, this policy must detail in firm terms what the penalties are for violating it's guidelines (no one will take it seriously otherwise).

This chapter is all about developing computer security policies and selling them to the employees. It also includes a mention of software piracy and an explanation of why you shouldn't copy that floppy. The chapter concludes with a few tips on what to do if all of your policies and other security measures should fail.

MAKE IT A POLICY TO PROTECT YOURSELF

> If you're a police dog, where's your badge?
>
> The question James Thurber (1894–1961) used to drive his
> German shepherd crazy

Computer security is considered a "people problem," in the sense that much of what passes for computer security could be made more effective if employees were aware of the need to follow certain security procedures and were trained to be on the alert for potential security loopholes. It stands to reason, then, that one of the ways to bolster security is to give employees a set of guidelines for computer use and outline the sorts of activities that the company considers proper and improper. Once you've done that, your next job will be to get the employees to buy into the policy.

Not for everyone   Many large companies also create comprehensive policies that spell out in great detail how computers are to be protected, who is responsible for the various sorts of data that the company creates, what security controls must be implemented, and so on. That's not something the typical small company needs to do, however. Large companies have professionals who do nothing but create security policies and then go around enforcing them. If you run a business, you're not going to have time for all that.

THE RIGHT AND WRONG OF USING COMPUTERS

> I learned years ago not to doze off or leave my wallet lying around in the
> presence of people who tell me that they are more moral than others.
>
> Carl T. Rowan
> "In the Name of Morality," *Washington Star,* Oct. 17, 1980

Many of the computer security policies I've come across have a section or two devoted to computer ethics before getting into the specifics. There has been a lot of talk about computer ethics in recent months—politicians spout about forming commissions to promote them, universities ponder the meaning of them, and law enforcers say there would be less crime if we had more of them.

May not know better   The reasoning behind promoting computer ethics is such that if an employee duplicates a copyrighted software package, it may not be because he is dishonest; it may be because he thinks that this sort of copying is basically harmless. That same employee would never consider rifling through the boss' desk drawers, but might not reckon that going through the boss's computerized files is pretty much the same thing.

I buy that notion, but not entirely. I've reported on too many instances where the employees did the most damnable things such as planting programs designed to destroy valuable data, and they were clearly aware of what they were doing. In any case, I pulled together two sample ethics statements that will help you formulate your own.

My friend Peter Tippett, who is president of the National Computer Security Association and a founder of the Computer Ethics Institute, says that too many people operate under what he calls the "The Nintendo Fallacy." Many users believe that if something is wrong or unethical, he says, there should either be a law against it, or the computer or system should prevent them from doing it. For example, many users believe that if a computer security system has a weakness, it should be exploited, or that, because writing a computer virus is not explicitly illegal, writing and trading in computer viruses is good, or at least okay.

Nintendo Fallacy

The Other Commandments

> I know the answer! The answer lies with the heart of all mankind! The answer is twelve? I think I'm in the wrong building.
>
> Charles Updike

Peter Tippett is the author of the Computer Ethics Institute's code of conduct, which includes the following admonishments (there are 10 in all, but these are the most relevant):

- Thou shalt not interfere with other people's computer work.

- Thou shalt not snoop around in other people's computer files.

- Thou shalt not use a computer to steal.

- Thou shalt not copy or use proprietary software for which thou hast not paid.

- Thou shalt not use other people's computer resources without authorization or proper compensation.

You can get more information about computer ethics from the Computer Ethics Institute at (310) 459-9565. If you have a Compuserve account, type GO ETHICS to visit their forum.

GO ETHICS

How to Conduct Yourself

Donn Parker is easily one of the most knowledgeable people on the planet when it comes to computer security. He's written several books, and the security heads of top international companies pay big bucks just to hear what he has to say about computer security. Donn, who is a consultant at SRI International, the famous

Silicon Valley thinktank, has defined five tests or considerations to use when trying to decide whether or not something is ethical. They are designed to be used by anyone to help them understand the ethical implications of something they are about to do. Chew on some of these considerations for conduct for a while:

1. *Informed Consent*—Try to make sure that the affected people are aware of your planned actions and that they don't disagree with your intentions even if you have the right to do these things.

2. *Higher Ethic in the Worst Case*—Think carefully about your possible alternative actions and select the most beneficial one necessary to cause the least harm under the worst circumstances.

3. *Change of Scale*—Consider that an action you take on a small scale or by you alone might result in significant harm if carried out on a larger scale or by many others.

4. *Owners' Conservation of Ownership*—As a person who owns or is responsible for information, always make sure that the information is reasonably protected and that ownership of it and rights to it are clear to all users.

5. *Users' Conservation of Ownership*—As a person who uses information, always assume it is owned by others and their interests must be protected unless you explicitly know it is public or you are free to use it in the way you wish.

By itself, a code of ethics will not keep computer systems safe from employees, well meaning or otherwise. Not everyone will follow a code of ethics, just as not everyone obeys the law. An ethics statement is, however, a key part of every solid security plan.

WHAT ELSE GOES IN THE POLICY?

> I believe in rules. Sure I do. If there weren't any rules, how could you break them?
>
> Leo Durocher
> *Nice Guys Finish Last*, 1975

Okay, now some nuts and bolts about developing a computer security policy. You have two aims: to state explicitly what you consider acceptable behavior and to state explicitly what you consider to be unacceptable behavior. Not much room for ambiguity, huh?

Top-Down View of Policies

> The world is divided into people who think they are right.
>
> Anonymous

I've sifted through several different policies and pulled out several key issues that these policies have in common. The end result is somewhat general, but you can use the following information as the basis for developing your own policies:

Up top, you should state that the company's goal is to protect its computer systems and the information stored in them from accidental or deliberate unauthorized disclosure, modification, or destruction. Add to that your intent to put appropriate security controls in place in order to achieve your stated goal. Finally, note that you also intend to hold employees personally accountable for the information resources entrusted to them. That should get their attention!

Before we go on, I'll tell you that any lawyer can punch holes through most **Hole puncher** policies. Having a written policy, however, protects you from having an employee claim that he or she did not know that certain activities were considered improper and that violations of the company's computer security policy could result in termination of employment. Once you have formulated your policy, ask your company's legal experts to take a look at it.

The following sections describe some key areas that you should address in your policy.

Permission

Use of computer facilities by an individual must be authorized by the owner of the information or a senior manager. Prior permission to use another user's computer account or userID must be acquired from the owner of the account, who is responsible for its use. All computer and electronic files belong to somebody. They should be assumed to be private and confidential unless the owner has explicitly made them available to others.

Responsibilities

You are the owner of your data, and it is your responsibility to ensure that it is adequately protected against unauthorized access. This means you must avail yourself of the access controls and other security measures that the company has provided and take prudent and reasonable steps to limit access to your accounts.

Keep passwords and accounts confidential. Users should change their passwords frequently and should avoid using their names, their spouses' or friends' names, or a password that could easily be guessed.

Do not leave terminals unattended without logging out first.

Unauthorized Access to Files and Directories

You must not engage in any activity that is intended to circumvent computer security controls. This means you must not attempt to crack passwords, to discover unprotected files, or to decode encrypted files. This also includes creating, modifying, and executing programs that are designed to surreptitiously penetrate computer systems.

You also must not access the accounts of others with the intent to read, browse, modify, copy, or delete files and directories unless they have given you specific authorization to do so.

Do not use an account for a purpose not authorized when the account was established, including personal and commercial use.

Unauthorized Use of Software

You are prohibited from loading any software on any computer system without approval. That includes commercial, shareware, and freeware software. Further, you are expressly prohibited from using company computers to make illegal copies of licensed or copyrighted software. Copyrighted software must only be used in accordance with its license or purchase agreement. You do not have the right to own or use unauthorized copies of software or to make unauthorized copies of software for yourself or anyone else.

You are prohibited from using software that is designed to destroy data, provide unauthorized access to the computer systems, or disrupt computing processes in any other way. Using viruses, worms, Trojan horses, and other invasive software is expressly forbidden.

The company has installed antivirus software on all of its computer systems, and employees are required to use it. You are prohibited from tampering with this software or turning it off. All disks that are inserted into the company's computers must first be scanned for viruses or signs of other forms of malicious software.

Use antivirus software   *Note:* If you haven't installed antivirus software and don't require employees to use it, read Chapter 2.

Use for For-Profit Activities

The company's computer systems are for the sole use of the company. You are prohibited from using the company's computer systems for personal or private financial gain unless that use has been specifically authorized.

Electronic Mail

The electronic mail system is to be used only for company-related business. You are prohibited from transmitting fraudulent, harassing, or obscene messages and files. You must not send any electronic mail or other form of electronic communication by forging another's identity or attempt to conceal the origin of the message in any other way.

Harassment

Do not use the company's computer systems to harass anyone. This includes the use of insulting, sexist, racist, obscene, or suggestive electronic mail; tampering with others' files; and invasive access to others' equipment. In addition, users of any electronic communication facilities such as electronic mail, networks, bulletin boards, and newsgroups are obligated to comply with the restrictions and acceptable practices established for those specific facilities. Certain types of communications are expressly forbidden. This includes sending obscene, harassing, or threatening material; and using the facilities for commercial or political purposes.

Attacking the System

You must not deliberately attempt to degrade the performance of the company's computer system or subvert it in any other way. Deliberately crashing the system is expressly forbidden.

Theft

All hardware, software, and computer-related supplies and documentation are the sole property of the company. They must not be copied or removed from the company without proper authorization. All hardware, software, and computer-related supplies and documentation must be disposed of within the guidelines established by authorized company computer system personnel.

Note: You also want to make sure that employees don't simply toss old **Not in the** manuals, floppy disks, and the like into a garbage bin. The manuals should be **garbage** shredded and the floppy disks erased, for example, to remove any information that could be used by an outsider to penetrate the company's computer systems. And while you're being prudent, don't overlook recycling laser toner cartridges, which can be used to offset the cost of buying new cartridges.

Waste and Abuse

You must avoid any activity around your workstation that may result in damage to your computer, software, or information. Eating, drinking, and smoking while seated at your computer are not permitted. The company's computer systems are a valuable resource, and they should not be abused or wasted. Be considerate of fellow workers if you must share computer resources. Avoid monopolizing systems and connect time, disk space, and other computer resources. Using the company's computer systems to store personal data and to play computer games is not permitted.

Networks

Do not use the company-owned or any other network accessible by company computers—whether local, national, or international—for any activity other than company-related business. This includes, but is not limited to, "surfing" the Internet, engaging in online discussions in newsgroups and bulletin board services, attempting to access other computer systems without authorization, posting commercial messages, and transmitting viruses, worms, or other invasive software.

Enforcement

The company will investigate any alleged abuses of its computer resources. As part of that investigation, the company may access the electronic files of its employees. If the investigation indicates that computer privileges have been violated, the company may limit the access of employees found to be using computer systems improperly. Further more, the company may refer flagrant abuses to senior managers or law enforcment authorities. Although the company wishes to ensure that the privacy of all its employees is protected, in the course of its investigation, the company may reveal private, employee-related information to other employees.

Your responsibility   You are responsible for your own actions and should you violate the company's computer-use guidelines, your position may be terminated in extreme cases of flagrant abuse or disregard of these guidelines. You also are required to participate in assuring the legal and ethical use of company computers and user accounts. Any violation of these guidelines should be reported to your supervisor or a senior manager.

Workplace Monitoring

The company has the obligation to ensure that its computer resources are used properly and within the guidelines established by the company. In pursuit of that goal, the company reserves the right to monitor the system for signs of illegal or unauthorized activity.

Last Rights and Wrongs

You'll also need to include somewhere in your policy a statement indicating that just because a particular activity is not expressly prohibited by the policy does not mean that it's okay for the employee to engage in it. Computer technology changes rapidly, as do the ways in which employees are able to use, and perhaps, abuse, the company's computer systems. No single policy can ever cover all of the possibilities.

A computer security policy is not a substitute for proper computer security controls like the ones we have been talking about for several chapters now. What it does is demonstrate that you're serious about protecting the company's computer resources and it induces employees to become part of the solution rather than part of the problem. It also defines the ground rules. In the event that you do have a problem, the policy gives you something to stand on, a foundation on which to base your corrective actions.

Caveat

Policy Helpers

> Originality is something that is easily exaggerated, especially by authors contemplating their own work.
>
> John Kenneth Galbraith
> *The Affluent Society,* 1976

Writing policies is tedious and just plain hard work, but I've got a tip for you that will make it as easy as stepping off a curb. Go out and get a copy of *Information Security Policies Made Easy,* by Baseline Software. It's a compilation of 600 policies for passwords, access control, viruses, disaster recovery, and more. This policy construction kit comes as a book and on disk. All you have to do is plug your company's name into each policy if you want to use them right out of the box, or you can create your own. It will cost you $495, but think of all of the time you'll save. I should mention that I don't get a nickel for recommending this to you. Charles Cresson Wood, who heads Baseline, is an expert's expert, and he knows more about computer security policies than anyone I know.

Fill in the blanks

The National Institute of Standards and Technology, through its National Computer Systems Laboratory, puts out several special publications about information systems security, including an executive's guide to information policies. A list of current publications is available from the Standards Processing Coordinator, National Institute of Standards and Technology, National Computer Systems Laboratory, Technology Building B-64, Gaithersburg, MD 20899. Telephone: (301) 975-2817.

GET THE BOSS BEHIND THE PROGRAM

> The power to define the situation is the ultimate power.
>
> Jerry Rubin
> *Growing (Up) at 37,* 1976

For any computer security program to succeed, it has to have the support of senior managers. Without the boss and his cohorts saying, "Everyone get with the program, or else," no one will take it seriously (at least not enough to be truly effective). Step one is to make sure that everyone knows that the company's computer security policies have the blessing of the men and women at the top.

Good for business

Why even bother setting up a computer security program? It's good for business. What could be a better reason than that? The main thing is that you have taken measures to protect the company's information and computers against fraud, disaster, and all of the other factors that could put the business out of business. Also, having a well-defined computer security policy can help boost the company's image with customers, suppliers, and other business partners.

Crude, but Effective

> Litigation, n. A machine which you go into as a pig and come out as a sausage.
>
> Ambrose Bierce
> *The Devil's Dictionary,* 1906

Still not convinced that formulating a policy is worthwhile? What if I told you that if you don't have an established, written policy, you could be held personally liable in the event of a security breach that has an impact on the company's earnings or on the privacy or even welfare of its employees?

Crude crime

Remember the *Exxon Valdez*? In March 1989, its hull was ripped open on a reef, gushing millions of gallons of black crude into Alaska's Prince William Sound. The ship's captain, alleged to have been napping in his bunk, faced criminal charges in the aftermath of the spill.

My friend Sanford Sherizen, who is president of Data Security Systems, Inc., a computer-crime prevention firm, says there are lessons to be learned from the Alaskan disaster that captains of industry would do well to heed, lest, like the captain of the grounded tanker, they be hauled into court. The charge? Failure to adequately protect their corporate computer systems against hacker attacks, viruses, and other serious breaches of security. Corporate and government computer systems are like the Exxon *Valdez*—unprotected, under inadequate leadership control, operating through dangerous channels, and loaded with valuable and messy stuff—Sanford says.

Increased crime

Several experts agree that the prospect of a serious computer security breach—one causing a company to go bankrupt or harming its employees or customers in some other way—is likely to increase. Distributed information systems and the networks that interconnect them have made corporations more competitive, but at the same time, they have made them more vulnerable to attack by disgruntled employees, hackers, and others. In the event of a computer-security breach that harms an individual or corporation, senior managers, officers, and directors are someday going to be held responsible, Sanford says.

Some legal experts tell me that it's only a matter of time until companies will be forced to adhere to certain minimum standards for computer security. The issue is whether those standards will be adopted voluntarily by corporations or foisted upon them by the law. A handful of states—Florida and California, for example—have passed legislation that would require state agencies to take measures to adequately protect their computer systems.

COMPUTER AWARENESS TRAINING

> Nothing so needs reforming as other people's habits.
>
> Mark Twain
> *The Tragedy of Pudd'nhead Wilson, 1894*

Once you have developed the policy, you need to communicate it to every employee. A copy of the policy should be given to new hires and explained to them in detail as part of their orientation. You will also need to give employees a refresher course, at least once a year.

Companies that foster security awareness say that the training must be regular and sustained and that a refresher course every six months is not too often. Also, new employees must be trained as soon they are hired in order to impress upon them the importance of security, perhaps before bad habits set in. Managers must be part of the training equation as well. Managers should be asked to participate in programs and to endorse programs to give them a stamp of legitimacy and importance.

Regular and refresher

Promoting Awareness

There are many ways to promote security awareness, including videotapes, seminars, posters, articles in company newsletters, and security awareness seminars. Mix and match the following campaign tools according to the audience's size and sophistication. The following tools are in use at AT&T Bell Laboratories, Metropolitan Life, and several other corporations that find them useful in waging a campaign to foster adherence to security procedures.

Mix and match

Talks

Nothing will ever take the place of face-to-face talks with employees. They present opportunities to make suggestions that are specific to the group or department, handle questions as soon as they arise, and gauge the attitudes and familiarity with protecting corporate assets and information systems. The best time to get the employees' attention is when they first begin working for your company. An explanation and discussion of the company's computer security policies should be made part of every orientation program. You'll also have to conduct refresher courses once a year for all employees.

Videos

Today's employee has been raised on television, so it's not surprising that videos on security topics can be an effective way to communicate security awareness to employees. One source for computer-security videos is Commonwealth Films in Boston, which markets training videos with titles like "Data Security: Be Aware or Beware," and "Invasion of the Data Snatchers." A discussion and handouts following the session help reinforce the security message.

Newsletters

Company newsletters can be an invaluable way of regularly promoting security awareness. Write articles on a variety of topics. Keep them brief, only a paragraph or two, and to the point. Supplement the articles with cartoons, puzzles, and other entertaining approaches.

Posters

Develop a security theme and support it with a series of posters that stand out from others that may be posted in your company. Keep the messages simple and direct. Use a variety of approaches, from the serious to the humorous.

Brochures and Booklets

A simple booklet or brochure can be used to reinforce the security message or serve as a reminder to employees. Keep them easy to read and avoid using an overly serious tone.

Trinkets

Everyone loves a freebie. Post-its notes, pens, mouse pads, stickers, and the like also spread the security message. If carefully chosen, the trinket will be both handy and readily in sight.

Awards

An award for fostering security or for implementing innovative security techniques is a positive approach to awareness. Make them valuable by giving them only when they are truly deserved.

Computer Security Awareness Day

> Mom and Pop were just a couple of kids when they got married. He was
> eighteen, she was sixteen, and I was three.
>
> Billie Holliday
> *Lady Sings the Blues*, 1958

Each year, on December 2, the Association of Computing Machinery, the National
Computer Security Institute, and other professional and industry organizations
sponsor Computer Security Awareness Day. That's the day they have chosen to
tout computer security and to try to stimulate businesses and universities into
going around and making sure all is quiet on the security front. They've published a list of activities that you can use to mark the day:

1. Display computer security posters.

2. Present computer security briefings.

3. Change your password.

4. Present a computer security video, film, or slide show.

5. Check for computer viruses.

6. Protect against static electricity.

7. Modify the log-on message on your computer system to notify users that the
   system will be monitored.

8. Vacuum your computer and the immediate area.

9. Clean the heads on your disk drives and tape backup systems.

10. Back up your data.

11. Delete unneeded files.

12. Demonstrate (to co-workers) computer security software.

13. Publicize existing computer security policies.

14. Issue new computer security guidelines.

15. Declare an amnesty day for computer security violators who wish to reform.

16. Announce Computer Security Awareness Day in your newsletter.

17. Examine the audit files on your computers.

18. Verify that the welcome message normally used on your computers is appro-
    priate for your organization.

19. Put write-protect tabs on disks that are not supposed to be written to.

20. Take the write-protect rings out of the tapes in your library.

21. Verify your inventory of computer applications.

22. Verify your inventory of computer utilities and packaged software.

23. Verify your inventory of computer hardware.

24. Verify your inventory of computer networks.

25. Inspect and install power protection equipment as appropriate.

26. Inspect or install fire and smoke detectors and suppression equipment in computer areas.

27. Eliminate dust from computer areas, including chalk dust.

28. Provide disk and water covers for personal and larger computers.

29. Post "No drinking," "No eating," and "No smoking" signs in computer areas.

30. Develop or review recovery plans for all computers.

31. Verify that passwords are not posted.

32. Verify that backup power and air conditioning exist to support computer operations.

Are we having fun yet?

33. Have a mini–training session to provide all computer users with a basic understanding of computer security.

34. Verify that all source code is protected from unauthorized changes.

35. Verify that each computer has its own trouble log and that it is being used.

36. Verify that appropriate off-site storage exists and is being used.

37. Remove all unnecessary items such as extra supplies, coat racks, and print-outs from the computer room.

38. Select a system on which to perform a risk analysis.

39. Begin planning next year's Computer Security Awareness Day.

40. Change the FORMAT command in MS-DOS to avoid accidentally formatting disk drives.

41. Protect the computer on your store-and-forward phone system.

42. Hold a discussion about ethics with computer users.

43. Volunteer to speak at a local computer club.

44. Collect Computer Security Awareness Day memorabilia to trade with others.

45. Register and pay for all shareware that you use regularly.

46. Apply all security-related patches to your operating systems.

47. Help novice users back up their files this week.

48. Attend an ACM Computer Security Awareness Day Seminar.

Here are a few more that come to mind:

49. Create a policy that forbids employees from using disks brought from home in company computers.

50. Install antivirus software on PCs and scan all new programs before they are installed.

51. Change voice mail passwords.

Don't Copy That Floppy

> I don't want to know what the law is, I want to know who the judge is.
>
> Roy Cohn
> *New York Times Book Review,* April 3, 1988

Software pirates steal in a year as much business software as McDonald's sells hamburgers. That's according to the Software Publishers Association (SPA), a trade group composed of top software publishers based in Washington, D.C. The SPA says that a total of $7.4 billion worth of business application software was illegally copied in 1993. Most of that thievery takes place in the U.S., the SPA adds.

Software is protected by the Copyright Act and the Software Copyright Protection Bill (there are other laws, but these two are the heavy hitters). Only the copyright owner has the exclusive right to reproduce the copyrighted work and to distribute copies of the copyrighted work. That's what it says in Title 17 of the Copyright Act. It also says that anyone who violates any of the exclusive rights of the copyright owner is breaking the law. You or your boss may have paid for a particular program, but the law says that you can't make copies or rent it to anyone. The only exception is that you are allowed to make backup copies of your programs as a way to protect your investment in case something bad happens to the original disks. **Exclusive rights**

The closest I ever got to law school was taking my LSATs, so I should be the last one you should listen to when it comes to legalisms. However, I can tell you that if you copy software that belongs to someone else, and they find out about it, you get in trouble, for sure. The law is pretty clear about what you can and can't do as far as copyrighted software goes, but not everyone understands plain English, or maybe they don't think the laws apply to them.

Lots of companies (lots of my friends, too) make more than just backup copies of their software. A company that I once worked for (who shall remain nameless) bought a bunch of new computers but only a single copy of three programs that it needed for the new machines. These were fancy page layout and graphics programs, the kind that cost hundreds of dollars apiece. From the company's point of view, it was saving money, which is good for the bottom line. Besides, if the **More than backups** company didn't make copies, it wouldn't be able to buy all that it needed. This is the sort of rationalization that will one day get my former employer a visit from the SPA, a.k.a. the Software Police.

Dim view   As you can appreciate, the SPA and its members take a dim view of getting ripped off. The SPA runs lots of hard-hitting magazine ads showing people in handcuffs and behind bars. In addition to admonishing readers "Don't copy that floppy," they urge employees to drop a dime on their bosses if they suspect them of illegally copying software. The SPA says that it gets 800 calls a week to its 800 hotline. They follow up on about 10 percent of the calls. If the SPA suspects that the employer is a large-scale software pirate, it calls the Federal Bureau of Investigation as well as local authorities and asks them to raid the place.

Knock, knock   If the SPA or the law ever comes knocking on your door, they will be looking for evidence that you have purchased all of the software that is on your workstations and LANs. If they find ten copies of Microsoft Word, but you can only provide a receipt for one copy, you'll be required to destroy the remaining copies and purchase nine replacements. Also, you may have to pay a penalty, which is typically equal to the retail price of the stolen software. Word sells for about $300 a pop, so you would be looking at forking over $5400.

Uh, oh . . .   If you're really blatant and operating with complete disregard for the law, the penalties are potentially a lot higher. Under the Copyright Act, the civil penalties can be as high as $100,000 for each infringed work and criminal penalties can go to $250,000 and five years in jail for each infringed work. The Software Copyright Protection Bill makes it a felony to illegally copy ten or more software programs or programs with a total retail value of $2500 or more. Criminal penalties include fines of up to $250,000 and imprisonment for up to five years. Not surprisingly, given the option of paying for the ripped-off software plus a penalty or getting embroiled in a complicated lawsuit, most companies settle out of court.

Copyright religion   A lot more companies these days are getting copyright religion and making sure that the software they buy is not illegally copied. Licensing and metering software for networks is one of the key ways that companies can get a handle on the software they have purchased.

The SPA has a free software auditing package called SPAudit. You can get that by calling (800) 866-6585. If you want to blow the whistle, the SPA's hotline is (800) 388-7478. The trade group also has a forum on Compuserve that you can go to by typing GO SPA.

Here are some tips to keep the Software Police at bay:

- Don't permit anyone to make illegal copies of software.

- Don't allow employees to load new software on their machines.

- Don't permit employees to download software from online services and bulletin board systems.

- Conduct an audit periodically to make sure that all of the software you're using is legit.

Hack Attack Aftermath

> Everybody is a potential murderer. I've never killed anyone, but I
> frequently get satisfaction from reading the obituary notices.
>
> Clarence Darrow, in an April 18, 1937, newspaper interview

Okay, despite your having taken everything that I've said thus far to heart, an intruder gets into your system, tampers with some files, steals your precious information, and sells it to your nearest competitor. Don't blame me, I never promised you perfect security let alone a rose garden. But let's see what we can do to nab the thieving, lowlife sneak and make sure that he goes directly to jail:

1. If you haven't done it already, now is the time to post a "No Trespassing" sign in the form of a systems greeting that warns all intruders that their activities will be monitored.

2. Gather evidence. Check your audit reports for signs of illegal activity. You need to know exactly when the intruder entered your system, how he got in, where he went, and what he did. If it's an insider, you'll also need to know who got in; if it's an outsider, that's going to take some trickery. In the interim, it's especially important that you shut down the security loophole and check the system for programs or files of suspicious origin. The last thing you need is a password-grabbing Trojan horse, logic bomb, or some other bit of rogue code on your system.

3. Contact the appropriate law enforcement agencies. Depending on the extent of the crime and the dollar loss (if any), you will need to contact local, state, and federal officials. The first thing they're going to ask you is for evidence. You'll also need to substantiate how you arrived at a dollar figure for your loss. The FBI, for example, will not intervene if the loss is under a certain amount, although they will deny that they need to cross a financial threshold before getting involved in computer crime cases.

4. Expect that no matter what law enforcement agency you deal with, the officers and agents will be well meaning but probably not well versed in technology, at least not as well as you are. Although law enforcement agencies are becoming more adept at investigating computer crimes, if you look at just how many cases nationwide have been successfully prosecuted, you'll see that it's not very many. A big part of this is a reluctance to investigate because the crimes are complex and cross local, state, federal, and even international

judicial boundaries. Another big part is making the case stick in court. Not many computer crime cases result in jail time for the offender. You're going to have a lot of explaining to do, and you'll need to bolster your case with clear-cut evidence of what happened and why it is even a crime.

5. Familiarize yourself with local, state, and federal computer crime statutes. Check to see if your state has a computer crime law and exactly what sorts of crimes are covered. Not every state expressly prohibits planting a virus in a computer system. Federal law enforcers will only get involved if the criminal used a "federal interest computer." There's a brief description of the federal laws at the end of this chapter, including a definition of "federal interest computer."

6. Set a trap. Lock down everything in sight except a few files that you want the intruder to go after. Then monitor system activity for signs of someone going in to look at those files. In Clifford Stoll's *Cuckoo Egg*, Stoll described how he nabbed three German hackers in the employ of the KGB by baiting them with tantalizing files purported to be about the Strategic Defense Initiative, or Star Wars.

7. As the LAN supervisor, it's your system and it's your responsibility. You'll act as the point man (er, point person) when dealing with the computer crime squad. Also, you want to be ready to provide whatever assistance investigators need to prosecute your case.

8. If the crime is a voice mail or PBX crime, contact your system vendor and regional and national telephone companies. The large companies maintain computer crime task forces that can assist you in setting up your electronic stakeout and gathering evidence.

9. Contact the Computer Emergency Response Team (CERT) at Carnegie Mellon University's Software Engineering Institute in Pittsburgh, Pennsylvania. In 1994, CERT handled more than 2000 incidents, which affected over 40,000 sites (half from a single attack); received over 3000 hotline calls; published 15 security advisories; and received over 29,000 e-mail inquiries. The Software Engineering Institute has a World Wide Web home page located at http://www.sei.cmu.edu that carries CERT advisories, which provide information on how you can obtain a patch or details of a workaround for a security problem. They're also available via anonymous FTP from info.cert.org. To be added to the CERT mailing list, send mail to cert-advisory-request@cert.org. You can get CERT contact information via a 24-hour telephone hotline for system administrators, 412-268-7090; by fax, 412-268-6989; or by e-mail, cert@cert.org.

COMPUTER CRIME STATUTES

I mentioned earlier that law enforcement is generally reluctant to investigate computer crimes. There are at least two reasons I can think of for this:

1. Computer crime resists definition. For one person, it is any crime directed at or taking place within a computer; for another, it is any crime in which a computer is a tool of the crime.

2. Businesses report only a small percentage—about 6%, by one estimate—of criminal acts aimed at their computer systems, for fear that publicity will be bad for business or attract copycat crooks.

Without any kind of national consensus on what computer crime is and how much it costs, there is no appreciation for the magnitude of the problem and thus no incentive on the part of business and government to do anything about it.

Compounding the problem is the propensity of industry and law enforcement to blame each other for failing to take stronger measures to combat computer crime. Information systems security managers complain that when they report crimes, the bulk of offenses go unpunished. Law enforcers often lack necessary skills and are too slow to investigate and prosecute computer crimes, they say. **Pointing fingers**

Computer crimes are difficult, time consuming, and costly to investigate, and in the face of other crimes, have a low priority, says an assistant district attorney I know. Computer crime just doesn't stack up against murder, he adds.

Federal-Level Computer Crime Laws

What follows is a brief summary of key federal statutes covering computer fraud and software piracy:

Copyright Law (Title 17 of the U.S. Code)

The law makes it illegal to make or distribute copies of copyrighted material without proper authorization. However, the law also states that you have the right to make a backup copy to protect your investment against damage or loss.

Computer Software Rental Admendments Act of 1990

It is illegal to rent, lease, or lend copyrighted software without the authorization of the copyright holder. The act does not apply to a nonprofit library or nonprofit educational institution.

Electronic Communications Privacy Act of 1986

The law makes it illegal for anyone to intercept telecommunications, such as cellular telephone calls and electronic mail without authorization.

Computer Fraud and Abuse Act of 1986

It is illegal to knowingly access a computer without authorization to exceed authorized access, to cause losses of more than $1000, or to prevent authorized users from using the computer. The law is restricted to "federal interest computers." That's not a computer owned by the government necessarily, but one that accesses federal data. It also applies to computers that are located in two or more states. In other words, if the hacker uses a computer in California to break into a computer in Oregon, the computers would be federal interest computers.

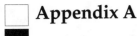

Appendix A
PC and Mac Antivirus Software

Alternative Computer Technology Inc.
7908 Cin-Day Rd.
West Chester, OH 45069
513-755-1957
PC Products: VSweep; OSweep; Vaccine; D-Fence

Application Configured Computers Inc.
P.O. Box 0433
Baldwin, NY 11510
516-623-6295
PC Products: Detekt; V-Phage/DOS

Command Software Systems Inc.
1061 E. Indiantown Rd., Ste. 500
Jupiter, FL 33477
407-575-3200
PC Products: F-PROT Professional

Datawatch Corp.
234 Ballardvale St.
Wilmington, MA 01887
508-988-9700
PC Products: Virex for the PC
Mac Products: Virex

M&T Technologies Inc.
1435 N. Hayden Rd.
Scottsdale, AZ 85257
602-994-5131
PC Products: Microsafe SIC/Virus Protect

New Castle International
P.O. Box 267
Rye Beach, NH 03871
603-431-6170
PC Products: Invircible

Norman Data Defense Systems, Inc.
3028 Javier Rd., Ste. 201
Fairfax, VA 22031
703-573-8802
PC Products: Armour/Norman Virus Control for Workstations;
ThunderBYTE Anti-Virus Utilities for Windows

OnTrack Computer Systems Inc.
6321 Bury Dr.
Eden Prairie, MN 55346
800-752-1333
PC Products: Dr. Solomon's Anti-Virus Toolkit for DOS;
Dr. Solomon's Anti-Virus Toolkit for Windows;
Dr. Solomon's Anti-Virus Toolkit for OS/2

RG Software Systems, Inc.
6900 E. Camelback Rd., Ste. 630
Scottsdale, AZ 85251
602-423-8000
PC Products: Vi-Spy Professional Edition;
Vi-Spy Professional Edition for Windows

Safetynet Inc.
55 Bleeker St.
Millburn, NJ 07041
800-851-0188
PC Products: Virusnet;
Drive-In Anti-Virus

Symantec Corp., Peter Norton Product Group
10201 Torre Ave.
Cupertino, CA 95014-2132
800-441-7234
PC Products: Norton AntiVirus 3.0 for DOS and Windows
Mac Products: Symantec AntiVirus for Macintosh

ThunderBYTE North American Headquarters
300-49 Main St.
Massena, NY 13662
800-667-8228
PC Products: ThunderBYTE Anti-Virus Utilities for Windows

Antivirus Shareware for PCs and Macs

McAfee Associates
2710 Walsh Avenue
Santa Clara, CA 95051
408-988-4004
PC Products: VirusScan—Available on Compuserve, American Online and many other commercial online services.

Thompson Network Software
2619 Sandy Plaines Rd.
Marrietta, GA 30066
404-971-8900
PC Products: The Doctor—Available on Compuserve and via FTP at thomnet.com.

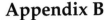

Computer Security Companies and Organizations

The following is a list of the major computer security companies and organizations mentioned in this book.

AccessData
560 S. State St., Ste. J-1
Orem, UT 84058
801-224-6970
800-489-5199
Password recovery utilities

The AG Group
2540 Camino Diablo, Ste. 200
Walnut Creek, CA 94596
510-937-7900
800-466-AGGO
Computer access controls

AllMicro
18820 U.S. Hwy. 19N, Ste. 215
Clearwater, FL 34624
813-539-7283
800-653-4933
Data recovery software

American Power Conversion
132 Fairgrounds Road
West Kingston, RI 02892
401-789-5735
800-788-2208
Power protection equipment

Anchor Pad Products
35 Hammond St.
Irvine, CA 92718
714-580-2555
800-626-2467
Antitheft devices

ASD Software
4650 Arrow Hwy., Ste. E-6
Montclair, CA 91763
909-624-2594
Access control software

Baseline Software
P.O. Box 1219
Sausalito, CA 94966
415-332-7763
800-829-9955
Password protection utilities
Information security policies

Casady & Greene
22734 Portola Dr.
Salina, CA 93908
408-484-9228
800-359-4920
Access control software

CKS
11 Parkway Ctr., Ste. 390
Pittsburgh, PA 15220
412-928-3000
800-321-9004
Access control software

COM&DIA
3000 Highwoods Blvd., Ste. 100
Raleigh, NC 27604
919-878-6503
Access control software

Commonwealth Films
223 Commonwealth Ave.
Boston, MA 02116
617-262-5634
Computer security videos

Communication Devices
1 Forstmann Court
Botany Village
Clifton, NJ 07011
800-359-8561
Access control hardware and software

Compu-Gard
36 Maple Ave.
Seekonk, MA 02771
508-761-4520
800-333-6810
Antitheft devices

CryptoCard
1250 W. Northwest Hwy.
Palatine, IL 60067
708-776-1108
Access control hardware and software

Curtis Manufacturing
30 Fitzgerald Dr.
Jaffrey, NH 03452
603-532-4123
800-955-5544
Antitheft devices

Cylink
910 Hermosa Ct.
Sunnyvale, CA 94086
408-735-5800
800-533-3958
Encryption hardware

Dantz Development
4 Orinda Way, Bldg. C
Orinda, CA 94563
510-253-3000
800-225-4880
Tape backup software

Enigma Logic
2151 Salvio St., Ste. 301
Concord, CA 94520
510-827-5707
Access control hardware and software

Exabyte
1685 38th St.
Boulder, CO 80301
303-442-4333
800-EXABYTE
Tape backup drives

Fischer International Systems
4073 Merchantile Ave.
Naples, FL 33942
813-643-1500
800-237-4510
Access control software

Frye Computer Systems
19 Temple Pl.
Boston, MA 02111
617-451-5400
800-234-3793
LAN utilities

FWB
2040 Polk St., Ste. 215
San Francisco, CA 94109
415-474-8055
Hard disk utilities

Globus Systems
1447 McAllister St.
San Francisco, CA 94115
415-292-6744
800-538-4701
Antitheft devices

Intrusino Detection
217 East 86th St., Ste. 213
New York, NY 10028
212-360-6104
LAN utilities

Kensington Microware
2855 Campus Dr.
San Mateo, CA 94403
415-572-2700
800-535-4242
Antitheft devices

LeeMah DataCom Security
3948 Trust Way
Hayward, CA 94545
510-786-0790
800-444-4309
Call-back modems

Maedae Enterprises
5430 Murr Rd.
Peyton, CO 80831
719-683-3860
Encryption software

Magna
1999 S. Bascom Ave., Ste. 810
Campbell, CA 95008
408-879-7900
800-80-MAGNA
Access control software

Mergent International
70 Inwood Rd.
Rocky Hill, CT 06067
203-257-4223
Access control software
Power protection equipment

MountainGate Data Systems
9393 Gateway Dr.
Reno, NV 89511
702-851-5556
Removeable hard drives

On Technology
One Cambridge Center
Cambridge, MA 02142
617-374-1400
800-767-6683
LAN utilities

Oneac
27944 N. Bradley Rd.
Libertyville, IL 60048
708-816-6000
800-327-8801
Power protection equipment

OnTrack Data Recovery
6321 Bury Dr.
Eden Prairie, MN 55346
612-937-5161
800-872-2599
Data recovery services

PC Integrity
301 N. Harrison St., Ste. 106
Princeton, NJ 08540
609-466-1700
800-742-7722
Software copying controls

Qualtec Data Products
47767 Warm Springs Blvd.
Fremont, CA 94539
510-490-8911
800-628-4413
Antitheft devices

Racal-Datacom
1601 N. Harrison Pkwy.
Sunrise, FL 33323
305-846-1601
800-RACAL-55
Encryption hardware

Racal-Guardata
480 Spring Park Pl., Ste. 900
Herndon, VA 22070
703-471-0892
800-521-6261
Access control hardware

RSA Data Security
100 Marine Pkwy., Ste. 500
Redwood City, CA 94065
415-595-8782
Encryption software

Secure-It
18 Maple Ct.
East Longmeadow, MA 01028
413-525-7039
800-451-7592
Antitheft devices

Security Dynamics
One Alewife Center
Cambridge, MA 02140
617-547-7820
Access control hardware and software

SecurTech
5755 Willow Ln.
Lake Oswego, OR 97035
503-636-6831
800-800-9573
Antitheft devices

Smart Disk Security
4073 Merchantile Ave.
Naples, FL 33942
813-263-3475
Access control hardware and software

SonicPro International
5201 Great American Pkwy.
Santa Clara, CA 95054
408-982-2568
800-848-0300
Antitheft devices

Square D
1660 Scenic Ave.
Costa Mesa, CA 92926
714-557-1636
800-344-0570
Power protection equipment

Stolen Computer Registry
P.O. Box 1490
New York, NY 10159
212-777-1291
Stolen computer registry service

Symantec/Peter Norton Product Group
10201 Torre Ave.
Cupertino, CA 95014
408-253-9600
800-441-7234
Access control software
Antivirus, backup, and data
recovery utilities

Tripp Lite
500 N. Orleans Ave.
Chicago, IL 60610
312-755-5400
Power protection equipment

usrEZ Software
18881 Van Karman Ave., Tower 17,
Ste. 1270
Irvine, CA 92715
714-756-5140
Access control software

ViaCrypt
2104 W. Peoria Ave.
Phoenix, AZ 85029 USA
602-944-0773
Encryption software

Z-Lock
P.O. Box 949
Redondo Beach, CA 90277
310-316-7709
Antitheft devices

Organizations

Computer Emergency Response Team
Software Engineering Institute
Carnegie Mellon University
Pittsburgh, PA 15313-3890
412-268-7090
(24-hour hotline)

National Computer Security
Association
10 South Courthouse Ave.
Carlisle, PA 17013
717-258-1816

Computer Security Institute
600 Harrison St.
San Francisco, CA 94107
415-905-2626

National Institute of Standards and
Technology
National Computer Systems Laboratory
Technology Building B-64
Gaithersburg, MD 20899
301-975-2817

Appendix C

Notes from the
Virus Front

THIS JUST IN . . .

While this book was on the way to the printer, I got word of an entirely new virus whose characteristics are so unique, I begged my publisher to hold up final production just long enough for me to stick in a few paragraphs about it.

What makes this virus so unusual is that it is the first to be found in the wild that infects documents instead of programs. What's more, it is also the first virus to be uncovered that is capable of infecting both PCs and Macintoshes. Fortunately, the virus is not destructive and spotting and removing it is easy, so there's no need to panic. It infects only documents written in Microsoft's Word 6.0 program (one of the most popular word processing programs).

Several virus hunters seem to have come across the virus, pretty much at the same time. As a result, the virus has been given a variety of names, including WinWord.Concept, WW6 and WW6Macro on the PC and Word-Macro-9508 on the Macintosh. Microsoft, who publishes Word, has dubbed the virus the Prank Macro.

The virus is written in Word Basic, the computer language used in Word to create macros. Macros are little programs that permit you to do a sequence of discrete steps, such as cutting and pasting text, by pressing only one or two keys. Prank consists of a set of these Word macros and is designed to infect Word documents that end with .DOC and templates that end with .DOT. Documents created in Word on either PCs or Macs are interchangeable, so the virus is capable of spreading from one platform to another.

PC users will know they have the virus if a small box pops up on screen with the number 1 in it, the first time they open an infected file. It appears only once, so it's easy to miss. Mac users will find infected files show up on the desktop with template icons rather than the usual document icons. In both cases, you can scroll through the list of macros installed on your machine under the Tools and Macros menu. If you spot all of the following files you have the virus: AAAZFS, AAAZAO, AutoOpen, Payload and FileSaveAs.

There are a variety of ways to get rid of the virus. You can delete the suspicious-looking macros on either the PC or Mac, for example. PC users with Internet access, can point their World Wide Web browsers to Microsoft's home page: http://www.microsoft.com and download a free fix. Also, anti-virus software publishers such as Datawatch and Symantec are providing free updates for their software designed to remove the Prank Macro.

Although this particular virus seems to have been contrived just to prove that writing a virus that feeds on macros can be done, it signals a whole new change in direction by virus writers. My guess is that it won't be long before we see more viruses capable of infecting data files and that the virus problem will become even worse than it already is. Don't fall asleep on your watch.

Index

Abuse, defined, 205
Access control, 46–47
  of laptop, 74–75
  levels of, 67
  programs for, 61–68
  remote, 80–85
Access control LAN right, 97
Acoustic couplers, 73
Adleman, Leonard, 138
AIDS Information Introductory Disk,
    Version 2.0, 40–41
Alarm
  burglar, 167
  for laptop, 78
  for office equipment, 168
alt.2600 newsgroup, 11–12
alt.security.pgp newsgroup, 132
ANI (automatic number identification), 83
Antiglare filters, 173
Antivirus software
  choosing, 36–37
  disinfectants, 35–36
  file-change detectors, 34
  importance of, xv, 5
  importance of for backups, 183
  for the Mac, 37–39
  scanners, 29–30, 33–34
  suppliers of, 101, 219–221
  types of, 32–33
  virus activity monitors, 35
  virus-infected, 40
Application-level firewall, 115
At Ease (Apple), 65
ATMs, 47
  debit cards at, 55–56
  security at, 49
  tips for using, 50
Attack scanners, 113
ATTRIB command (DOS), antivirus use of, 39

Auditing
  software, 100
  user, 67, 99
Automated Systems for Contingency Planning
    and Disaster Recovery (Institute of Internal
    Auditors), 155
Automatic number identification (ANI), 83
Availability, defined, 2
Awareness training, 209–216

Baby monitors, security concerns with, 128–129
BACKUP command (DOS), 188–189
Backups
  onto floppies, 188–190
  importance of, xv, 3–4, 176
  incremental, 181–182
  of LAN, 101–102
  of laptop, 74
  onto magneto-optical drives, 194
  procedures for, 184–185
  reasons for, 176–177
  onto secondary hard drive, 190–191
  software for, 180–181
  strategies for, 186–188
  tape, 177–180, 183–184
  tips for making, 182–183
Battery, conserving, 75
Bellovin, Steven, 115
Bernoulli removable cartridges, 192–193
Bernoulli Zip drives, 193
Biometrics, 59–60
  drawbacks to, 60–61
Blackouts, 159
Blurred vision, from monitor, 172
Bob (Microsoft), password protection in, 64
Boot disk. See Rescue disk
Boot record, saving, 71
Boot sector viruses, 28
  repairing damage of, 36

Broderick, Matthew, 12
Brownouts, 159
Burglar alarm, 167
Burn data wiper (Watson and Jensen), 197

Cables, integrity of, 158
Call-back modems, 82
Call-sell operators, 129
Caller ID, 83
Cannabis virus, 29
Carpal tunnel syndrome, 170, 174
CD-Recorders, 194–195
CDEF virus, 26
Cellular telephone
   cloning of, 126–127
   digital future of, 127–128
   as disaster backup, 154
   eavesdropping on, 125–126
Central Point (Symantec), 121
CERT (Computer Emergency Response
   Team), 109, 216
Chair, ergonomically designed, 171
Challenge and response, 57
Cheswick, William, 115
CHKDSK command (DOS), 70
Circuit-level firewall, 115
Clean Sweep uninstaller program, 198
Clipper encryption scheme, 145
CMOS setup
   saving, 71
   security in, 64
Cohen, Fred, 26–27
Cold sites, 153
Competitive intelligence (CI), 17
Compressed software, 33, 34
Computer literacy, importance of, 6
Computer Emergency Response Team, 109, 216
Computer Ethics Institute code of conduct, 201
Computer Fraud and Abuse Act of 1986, 218
Computer Insurance Agency, 169
Computer Software Rental Amendments Act
   of 1990, 217
Conduct, guidelines for, 202
Confidentiality, defined, 2, 21–22
CONFIG.SYS module (DOS), 76
Cook, Bill, 122
Copy inhibit LAN attribute, 96

Copyright laws, 99–100, 213, 217
   penalties under, 214
Cordless telephone, security problems with,
   128–129
Crack, password-cracking program, 12, 51
CrackerJack, password-cracking program, 12, 51
Create LAN right, 97
Credit card fraud, 129
Credit reports, fraudulent access to, 14
Crime
   employee, 8, 9, 201
   information theft, 8, 17
   risk of, 4,5, 208–209
   statutes defining, 217–218
   theft, 68–70, 77, 166–167, 205
Crypta card (Telequip), 58
Ctrl-Alt-Del, defeating, 68
Curve Encrypt, drive-locking system, 146

DAT drives, 179–180
Data diddling, 8
Data Encryption Standard. See DES
DC/DREP (Kingswell), 155
DDS-2 drives, 179–180
Decryption, defined, 133
Delete inhibit LAN attribute, 96
DES, xv, 66
   advantages of, 138
   mechanism of, 136–137
Desk height, 172
DiaLOCK (COM&DIA), 64
DiaLOCK BOOT (COM&DIA), 97
Diffie, Whitfield, 134
Digital audio tapes, 179–180
Digital signature, 135
Digital telephone systems, drawbacks of, 73–74
Disaster recovery, 18, 149–150
   from electrical damage, 159–166
   emergency disks for, 195
   employee involvement in, 155–156
   insurance, 168–169
   planning for, 150–152, 155–156
   prevention, 158, 195–196
   services, 153
   survival equipment, 157
   from theft, 166–168
   undeleting files, 196–198
   from water damage, 157–158

Dishonesty, 7–8
Disinfectant, Mac antivirus software, 26, 38
Disinfectants, 35–36
Disk locking, 68–75
Disk Ogre virus, 36
Disk Tools (Mac), 71
DiskFit Direct (Dantz), 182
DiskFit Pro (Dantz), 182
DiskGuard (ASD), 64
DiskLock (Symantec), 64
Documents, disposal of, 18
DoD wipe, 146
DTMF decoder, 126
Dukakis virus, 38
Dumpster diving, 10, 14–15

E-mail
   eavesdropping on, 8
   ethics of, 204–205
   Internet, 112–113
   problems with, 103–104
   security tips for, 104–105, 108
   sending files by, 74
   virus in attachment to, 119
Eavesdropping, 8
   on cellular phone conversation, 125
   on cordless phone conversation, 128
   on encrypted message, 133–134
   on wiring, 89–90
1813 virus, 29
Electrical damage
   from blackouts, 159
   from brownouts, 159
   from line noise, 160
   from spikes, 159–160, 161–162
   from surges, 160, 161–162
Electronics Communications Privacy Act of
      1986 (ECPA), 84–85, 126, 218
ELF radiation, 173
Embezzlement, 8
Emergency equipment, 72–73
   rescue disk, 70–71, 158
Emissions, from monitors, 170, 173
EMM386 command (DOS), 71
Employees
   disaster recovery by, 155–156
   dishonesty of, 7–8

Internet problems of, 116–117
   monitoring behavior of, 199
   monitoring and controlling access of, 93–95,
      96–97
   sabotage by, 7
   as security threat, 1, 3
Encryption, 131–132
   for backups, 181
   defined, 133
   government regulation of, 132, 145
   hard disk, 145–146
   importance of, xv, 18, 66
   keys of, 133–134
   private-key. See Private-key cryptography
   products that use, 146–147
   public-key. See PGP; Public-key cryptography
Enigma, drive-locking system, 146
Ergonomics, 170–174
Espionage, industrial, 17
Ethics, 200, 202
   code of, 201
Excel (Microsoft), 62
   password protection in, 63
Execute only LAN attribute, 96
Eye strain, 172–173

Fax machines, security concerns with, 129–130
FDISK command (DOS), 70
FDISK /MBR command (DOS), 36
Federal Crime Insurance Program, 169
File infectors, 28
File scan LAN right, 97
File-change detectors, 34
FileGuard data wiper (ASD), 197
Files
   deleting and undeleting, 68, 71, 143
   locking, 65
   unauthorized use of, 204
Fingerprint analysis, 60, 61
Firewall
   setting up, 113
   types of, 114–115
Floppy disks
   backing up onto, 188–190
   proper care of, 189–190
FolderBolt Pro (Kent Marsh), 65
Folders, locking, 65

FORMAT command (DOS), 70
Fortress antivirus program, 43
4096 virus, 36

Gatekeeper, Mac antivirus software, 38–39
Genetic pattern analysis, 60
Glare, minimizing, 173
Good Times hoax, 118–119
Greed, as motivation, 7–8
GuardIT! (Infinite Technologies), 97
Guest accounts, 67
    on LAN, 91–92

Hackers, 9
    characteristics of, 10–12
    dealing with, 215–216
    on Internet, 111–112
    risk of, 4–5
    techniques of, 12–13
Hand geometry, 60
    drawbacks to, 61
Handset adapters, 73
Harassment, 205
Hard drive
    backing up of, 175–197. See also Backups
    backing up onto, 190–191
    encryption of, 145–146
    locking, 64, 168
    removable, 191–192
    setup, security in, 63
Hard Pass (Data Tech), 65
Headache, from monitor, 172
Hellman, Martin, 134
Hidden LAN attribute, 96
HIMEM.SYS (DOS module), 71, 76
Hot sites, 153

IDEA (International Data Encryption
    Algorithm), 139
Incremental backups, 181–182
Industrial espionage, 17
Information
    classifications of, 21–22
    defined, 20
    need to know, 20–21

responsibility for, 22–23
theft of, 8, 17
value of, 19–20
Information Security Policies Made Easy
    (Baseline), 207
Integrity, defined, 2
International Data Encryption Algorithm
    (IDEA), 139
Internet
    commercial hookups to, 110
    e-mail on, 112–113, 118–119
    employee indiscretions on, 116–117
    etiquette on, 109
    firewall for, 113–115
    password sniffing on, 111
    pervasiveness of, 109
    privacy-enhanced, 144
    routers to, 114–115
    security concerns on, 110–111
    security tips for, 116
    spoofing on, 111–112
    tips for using, 117
    virus dissemination on, 27, 41, 87, 116
Intruder Detection (Novell NetWare), 93–94
Intrusion detection, 98–99
Inventory, taking, 154–155
IP spoofing, 111–113
Israeli virus, 29

Jerusalem virus, 29, 36
Johnson, Chris, 38
Joshi virus, 36

Kane, Robert, 94, 98
Kane Security Analyst (Intrusion Detection), 98
Kerberos encryption program, 144–145
Keyboard
    correct posture at, 173
    locking, 68
Keys
    PGP, 139, 141
    public vs. private, 133–134, 136
    revocation of, 143
Keystroke analysis, 60
KSA [Kane Security Analyst (Intrusion
    Detection)], 98

LAN
  access control on, 94–95
  attributes on, 95
  automatic password administration on, 97–98
  backing up, 101–102
  defined, 88
  hacking onto, 81, 101
  intrusion detection on, 98–99
  passwords on, 93–94
  physical security of, 89–90
  rights on, 96–97
  security checklist for, 102–103
  security concerns on, 12, 80–81, 87
  security options for, 82–85, 90, 97
  supervision of, 91–93
  unauthorized use of, 206
  viruses on, 100–101
  wiring of, 89–90
Laptop
  access control for, 74–75
  alarms for, 78
  backing up, 74
  locks for, 77–78
  privacy screens for, 78–79
  rescue disks for, 70–71
  security for, 79–80
  survival kit for, 70
  theft of, 68–70, 77
Law enforcement agencies, 215–216
Lazarus Data Recovery, 157
Lighting, of monitor, 172–173
Lightning damage, 160
Line noise, 160
Local area network. See LAN
Lock 'M Up (Bill Travis), 65
Lockout
  disk, 68, 75, 168
  timed, 67
Locks, 47
  for LANs, 89
  for laptops, 77–78
  for office door, 167
Log
  network, 99, 112
  user, 67
Logic bomb, 7, 17, 42
Lotus 1-2-3 (Lotus), password protection in, 63
LZEXE compression software, 33

Mac Control (BDW), 65
MacPerfect (Hi Resolution), 65
Magnetic stripe cards, 55–56
Magneto-optical drives, 194
Mail lists, 105
Manual
  importance of reading, xv
  proper disposal of outdated, 18
Master Boot Record, repairing, 36
MasterKey (New Visions), 63
MBDF virus, 38
Media vault, 185
MEMMAKER command (DOS), 71
MerryXmas virus, 38
Michelangelo virus, 28
MicroSAFE Laptop Information Security System (M&T), 74
Microsoft Antivirus, 33
Misfortune, defined, xiii
Mitnick, Kevin, 9
Modem
  call-back, 82
  savers, 73
  secure, 82
Modify LAN right, 97
Monitors
  emissions from, 170, 173
  filters for, 173
  maintenance of, 173
  positioning of, 172
  privacy screens for, 78–79
Moonlighting, using company equipment, 8, 204
Morris, Robert T., 41, 87
MPR-II limits on ELF radiation, 173
MSAV (Microsoft Antivirus), 33
MSBACKUP command (DOS), 188–189
MSD diagnostic program (Microsoft), 196

National Computer Security Association, 177
National Computer Systems Laboratory, 207
National Institute of Standards and Technology, 207
Netcrack, hacking program, 101
NetWare (Novell)
  passwords on, 93–94
  security on, 90
NetWare Loadable Modules (NLMs), 90

Network. See LAN
Nintendo Fallacy, 201
NLMs, 90
Norstad, John, 38
Norton Desktop (Symantec), 182, 197
Norton Utilities (Symantec), 197
  rescue disk utility, 71
  unerase command of, 68
  wipeinfo utility, 197
Notebook computer. See Laptop

On Guard (Power On), 65
On Track Data Recovery, 157

Packet-filtering routers, 114
Parker, Donn, 201–202
Partition table, saving, 71
Pass phrase, in PGP, 141–142
Password, 48
  adjuncts to, 54–61, 98
  automatic administration of, 97–98
  built-in, 64
  challenge and response, 57
  choosing of, 1, 4, 10, 19
  cracking, 12, 51–53, 81
    on Internet, 111
  hacker-proof, 54
  insecurity of, 5, 10–12, 45, 49
  on LAN, 93–94
  management of, 66
  obtained by fraud, 10
  periodic change of, 94
  physical security of, 19, 49–50
  protection of, xvi, 65–66
  sharing of, 50–51
  SSO, 105–109
  token, 57–59
  for voice mail, 124
  unique, 94
  on UNIX, 11–12
Password (Ray Dittmeier), 65
Password Coach (Baseline), 98
Password Recovery Utilities (AccessData), 63, 147
PB Guard (ASD), 74
PC/DACS (Mergent), 67
PC Tools, 121
  rescue disk utility, 71

PCMCIA cards, 58
Periodic Change in Passwords option
  (NetWare), 94
Permission, defined, 203
PersonaCard (National Semiconductor), 58
Personal identification number. See Password
Personal NetWare (Novell), security on, 90
PGP encryption program, xv, 139
  digital signature in, 139
  distribution of, 140
  mechanism of, 141–143
  security of, 141–142
  setting up, 140–141
  signature function of, 143
  wipe option of, 143
Phreaking, 11, 15–16
  counteracting, 124–125
  via voice mail, 123
Physical damage
  electrical damage, 159–166
  smoke damage, 150
  spills, 5, 158
  water damage, 157–158
  weather-related, 151
PIN. See Password
Piracy of software, 100, 200, 204, 213–215
  penalties for, 214
PKLite compression software, 33
PKZIP, as rescue tool, 71
PLO virus, 29
Policies
  employee rights, 206
  ethics and, 200–202
  implementation of, 207–208
  monitoring, 199
  security, 202–207
  self-protective, 200
  writing of, 207
Polymorphic viruses, 29
Portable computer. See Laptop
Posture, 171–172
Power problems, 159–160
  dealing with, 160–161
Power surges, 160
  guarding against, 161–162
Pretty Good Privacy. See PGP
Privacy screens, 78–79
Privacy-Enhanced Mail standard, 144
Private, defined, 22

Private-key cryptography, 136
Public-key cryptography, 134–136. See also PGP
  keyring for, 142–143

QIC-80 (quarter inch cartridge), 178–179

RAM disk, 75, 76
RAMDRIVE.SYS (DOS module), 76
Read LAN right, 97
Read only LAN attribute, 96
Read/write LAN attribute, 96
Remote access, control over, 80–85
Removable hard drives, 191–192
Repair people, unauthorized telephone use
  by, 124
Repetitive-motion disorders, 170, 174
Rescue disk, 158
  for laptop, 70–71
Responsibilities, defined, 203
Retina scanners, 60
  drawbacks to, 61
Retrospect (Dantz), 182
RIPEM encryption program, 144
Ripper virus, 29
Risk assessment, 23
Rivest, Ron, 138
Router, packet-filtering, 114–115
RSA encryption program, xv, 137–139, 143
  advantages of, 138
RSA Secure encryption program, 139
RSI (repetitive strain injury), 174

Sabotage, 8
Safeware, 166, 169
Salami slicing, 8
SCANDISK command (DOS), 70
Scentinel (Bloodhound Sensors), 60
Screen savers, 62
Secret, defined, 21
Secure modems, 82
Secure-View (Kantek), 79
SecureID card (Security Dynamics), 57
Security
  assessment of, 23
  awareness, 209–216

cost of breaches of, 2–3
defined, 2
organizations dealing with, 231–232
physical, 18, 47
threats to, 3
vendors of equipment, 223–231
Security Administrator Tool for Analyzing
  Networks (SATAN), 12, 113
Sentinel (Brian Booker), 65
Server, physical security of, 89
SET command (DOS), 141
Shamir, Adi, 138
Sharable LAN attribute, 96
Sherizen, Sanford, 208
Shredder data wiper (Jeff Prosise), 197
Signature dynamics, 60
Signatures, virus, 34, 37
Simply Everything (Deadbroke), 65
Smart cards, 56
  for modems, 82–83
SmartDisk, 58–59
SMARTDRV command (DOS), 75–76
Smoke damage, 150
Sniffer programs, 12, 53
  used on Internet, 111
Social engineering, 10, 13–14
Software
  installing, 158
  piracy of, 100, 200, 213–215
  sources of, xvi
  unauthorized use of, 204
Software Copyright Protection Bill, 213, 214
Software metering, 100
Software Publishers Association, 213–214
SPAudit (SPA), 214
Spikes, 159–160
  guarding against, 161–162
Spills, 5, 158
Spoofing, 111–113
SSO (streamlined sign-on), 105
  benefits of, 106–107
  disadvantages of, 107–108
  guidelines for, 108–109
Standby power system, 164
Static, threat of, 5
Stealth virus, 18, 30
Stolen Computer Registry, 168
Stoplight 95 (Security Integration), 97

Stoplock V smart card, 56
Storage
  CD-R, 194–195
  floppy, 188–190
  hard drive, 175–197
  magneto-optical, 194
  removable cartridge, 192–193
  removable hard-drive, 191–192
  tape, 177–180, 183–184
Storm Windows (Cetus), 65
Streamlined sign-on, 105
  benefits of, 106–107
  disadvantages of, 107–10
  guidelines for, 108–109
Supervisor LAN right, 97
SUPERVISOR account on LAN, 91–92
  powers of, 95
Surge suppressor, 160, 161
  types of, 162
  vendors of, 162
SyQuest removable cartridges, 192, 193
SYS command (DOS), 36, 70
SYSTEM.INI (Windows module), 71

Tape drives, 178–179
  internal vs. external, 183–184
Technoshock, xiv
Telephone
  cellular, security problems with, 125–128
  cordless, security problems with, 128–129
  handling queries on, 14
  jacks and wiring for, 72–73
  phreaking of, 11, 15–16, 123–125
  security tips for using, 129
Telephone system
  back doors to, 122–123
  described, 121
  digital, 73–74
  monitoring of, 123–124
  risk assumption by user of, 122
Terminate and stay resident programs (TSRs), 35
Three Tunes virus, 38
Time bomb, 17, 42
Timed lockout, 67
Tippett, Peter, 201
Token password generators, 57–59
Tokens, 55
ToneLoc, war dialer, 13

Total Recall data recovery, 157
TraqNet (LeeMah DataCom Security), 82–83
Trashing, 10, 14–15
Triple DES, xv, 66, 137
Trojan horses, 17, 40–41
  password-stealing, 52–53
Tropez phone, 128
TSRs, 35

Unauthorized use, monitoring of, 5
Unclassified, defined, 22
UNDELETE command (DOS), 68, 71
  using, 196–197
UNFORMAT command (DOS), 71
Uninstaller (MicroHelp), 198
Uninterruptible power supply (UPS), 160,
    163–164
  tips for using, 165
Unique Password option (NetWare), 94
UNIX, viruses on, 43
User log. See Log
UUencode/UUdecode, 74

ViaCrypt, encryption program, 139, 144
Virus
  access control and prevention of, 67
  activation of, 29
  on backups, 183
  boot sector, 28, 36
  cross-platform incompatibility of, 42–43
  defined, 27–28
  file infectors, 28
  on LAN, 100–101
  on Macintosh, 37–39
  mechanism of, 29
  origin of, 26–27
  planting of, 8
  polymorphic, 29
  prevention of infection, 39–40
  risk of, xv, 3, 25–26, 27
  route of infection by, 30–31
  signature of, 34, 37
  stealth, 18, 30
  symptoms and signs of, 31–32
  treatment of, 32–36. See also Antivirus
      software
  types of, 17–18

Virus activity monitors, 35
Voice mail
  eavesdropping on, 8, 16
  phreaking via, 123
  passwords on, 124–125
Voice verification, 60
  drawbacks to, 61
Voltage regulator, 160, 163
VSafe antivirus software, 33
Vue-It (Chi/Cor), 155

War dialers, 13, 81
Warning banner, importance of, 18, 83–84, 215
Waste, defined, 205–206
Watchdog SecureID (Fischer Int'l), 67
Water damage, 157–158
Weather, disaster caused by, 151
WIN.INI (Windows module), 71
WinBolt (Tritech), 65
Windows 95, antivirus considerations of, 43
WinGuard (Cetus), 65

WinGuard Access (Communications Devices), 82
Wiping files, 143, 146, 197
Wiring, eavesdropping on, 89–90
Word (Microsoft), password protection in, 62
Wordperfect (Novell), password protection in, 63
Workplace monitoring, 206
World Wide Web (WWW), 119
  security problems on, 119–121
Worms, 17
  case study of, 25, 41
Wrist rests, 174
Write LAN right, 97
Write-protecting disks, 39
WWW (World Wide Web), 119
  security problems on, 119–121

X-ray machines, laptops and, 79

Zip drives (Bernoulli), 193